Journal of Qualitative Research in Sports Studies

Journal of Qualitative Research in Sports Studies

Volume 17, Issue 1, December 2023

ISSN: 1754-2375 [print]

ISSN: 2755-5240 [online]

Published by:
Sport and Wellbeing Press
University of Central Lancashire
Preston UK
PR1 2HE

Journal of Qualitative Research in Sports Studies
Volume 1 (2007)   Liverpool Hope University and Write Now CETL
                  (Centre of Excellence in Teaching and Learning)
Volume 2 (2008)   University of Central Lancashire and SSTO (School of Sport, Tourism and The
                  Outdoors) and CRIT (Centre for Research Informed Teaching)
Volume 3 (2009)   University of Central Lancashire: SSTO Publications and CRIT
Volume 4 (2010)   University of Central Lancashire: SSTO Publications and CRIT
Volume 5 (2011)   University of Central Lancashire: SSTO Publications and CRIT
Volume 6 (2012)   University of Central Lancashire: SSTO Publications
Volume 7 (2013)   University of Central Lancashire: SSTO Publications
Volume 8 (2014)   University of Central Lancashire: SSTO Publications
Volume 9 (2015)   University of Central Lancashire: SSTO Publications
Volume 10 (2016) University of Central Lancashire: Sport and Wellbeing Press
Volume 11 (2017) University of Central Lancashire: Sport and Wellbeing Press
Volume 12 (2018) University of Central Lancashire: Sport and Wellbeing Press
Volume 13 (2019) University of Central Lancashire: Sport and Wellbeing Press
Volume 14 (2020) University of Central Lancashire: Sport and Wellbeing Press
Volume 15 (2021) University of Central Lancashire: Sport and Wellbeing Press
Volume 16 (2022) University of Central Lancashire: Sport and Wellbeing Press
Volume 17 (2023) University of Central Lancashire: Sport and Wellbeing Press

Notice

The discussions, statements of fact and opinions contained in the articles of The Journal of Qualitative Research in Sports Studies are those of the respective authors and cited contributors and are set out in good faith for the general guidance of student supported research and the promotion of pedagogical discussion in teaching and learning contexts. No liability can be accepted by the Editor, Editorial Board, Advisory Board, the reviewers or the authors/submitters for loss or expense incurred as a result of relying upon particular statements or circumstances made in this journal.

Journal created by Clive Palmer (2007)
JQRSS logo design by Mervyn Clarke (2014)
Cover Artwork: *Up and Down* by David Pryle (1975)

ISBN: 978-0-9955744-9-6
Sport and Wellbeing Press
Lancashire

UK

Journal of Qualitative Research in Sports Studies

Volume 17, Issue 1, December 2023

ISSN: 1754-2375 [print]

ISSN: 2755-5240 [online]

Peer Reviewers

I would like to thank the reviewers and board members for their conscientious efforts to support the authors' research. Reviewers' comments are very much appreciated, their constructive feedback being invaluable for improving the quality of articles and what might be learned from them. Collectively your shared wisdom has contributed to the educational experience of the wider readership. On behalf of submitters and readers, thank you.

Clive Palmer

Journal of Qualitative Research in Sports Studies

Volume 17, Issue 1, December 2023

Contents

Presentation Details:

Title: **14pt Tahoma - Bold**

Names: **11pt Tahoma-Bold**

Affiliations: 11pt Tahoma (in brackets)

Section headings: **11pt Tahoma - Bold**

(Main section headings are - Abstract, Conclusion, and References)

Sub-headings: **11pt New Times Roman – Bold**

(Sub-headings devised by the authors as appropriate)

Main body of text: 11pt Times New Roman (14pt line space)

Quotes of more than 3 lines: indented and 10pt Times New Roman (12pt line space)

No footnotes or endnotes

Harvard referencing only

Name and date in text with page number if citing a direct quote e.g. (Atkinson, 1991:79). All references to be placed in one alphabetical list.

Books:

Atkinson, P. (1991) *The Ethnographic Imagination.* Falmer Press, London.

Kreider, R.B., Fry, A.C. and O'Toole, M.L. (1998) *Overtraining in sport.* Human Kinetics, New Zealand.

Journals:

Annells, M. (1999) Evaluating phenomenology, usefulness, quality and philosophical foundations. *Nurse Researcher*, 6, 2, 5-19.

Cote, J., Salmela, J.H., Baira, S. and Russell, S. (1993) Organising and interpreting unstructured qualitative data. *The Sport Psychologist*, 7, 1, 127-137.

Edited Books:

Alder, P.A. and Alder, P. (1994) Observational techniques (pp.377-392). In, Denzin, N.K. and Lincoln, Y.S. (Eds.) *Handbook of Qualitative Research.* Sage, Thousand Oaks, CA.

Websites:

Bauer, J.A. (1996) Russian men's team on Floor, 1996 Olympics, *Gymnastics Photos* [online]. Available at: http://www.geocities.com/Colosseum/Field/7979/ (Accessed 10th October 2001).

Submissions process

Articles submitted should be original and not be under consideration for another publication at the same time. Inform the editor of a potential submission by sending in an abstract. See notes in Editorial; Open Call for Papers for further advice. Follow the format of the journal for general guidance on topics, themes, working with data and presentation of your text. This is an open access journal. There are no subscription or membership fees to JQRSS. Hard copy volumes are available from online booksellers, such as Amazon.com. PDFs of all articles and volumes are available free of charge at the Editor's web-profiles:

Academia.edu: https://uclan.academia.edu/ClivePalmer
ResearchGate: https://www.researchgate.net/profile/Clive_Palmer
BePress: https://works.bepress.com/clive_palmer/

JQRSS also indexed at:

EBSCO Host and Google Scholar

Structure – general guidelines

Title
Contributor names and affiliations/Institutions
Abstract (150-200 words)
Keywords (4-6 one line)
Introduction
Subheadings as appropriate
Conclusion
References
Length of final submission 4000-6000 words textual (not including references)

JQRSS Author Profile

Author Name[1] brief overview of background/degree, institution, professional and research interests, roles, duties and aspirations. Typically, the student, or instigating author is first named.

Author Name[2] brief overview of [as appropriate] degree, institution, professional and research interests, roles, duties and aspirations. Staff/supervisor/co-writing academic may also [or alternatively] include: job position, recent project or publication, any other relevant detail for context.

Reviewer's comments

All papers are externally peer reviewed. There is a JQRSS proforma for reviewers to return their feedback and recommendation to the editor, and anonymously to the authors. Since 2011 a brief summary comment from the reviewer about the research has usefully been included at the end of the paper. The purpose of this is to demonstrate peer critique of the research to support further pedagogical discussion.

Journal of Qualitative Research in Sports Studies

ISSN: [print] 1754-2375
ISSN: [online] 2755-5240

Peer Review Recognition Certificate

Name, Name, Name, Name

....

JQRSS est. 2007
© *Sport and Wellbeing Press*

Dear Reviewer,

Thank you for your conscientious efforts to support the authors' research through your critique and learned review. Reviewer's comments are very much appreciated, your constructive feedback being invaluable for improving the quality of the articles and what might be learned from them. Collectively your shared wisdom has contributed to the educational experience of the wider readership and to the pedagogical mission which is central to JQRSS. On behalf of submitters and readers, thank you.

Dr Clive Palmer
JQRSS Editor In Chief
NTF, PFHEA

National Teaching Fellow 2019

UK Council for Graduate Education
RECOGNISED RESEARCH SUPERVISOR
UK Council for Graduate Education

Higher Education Academy

Association of National Teaching Fellows

University of Central Lancashire
UCLan

Previous Publications

The sporting image: sports poetry and creative writing

Edited by Clive Palmer (2009)

With a *Foreword* by John Lindley and contributions from:
Billy Wilson *aka* Mr Mouse, *Financial Security* and Paul Hall, *Casualski.*

Published by the Centre for Research Informed Teaching,
Preston, UK.
ISBN: 978-0-9562343-2-2

Available at:
https://uclan.academia.edu/ClivePalmer

This book contains sixty-five poems from students studying for a Sports Journalism degree and two short stories from outside the student cohort. A poetry workshop was led by John Lindley, a professional writer and former *Cheshire Poet Laureate* with final poems being inspired by a wide range of sporting incidents and personalities. The content of the poems are indicative of social phenomena which can be researched in sport studies, but may also begin to reveal the auto-biographical challenges of writing in a poetic form for the authors, who in some cases found a new and rich mode of personal expression.

Journal of Qualitative Research in Sports Studies
Volume 16, Issue 1, 2022
ISSN [print]: 1754-2375
ISSN [online]: 2755-5240

Editor in Chief: Clive Palmer
Published by Sport and Wellbeing Press,
University of Central Lancashire,
Preston, UK.
ISBN: 978-0-9955744-8-9

Past papers from all volumes are available at:
https://uclan.academia.edu/ClivePalmer

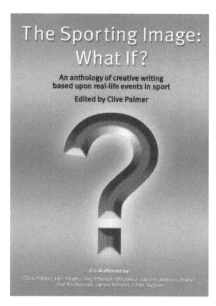

The sporting image: what if? - An anthology of creative writing based upon real-life events in sport

Edited by Clive Palmer (2010)

With a *Foreword* by Philip Caveney (Royal Literary Fellow) and individual contributions from Paul Hall *(North) Korean Odyssey* and John Metcalfe *Act now, think later*.

Published by: SSTO Publications, Preston, UK.
ISBN: 978-0-9566270-0-1

Available at:
https://uclan.academia.edu/ClivePalmer

Co-authored by Clive Palmer, Iain Adams, Ray Physick, Mitchel J. Larson, Anthony Maher, Joel Rookwood, James Kenyon and Chris Hughes. This book comprises 30 chapters; each chapter having a research preface to create context and/or plausibility for the creative story that follows.

This publication originates from a module at the University of Central Lancashire called *The Sporting Image*. The focus of the book was to take a sideways look at iconic features in sport; characters, events, artefacts and general goings-on. By considering the notion of 'what if?' reality has been re-interpreted and presented differently through a medium of creative writing. Each chapter has some underpinning research which is intended to illustrate where the creative story departs from reality. The research aspect is also to give a sense of plausibility for a range of different outcomes which are ostensibly possible for some famous people in sport. Through the conflict created for these characters we find many 'good apples' in sport who may have been rotten to the core (and vice-versa) and some 'juicy' dialogue leads them to novel endings, altered events and new milestones in an augmented life-history. These are the kind of things envisaged by the authors in *What If?* always for dramatic effect and often with moral tales lurking not too far behind the scenes.

Included in *What If?* are trials and tribulations for:

Muhammad Ali, Edmund Hillary and Sherpa Tensing, Mike Tyson, Thierry Henry, Rubin 'Hurricane' Carter, Jesse Owens and Hitler, Rio Ferdinand, Duncan Edwards, Dame Kelly Holmes, Roman Abramovich, Michael Schumacher
and many more…

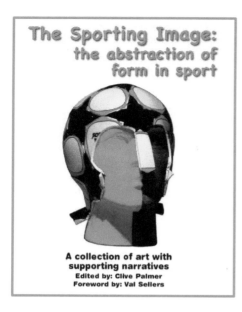

The Sporting Image:
the abstraction of
form in sport

A collection of art with
supporting narratives
Edited by: Clive Palmer
Foreword by: Val Sellers

The sporting image: the abstraction of form in sport: A collection of art with supporting narratives

Edited by Clive Palmer

Foreword by Val Sellers: *I plead guilty*.
Co-authored by Clive Palmer, Iain Adams
and Ray Physick

Published in 2011 by:
SSTO Publications,
Preston, UK.
ISBN: 978-0-9566270-2-5

Available at:
https://uclan.academia.edu/ClivePalmer

This book exhibits the final artworks from a teaching initiative in aesthetic education which spanned one academic year, 2010-11. The project, fundamentally, was to explore one way of educating students to become critical thinkers about issues in sport and then, to experiment with means of communicating their ideas to others through a mode of artistic representation. The key-note lecture from Val Sellers along with his practical workshop on abstraction (Chapter 2) at the start of the year was the basis for producing the final artworks, in conjunction with follow-up lectures and discussion of ideas. Consequently, the groundwork for moving from aesthetic theory to artistic practice is set out in the opening chapters to provide a clearer understanding of the challenge set before the students and how they were equipped to engage with it.

It is interesting to highlight that once students began to realise how academically free they were within the bounds of this intellectual task, their imaginations thrived seemingly like never before at university and there was a noticeable leap forward in creative awareness demonstrated by some students when devising and refining their artwork. Therefore, the educational value of this task may have been all the greater for these students who discovered a new sense of confidence in their reasoning to make a bold statement about sport, in this case, an artistic one. There are 49 chapters of student and staff artwork in chapters, split into 4 galleries: The Palmer Gallery, The Adams Gallery, a Viewing Gallery and a Cameo Gallery. The Viewing Gallery displays 23 artworks by students but without supporting narratives.

The sporting image: unsung heroes of the Olympics 1896-2012

Edited by Clive Palmer

Foreword by Professor Stephan Wasssong

Olympic Preface by Paul Hall (M.B.E.)
London 2012 - We could be heroes...

Published in 2013 by:
SSTO Publications,
Preston, UK.
ISBN: 978-0-9566270-4-9

Available at:
https://uclan.academia.edu/ClivePalmer

This is the fourth book in the Sporting Image Series compromising 32 chapters from students and academic staff, discussing Olympic culture across the genres of short story, poetry and artworks.

At its heart it's a philosophy book about the ethics of human behaviour; a moral philosophy explored through research and artistic representation about how people [Olympians] felt they ought to act, or not act in certain circumstances. Interestingly, it is the breadth of these circumstances outside of sport; wars, racism, discrimination and other social conflicts, that have been the stimulus for the Sporting Image students to research 'special' Olympians.

What identifies the few Olympians from the many for special attention are their personal responses to these broader socio-political tensions, as acts of unsung heroism which have been represented artistically – in artworks, poetry and short stories. Unsung in this context alludes to actions beyond the medals and beyond the gaze and glare of sports settings for which some Olympians may be popular or even considered famous. They may be unsung and heroic for acts of truly unselfish giving, going beyond the call of duty expected from a sports personality, unsung; uncelebrated in some way, for acts of sacrifice, acts certainly not recognised as being part of sport, but nevertheless, heroic in the true sense of the word.

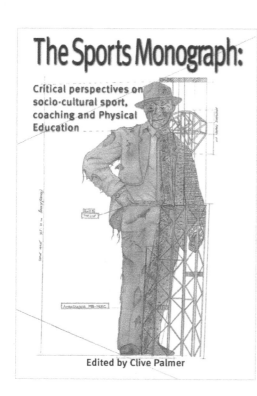

The Sports Monograph:

Critical perspectives on socio-cultural sport, coaching and Physical Education

Edited by Clive Palmer

The sports monograph: critical perspectives on socio-cultural sport, coaching and Physical Education

Edited by Clive Palmer

Foreword by Mr Val Sellers
Learning to listen in PE

Published in 2014 by:
SSTO Publications,
Preston, UK.
ISBN: 978-0-9566270-6-3

Available at:
https://uclan.academia.edu/ClivePalmer

With over 120 contributors across 60 chapters, their ages ranging from 6 months to 60 years, the Sports Monograph represents a compendium of voices; telling experiences and rich perspectives, all stimulated by personal involvement in sport, Physical Education and sports culture. Consequently, the volume has a broad remit but a common theme. This has permitted a refreshing degree of freedom for people across a wide spectrum of education to register their thoughts and feelings about physical culture as they may have experienced it. Chapters are generally of two styles; first, academic essays of sporting interest with critical and factual discussion, and second, creative stories, poems and other biographical reflections which bring to the fore the realities of sport and PE. The latter conspicuously holding up a mirror to those theorised experiences, revealing quite vividly the primacy, sensuality and emotional importance of being physically educated, but through the medium of literature.

Arts-based Education in Outdoor Learning

By Clive Palmer

Foreword by Myles Farnbank
Outdoor learning – an external perspective

Preface by Val Sellers
The trained eye: aesthetic education for outdoor learning

Aesthetics Reader by Warren Stevenson

Published in 2021 by:
Sport and Wellbeing Press,
Preston, UK.

ISBN: 978-0-9566270-6-3

Available at:
https://uclan.academia.edu/ClivePalmer

This innovative volume for Outdoor Learning comprises 40 chapters of artworks and discussion, prompting critical thinking and reflection on issues in society, from an Outdoor perspective or with Outdoor motives at their core. From local to global concerns, the range of 'issues' chosen were put to work as stimuli for the art that would emerge, and the learning to take place, over the course of an academic year. Topics include, among others; environmental damage and pollution, impacts of modern lifestyle, personal challenge on expeditions, outdoor fashion, personal identity and the outdoors, and human attitudes on life - from extinction to rebirth.

The chapters are from a university module called The Outdoor Image, spanning three cohorts of learners on BA (hons) Outdoor degrees (2014/15, 2015/16 and 2016/17). Adopting an arts-based pedagogy has allowed these students to explore their thoughts and present their ideas in a vibrant and engaging way, which they ably and confidently demonstrate in their art and in their writing. There are a number of contributions early in the volume which set the scene and explore some aspects of aesthetic theory, helping to establish a context for the chapters that follow. The volume closes with a chapter of 'student voices' helping to impart and confirm the pedagogical mission of this work and the impacts that this opportunity for art-based learning has had in their education.

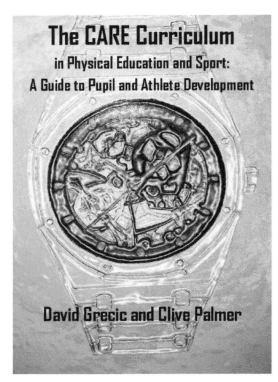

The CARE Curriculum in Physical Education and Sport: A Guide to Pupil and Athlete Development

By David Grecic and Clive Palmer

Foreword by Myles Farnbank
Outdoor learning – an external perspective

Preface by David Grecic
Developing an Alpha model to explore PE's human development potential

Published in 2021 by:
Sport and Wellbeing Press,
Preston,
UK.

ISBN: 978-0-9566270-6-3

The CARE Curriculum in Physical Education and Sport is a holistic model of learning which encompasses Cognitive, Active, Relational and Emotional domains of development. Across the sixteen chapters, PE teachers and Coaches are guided through the inner workings of the CARE Curriculum: its theoretical and practical applications for learning. Interactive reflection is encouraged throughout the book, with constructive lesson examples and user-friendly methods of recording progress are provided. Equipped with new ideas for planning learning activities, the reader is encouraged to shape their own ideas into a personalised plan of education that is informed by the CARE Curriculum concept.

Editorial

Creative, courageous, and confident...

Introduction

Welcome to Volume 17 (2023) *Journal of Qualitative Research in Sports Studies* (JQRSS) comprising papers from first-time authors alongside more experienced writers, all wishing to share their ideas stemming from primary research or through critical discussion articles. A glance down the contents page reveals a range of contributions which may be informative and thought provoking for people at different points on their journey through education and/or research experience. Reviewers' comments have been incorporated at the end of papers with a view to stimulating further discussion about a given topic. I hope readers will gain as much from browsing the experiences of others formulated through these pages as much as I have enjoyed working with the authors and editing this volume. Below, an *Overview of [current] Submissions* is followed by the *JQRSS Qualitative Researcher Award* for the previous year. Then an explanation of the *Scope and Purpose of the Journal* is followed by an *Open call for papers* and *JQRSS Operational Guidance*, which provides both an invitation to submit work and further advice to potential authors. In closing, there are summative comments and editorial acknowledgements.

Overview of submissions

Creativity, courage and confidence are stand-out qualities in the submissions to JQRSS this year, or to be more precise, qualities in the authors to write, present and share their research in such engaging ways. Across the papers a vibrant landscape of deep reflective thinking is evidenced, revealing not only their personal motivations and educational purpose for conducting research, but also, and judging from the reviewers' comments, the impact on others beyond education that will be achieved by presenting their work in such an accessible and engaging manner.

This reminds me of my *'Clive's 5Cs'* theory which was a product of my own deep reflection about what it was I was actually teaching in Higher Education. That is, after 25 years of teaching named modules around Sport and PE, such as Teaching and Coaching Methods, Coaching Practice in Athletics, Art in Sport's Journalism, Gymnastics, Research Methods, or Outdoor Education in the National Curriculum etc etc ... the list is long, I took stock and wondered what it was I was doing to people at university. I reasoned I was trying to teach them how to become, or show:

1. **Confidence,** 2. **Curiosity,** 3. **Creativity,**

4. **Critique,** 5. **Communication.**

As my teaching has moved predominantly into supervising doctoral students conducting their research[1], I no longer have 'things' to provide such as handouts and PowerPoints in a classroom setting, but I do strive to instil these qualities to enable colleagues to produce and share what is now manifest in these pages of JQRSS.

From: Clive Palmer (2019) *Research in Physical Education: Bridging cultures through shared practice–A collaboration for learning* 体育研究: 实践共享、学习合作、文化互通. Visiting Professor in Sport and Physical Education: keynote 运动与体育访问教授. Hunan Normal University, Changsha, China. 12-18th May.

So, a potential 6th C might be for *courage* which I believe all the researchers have shown in these articles for volume 17, as have the majority of previous submitters to JQRSS since 2007. The 5 letters of my name *Clive* serves to usefully limit my pedagogical theory from running away with itself. I prefer to think that this quality, courage, might be a product of *Clive's 5 Cs,* not a feature of the process. For those who bravely publish in JQRSS, having the courage to do something different in their learning should not be an issue or barrier we have to tackle as educators.

Jez Welch opens the running order in JQRSS vol. 17, by *Talking Rubbish* along with his PhD supervisors. This fascinating study on littering has the potential to scour the depths of ethical and moral behaviour in society, perhaps to an extent that we are not prepared for. Jordana Stringer in her article on *Fitspiration* looks at the impact of social media use to encourage fitness, and for people to share and create fitness-related content online. Then, Samantha Pywell is the first of four authors in this volume to

---

[1] **Palmer, C.** (2021) *Fostering freedom in PhD students: how supervisors can shape accessible paths for doctoral research.* THE Campus. Times Higher Education, posted: 16th November [online]. Available at: https://www.timeshighereducation.com/campus/fostering-freedom-phd-students-how-supervisors-can-shape-accessible-paths-doctoral-research (Accessed 17th November 2023).

concentrate on reflexivity as a central feature of their writing. This has the effect of placing the researcher at the centre of attention, and operations, making them visible, present and accountable in the research process. These are some outcomes noted in Samantha's study around language use, particularly the terms stress and anxiety in the clinical setting of palliative care. Then, Gail Keech's research to design and implement a nature-based learning programme in her International School in Luxembourg is set out in detail. A strong case is made here for the benefits of such a programme for school populations in inner-city or built-up areas, who are nature-deprived in their education. Next, we are transported to *Being in the world of fooball scouting* with Craig Lawlor who offers a powerfully storied account of his fieldwork observations, which are further refined, and performed into song. Rugby Union and coach education is our next destination, this research building upon the researcher voice in reflexive accounts of Darren Cunningham to look at decision making in rugby coaching. Then Pete Carruthers takes us off to the movies to consider *Empathy Machines* as part of his doctoral research into the use of theatre and film in training health care professionals, specifically around mental health nurse training. Like Craig Lawlor's research, Pete Carruthers' article has a participatory element to its presentation; it is also a visual feast to communicate this highly impactful research in a clinical and educational setting. Finally, Glenn Smith *Bares his soul in narrative health research* to tell his story of becoming a health professional alongside his enculturation into an island population on the Isle of Wight. Glenn's turn to autoethnography to achieve this, which is new to him as a doctoral student, signals his passion for learning and his motives to bring about positive change in his professional context. While creativity, courage and confidence are visible ingredients in all the papers in this volume, Glenn Smith's and Pete Carruthers' methodological choices are to be celebrated for the new insights they will afford to the communities that their research wishes to help. Bringing JQRSS volume 17 to a close is David Grecic writing with an international consortium of experts from across Europe, sharing their insights about the 'Fire Souls', who are community activists, advocates, and leaders of sport for health and wellbeing in their respective countries. This Sport *for* Development research is highly impactful, not lapsing into a numerical survey or report of actions and activities, but highlighting the work of the Fire Souls through their voice and the impact for good they are achieving on the ground.

The JQRSS Qualitative Researcher Award for Volume 16, 2022

The Editor's academic award for outstanding qualitative research; the *JQRSS Qualitative Researcher Award* (no.16, 2022) was awarded to Joanne Keeling (co-authored with Clive Palmer, at the University of Central Lancashire). The paper: *Rugby Mum's perspective: a story of care and chronic social damage observed from the touchline*, explores the phenomena of social behaviour around rugby league, from the situated, grounded position of the Rugby Mum. This award recognises the recipient's efforts to conduct high quality primary research and then, to communicate their discoveries in an engaging manner. It is hoped this award will have a positive impact upon the recipient's development and encourage them to continue with their research in the future. Accessed through various online platforms, this article is already making significant contributions to learning, regionally, nationally and across the globe. The award for 2023 (Volume 17) will appear in 2024 (Volume 18).

Scope and purpose of the journal

The *Journal of Qualitative Research in Sports Studies* presents a valuable opportunity for researchers at all levels including students; Undergraduates and Postgraduates alike, and all levels of academic staff from Demonstrator to Professor, to write and publish articles of their research activities in relation to the sport's world. The papers are peer reviewed by academics from the UK and overseas who have a mutual interest in researching sport, health, exercise and Physical Education. They also share enthusiasm for experimental writing and research design from a qualitative standpoint. Towards these ends the journal identifies the aims below, which the Advisory Board hope the reader will recognise as being educationally valuable for academic quality and student-centred learning:

(a) To showcase and share research at all levels; undergraduate, postgraduate, early career researchers and more seasoned academics.

(b) Through a process of mentoring and external review, help to improve new writers' confidence to present their ideas formally.

(c) To create a contemporary resource of qualitative research within the sports world which is accessible to all and can inform ongoing investigations.

(d) To create a stage for experimental designs in qualitative research which are exciting, engaging and pedagogically stimulating for the study of sport.

From the combined efforts of the authors, their mentors and the reviewers' feedback, the Advisory Board feel that these aims are achieved in some considerable measure through the papers comprising each volume. In working towards these aims I believe we bring significant meaning to the phrase Research Informed Teaching and hope that the readership will benefit from its contents.

Open call for papers and JQRSS operational guidance

There is an open call for papers to JQRSS and potential submitters are encouraged to contact the Editor with their ideas. Guidelines for layout and referencing are detailed in the opening pages of this journal. Deadlines for submission should be discussed with the Editor as they may be determined by a number of factors including the degree of mentoring required, reviewing possibilities and general readiness of the article for publication. Please use this current volume and earlier volumes as a guide to context, layout and appropriateness of content, and then, contact the Editor.

How it works: in many cases papers are dual authored, usually by the student who is first named with a mentor or supervisor as co-author. This helps to preserve both the identity of the original work and the integrity of the reviewing process. Most importantly, it reflects the student-teacher relationship in supervised research and mentored writing, which as a pedagogical principle is at the heart of what this journal is about. However, increasingly there are a number of sole-authored papers appearing from authors whose writing has been free of supervision, usually post-doctoral and independent researchers, which is a healthy sign of evolution in JQRSS, serving its readership and application of its contents.

Reviews of various forms are also invited for publication and may be sole authored by students or supported by a mentor. The aim of a review in this journal is that the criticisms offered are usefully directed at teaching and learning in some way and are therefore subject to editorial control. The norm in many journals is to feature book reviews predominantly, however, because of the mandate for JQRSS we wish to extend the act of reviewing to include reviews of not only books, but book chapters and journal articles. It is hoped that this may encourage students and staff to share their ideas by focusing more closely, and perhaps more usefully, on a single source of information, rather than offering general comments about a larger body work which in itself, may be more deserving of deeper critical review elsewhere. JQRSS reviews would typically be 500-1000 words in length. Please contact the Editor if you wish to submit a review.

In closing...

A journal should, arguably, serve the needs and interests of its readership and JQRSS strives to do just this. JQRSS has no society or paying membership and does not wish for one at this stage but sees the needs of its readership as defining its purpose; that of helping learners and researchers to develop their interests in and around qualitative research in sport. The educational remit of the journal is two-fold encompassing both the production of the contents through staff and student collaboration as well as the sharing of information to facilitate teaching and learning. Both may be a sign of its 'impact' in education. For example, the papers feed directly back into supervision tutorials, lectures, VLEs, Staff Profiles, online research sharing and CVs, as well as guiding initial research endeavours of many students at all levels.

Production costs and the distribution of JQRSS is an ongoing concern, however the journal continues this year to be produced via a Print on Demand service. It is therefore available online through companies such as Amazon or Play.com or can be ordered through any booksellers world-wide. Consequently, JQRSS in hard copy is widely available to support teaching and learning. In addition, PFD electronic copies of all back issues are freely available online at the open access websites:

Indexed at: Academia.edu / ResearchGate / Google Scholar / EBSCOhost

The price of the journal is set to cover print and initial production costs and is hopefully affordable for individuals and institutions. Please note also that authors elect to publish their work for publication in JQRSS on the understanding that there are no royalties, but as yet, there is no submission fee either. To these ends, a debt of thanks is owed to Professor David Grecic, the Director of the Institute for Coaching and Performance, University of Central Lancashire, for his continued support of JQRSS as it has developed into Volume 17. On behalf of all those who use JQRSS, thank you.

Thank you also to Mrs Mary Pryle and Dr Joseph Pryle and the David Pryle estate, for sharing the artwork *Up and Down* (1975) from David Pryle's Rainbow Collection[2], as frontispiece for this volume. In this picture, what appears at first glance to be a normal scene of outdoor living, upon closer inspection is not quite the case. The composition is both metaphor and motivation for qualitative research, inviting us to observe more closely what is going on around us, to reflect upon and reconsider things we may take for granted, and to remember that David Pryle conceived of this artwork as a reflection of the world he saw, one which we are already a part of and have an impact upon. For further interest please visit the following chapter:

David Pryle and Joseph Pryle (2021) The Relevance of Art in Education (Chapter 30: pp.196-221). In, Palmer, C. (Ed.) *Arts-based Education in Outdoor Learning*. Sport and Wellbeing Press, Preston, UK. ISBN: 978-0-9955744-1-0.

Finally, I would like to thank the authors, mentors and the reviewers for their valued contribution to JQRSS. In all cases you have freely shared your enthusiasms for learning through research, collaborating and sharing specialist knowledge to raise the quality of learning for all who access these pages. As Editor I thank you all most sincerely for supporting JQRSS.

Dr Clive Palmer

National Teaching Fellow

Principal Fellow Higher Education Academy

University of Central Lancashire

2023

---

[2] 'Rainbow' was a British children's television series, created by Pamela Lonsdale, which ran from 16th October 1972 until 6th March 1992, made by Thames Television.

JQRSS Qualitative Researcher Awards

Congratulations to the following researchers who have been recognised by the JQRSS Editorial Board for their outstanding research activities, scholarly conduct and valuable contribution to the journal.

Joanne Keeling: Volume 16, Issue 1, (2022)
Keeling, J. and Palmer, C. (2022) Rugby Mum's perspective: a story of care and chronic social damage observed from the touchline. *Journal of Qualitative Research in Sports Studies*, 16, 1, 87-106.

Susan Thomas: Volume 15, Issue 1, (2021)

Thomas, S. and Palmer, C. (2021) When nature and tech connect a case for using Augmented Reality in the Outdoors. *Journal of Qualitative Research in Sports Studies,* 15, 1, 1-28.

Hazel Isaacs: Volume 14, Issue 1, (2020)

Isaacs, H. and Palmer, C. (2020) Let's waste some time: an autoethnographic study of procrastination. *Journal of Qualitative Research in Sports Studies,* 14, 1, 1-48.

Maksim Berdnikov: Volume 13, Issue 1, (2019)

Berdnikov, M. and Krieger, J. (2019) Education facilitators at youth mega-events: practical and methodological considerations. *Journal of Qualitative Research in Sports Studies*, 13, 1, 111-126.

Carmen Byrne: Volume 12, Issue 1, (2018)

Byrne, C. and Palmer, C. (2018) Hero, heroine or outcast? A quest for understanding through critical dialogue: the Research Goddess and me. *Journal of Qualitative Research in Sports Studies,* 12, 1, 1-34.

David Grecic: Volume 11, Issue 1, (2017)

Grecic, D. (2017) Making sense of skill – a personal narrative of becoming more skilled at skill. *Journal of Qualitative Research in Sports Studies*, 11, 1, 33-48.

James Edwards: Volume 10, Issue 1, (2016)

Edwards, J. and Palmer, C. (2016) Getting home. *Journal of Qualitative Research in Sports Studies,* 10, 1, 127-156.

Sheri Treadwell: Volume 9, Issue 1, (2015)

Treadwell, S. and Stiehl, J. (2015) Advocating for change in rural Physical Education: a middle school perspective through Photovoice and student SHOWeD analysis. *Journal of Qualitative Research in Sports Studies*, 9, 1, 107-162.

Nicola Hamilton: Volume 8, Issue 1, (2014)

Hamilton, N. and Palmer, C. (2014) Learning to ride a bike-a qualitative study of cycling and the Bikeability programme. *Journal of Qualitative Research in Sports Studies*, 8, 1, 17-88.

Joseph Pryle: Volume 7, Issue 1, (2013)

Pryle, J. and Palmer, C. (2013) Cricket provision in schools – is the system flawed? An ethnographic investigation. *Journal of Qualitative Research in Sports Studies*, 7, 1, 27-86.

Sarah Nickless: Volume 6, Issue 1, (2012)

Nickless, S. and Palmer, C. (2012) Crawling through experience. *Journal of Qualitative Research in Sports Studies*, 6, 1, 1-12.

Beki Price: Volume 5, Issue 1, (2011)

Price, B. and Varrall, S. (2011) Doing and representing qualitative research: a human perspective (Part 1: visual). *Journal of Qualitative Research in Sports Studies*, 5, 1, 59-86.

Price, B. and Gilbourne, D. (2011) Doing and representing qualitative research: a human perspective (Part 2: textual). *Journal of Qualitative Research in Sports Studies*, 5, 1, 87-100.

Chris Hughes: Volume 4, Issue 1, (2010)
Hughes, C. and Palmer, C. (2010) Examining a coaching philosophy through ethnographic principles – Winter with Woolton. *Journal of Qualitative Research in Sports Studies*, 4, 1, 23-48.

Keith McGregor: Volume 3, Issue 1, (2009)
McGregor, K. and Palmer, C. (2009) It's not the falling I'm worried about it's hitting the ground - investigating the fear of falling, comfort zones and camaraderie between extreme grade rock climbers. *Journal of Qualitative Research in Sports Studies*, 3, 1, 127-146.

Paul Gow: Volume 2, Issue 1, (2008)
Gow, P. and Rookwood, J. (2008) Doing it for the team - examining the causes of contemporary English football hooliganism. *Journal of Qualitative Research in Sports Studies*, 2, 1, 71-82.

Rachael Lear: Volume 1, Issue 1, (2007)
Lear, R. and Palmer, C. (2007) Is there life after playing football? Investigating the perspectives of football coaches at a club in the Northwest of England. *Journal of Qualitative Research in Sports Studies,* 1, 1, 19-32.

Welch, J., Palmer, C., Pryle, J. and Byrne, C. (2023) Talking rubbish: instigating a change in behaviour and attitude in primary school children. *Journal of Qualitative Research in Sports Studies*, 17, 1, 1-14

Talking rubbish: instigating a change in behaviour and attitude in primary school children

Jez Welch, Clive Palmer, Joe Pryle and Carmen Byrne
(University of Central Lancashire)

Keywords: *littering; observation; behaviour change; education; intervention*

Abstract

This article provides an insight into a volunteer's introduction into the world of litter picking and the personal reflections made. Those reflections centre around who the perpetrators are, why they drop litter and what can be done to tackle the issue. Through field observations whilst undertaking litter picks, information is gathered to try and understand the 'who' and 'why'. Canvassed opinion from interested parties suggested the blame lies with children, however, such is the extent of the problem it is difficult to pinpoint where the blame lies with litter ranging from sweet wraps to vodka bottles. Evidence, through observations of litter types at locations and the timing of the littering indicated that some children did drop litter. As a result, a short discussion was held in a rural primary school. The initial aim of the discussion was to make the young audience aware of the littering problem in their local environment. Having delivered awareness by showing them what had be discarded on the streets the hope was to empower the children to act and become anti-littering heroes. Whether one half-hour intervention made any significant change towards behaviour is very much open to debate. However, some of the children have volunteered to pick up litter (with their parent's help) so perhaps it is a start and further widespread education is needed to be the enabler to change littering behaviours.

Introduction

Rubbish. Litter. Garbage. Trash. Four nouns, defined in volume 1, page 2 of the *Journal of Litter and Environmental Quality*, June 2017, as 'waste products that have been disposed of improperly, without consent, at an inappropriate location', that can all too often, and sadly reflect a walk through our towns and countryside. Data sourced by Roper and Parker (2008) from a study in 2005 suggests in Britain alone there was in excess of 2.25 million pieces of litter dropped each day. Research conducted by Campbell (2007) on behalf of Keep Britain Tidy reflected Roper and Parker's findings by suggesting that there was a worrying increase in people who were happy to drop litter from their cars and to neglectfully dispose of their fast-food packaging. A decade on from Campbell's study and my observations in early field work on my 'Rubbish PhD' would suggest that the trend has continued. The question

JQRSS Article No: 1/9-17-1-2023-PG[106]-162
ISSN: 1754-2375 [print] ISSN: 2755-5240 [online] Copyright ©: CC-BY-NC-ND
Web: https://uclan.academia.edu/ClivePalmer/Journal-of-Qualitative-Research-in-Sports-Studies

arises, how can the socio-cultural phenomenon of littering be curbed or stopped? This article is early-stage reporting as part of my PhD research which is intended to explore and offer a suggestion that may lead to a change in littering behaviour.

In the United Kingdom legislation exists (Environmental Protection Act 1990 and Clean Neighbourhoods and Environment Act 2005) which sets out the main laws relating to pollution and other activities considered as anti-social, including littering. Littering is covered in section IV of the 1990 Act and Part 3 in the 2005 Act. Accompanying the 1990 Act is a publication from the Department of the Environment (Environmental Protection Act 1990: Code of Practice on Litter and Refuse, 1991, p.1), which, on its pages of recycled paper offers further insight into the Act. The Code of Practice concedes in its Introduction that littering will never be eliminated until a time when 'there is a universal realisation that dropping litter is fundamentally anti-social and unacceptable'. Since those words have been committed to print almost 30 years have now elapsed and the data from Roper and Parker (2008) would indicate that as a society we are still waiting on the 'universal realisation' they mentioned. Indeed, it could be argued that, for some, littering has now become part of our culture, an accepted bad habit which is a concept already suggested by Madhani, Dawes and Brown (2009) in Australia. In addition, littering culture was one of the social issues highlighted in research by Prasetio, Rambito, Yudhistira, Aulia and Chowanda, A. (2018) which resulted in their creation of a desktop computer *Horror Myth Game* that sought to teach adults about the social problems of littering, and an attempt to address the issues.

A third Code of Practice on Litter and Refuse (Department for Environment, Food and Rural Affairs, 2006) replaced its 1991 and 1999 predecessors. The admission that littering will not be eliminated as described in 1991 has gone (along with its recycled paper pages) and replaced with an online plea from the government for the public to take more responsibility and to encourage volunteer litter picking in local groups. This is where my littering story begins, as a volunteer activist trying to clean up my community. What follows is an ethnographic account of an intervention I delivered in a Primary School, in a hope that littering behaviour may be changed by educating the young.

I have become increasingly aware of the issue of littering through my own observations and through the current outpouring of media coverage, such as the hugely successful *Our Blue Planet* (2017). As stated above, I have for the last 4 to 5 years, voluntarily carried out with support from my local council, many litter picks in my local area. My strong feelings regarding this issue have seen me start up a local volunteer group through Facebook and embark on a PhD aimed at studying littering behaviours. My motivations to pick up other people's litter centre around my own ethical beliefs and a desire to live in an area that is pleasant and free from litter. As a youngster I was brought up by my parents and extended family to respect the outdoors and to essentially do the right thing. I hold these values dear and they are values I have imparted to my own children. I feel I owe it to my mentors, some who sadly are no longer with us, to continue to do the right thing. Getting involved in litter picking, highlighting litter related issues, and perhaps influencing a change in behaviour is my contribution to the community. In my PhD, my original *contribution to knowledge*, may be in helping to bring about this change.

As had been expected, the first litter pick I completed saw a significant amount of rubbish collected from the streets, shrubs and even some placed in trees. However, since that initial pick, what was truly surprising was that even in a small rural town, I continued week on week to encounter a high level of littering. My observations have shown that no sooner an area be cleared then new litter takes its place, this being contrary to the concept proposed by Spehr and Curnow (2015) that 'cared for' areas are less likely to be littered so quickly. Members of the volunteer group I am involved with have also communicated the same observations on the group's Facebook page. Recently the group undertook a litter pick over a two-hour period on a Saturday morning in September. The 25 volunteers removed 80kgs of litter during the two-hour period: figure 1. Calculations suggested that the volunteers expended around 35 personnel hours during the event. Indeed, less than 24-hours later the recently cleaned area had again been littered.

Figure 1: 80 kgs of litter collected in a local setting – re-littered within 24 hours.

As reported by Gray (2010), the best-selling author Bill Bryson and president of the Campaign to Protect Rural England, observed that 'the British countryside is being *trashed* by litter'. As a resident of rural England, I can but only agree with this statement. Following that first litter picking experience and during subsequent outings I have taken the opportunity to reflect on the issue and as a result two initial research questions are being followed up:

1. Who is littering?

2. Why is littering happening?

Towards answering these 'big' questions, small steps have been made in gathering information that, allied with further research about changing behaviours and preventing littering in the future, may provide an insight to answering them.

The Who?

To answer the *who* question, I have analysed the litter in figure 1, and surveyed its location many hours of walking and observing, alas, I concede that at this moment in time I have no specific evidence relating to individuals or groups. This is something I hope to investigate further during future studies. At times throughout my litter picks, as I fill yet another bag, it would be easy to suggest a flippant answer that everyone drops litter. However, as I pass the bins in my town (of which there are 50 or so) I see that they are being utilised well and I am therefore encouraged that most people dispose of litter in a responsible manner.

When discussing the issue of littering with friends, family and members of the wider community a common response is 'it's the kids' and this is also suggested by Campbell (2007). Indeed, many of the items I have personally picked from the streets could lean towards that hypothesis. However, I would tend to support the argument made by Williams, Curnow and Streker (1997) that those least likely to litter are those aged around 10 to15 years. In support of this argument, I would point to the numerous discarded beer cans, wine bottles, cigarette packaging and scratch cards I have found whilst litter picking, all of which are items not typically associated with children of this age. My bag of litter is mixed, as are my thoughts on the *who*. There are items seemingly dropped by children but there are also items that are certainly adult by nature. As noted above, the research conducted by Campbell (2007) suggests that school children are the main protagonists, however, given Campbell's research is now more than a decade old, could it be the case that the littering children of 2007 are now the littering adults of today in 2023, who are now becoming the role models for today's children.

The observations relating to place suggest glimpses of the *who*. For example, schools and parks are hotspots, which may suggest children littering. However, littering is not confined to just those locations. There seems to be a specific problem around the local supermarket and disappointingly the hedgerows that line the country lanes are not immune either. Such was the variety of litter found around the supermarket it did little to pinpoint the *who*, though, the plethora of items in the country lanes offered much more of an insight. The vast majority of items laid to rest in the hedgerow were fast food cartons, beer cans, vodka bottles and wine bottles (ironically, many of which were Fair Trade). Most items were quite a distance from the town, so it may be assumed that these are items tossed from motor vehicles. These items, coupled with the likelihood that they may have been thrown from cars would suggest an adult approach to littering.

Observations relating to the timing of when the litter occurs again offers some clues as to who the culprits may be. For example, fast food containers and beer bottles that appear over-night suggest adult littering and the amount of litter around a school that appeared to reduce during half-term holidays may suggest littering by children. Again, from this limited data it is not possible to state exactly who is littering. I would suggest, as does Geller (1995), those who litter reveal a disconnect with their environment through apathy and ignorance resulting in the destructive action of littering. This, I believe, is key to tackling the problem.

The Why?
Prior to affecting change, consideration needs to be given to understanding why the problem exists in the first place. It is not as simple as saying 'people drop litter', it is getting to the crux of the problem and answering the question of 'why do people drop litter?' I used social media to canvas opinion on why people litter. The consensus was that littering is a learnt behaviour and it was suggested to be a result of 'lazy parenting'. As discussed by Martin, Breunig, Wagstaff and Goldenberg (2017), the social learning theory originally proposed by Bandura (1977, 1986) suggests a learnt behaviour is a result of observing a certain behaviour from others and copying it. It is also referred to as modelling. The modelled behaviour displayed by the parent can then become normalised and subsequently passed on to their children or any other impressionable person who may observe and interpret that 'it's ok' to drop litter. In time it may become an adopted culture.

A further consideration of why littering exists could relate to a need to fit in, or peer pressure. Conformity was researched by Asch (1951), whose results suggested that people want to fit in and be part of a group. In order to fit in, certain behaviours are mimicked, such as the act of dropping litter. If the group feels that 'it's ok' to drop litter then permissions to follow suit by individuals within the group seemingly may proliferate. The research conducted by Williams *et al.* (1997) concluded that people with certain demographics, such as those aged 15 to 24 are more likely to litter when they are in groups, with their peers rather than alone.

Another possible answer to the question of why littering exists could be that there is no real personal consequence, no risk. Risk as defined by Priest and Gass (2018) can relate to social embarrassment or financial loss. If there were penalties associated with dropping litter that may cause financial loss or embarrassment. While the reintroduction of the pillory or stocks may be deemed as heavy-handed or inappropriate for community littering, there may be other means in the modern day that work towards similar ends. It will be part of my research to consider these, such as social media notifications of littering behaviour, community service, and impact education for the young. Granted there is a law (Environmental Protection Act, 1990) in the United Kingdom that does carry a maximum fine of £2,500. The law states that it is a criminal offence for a person to drop litter in a public place. However, statistics would suggest that the enforcement of the law is negligible and as such poses little personal risk. Government figures, available at www.parliament.uk in relation to enforcement of the law show that in 2013 just 5,500 convictions were made for littering through the magistrate's court with the average fine being £140. The preferred route for conviction, as per the www.parliament.uk link, for most local authorities is through fixed penalty notices. The last available data covers 2008-09 and states that just 30,678 notices were issued of which only 19,039 were paid.

As alluded to above, the culture of littering can be considered a learnt behaviour. It is suggested by Shook (2010) that to bring about a cultural change there is a need to deeply embed values and behaviours, which change what individuals do. If the modelled behaviour becomes one of disposing of litter responsibly, as suggested by Bandura (1977, 1986), then others, through a cognitive process may follow and replicate that behaviour and choose not to litter.

The Plan

As noted above, without further investigation it is very difficult to say who exactly dropped the litter I found in figure 1. It is evident from my observations that one group, and I emphasise one group, that may be prone to dropping litter is children. It is suggested by Maynard and Stuart (2018) that before a change can take place there needs to be an awareness of the problem. Once awareness has been increased there lies the choice, a choice to change or not to change. The plan therefore was to try and educate children of Primary School age, who offer a degree of diversity, through age and social background, about this issue in a hope that their behaviour and outlook can be modified. In addition, this may enhance their emotional connection to where they live (Jarrett, 2015), boosting their motivation to responsibly dispose of litter. Essentially, in a very simplified way, the hope was to fast track the children to the fourth stage - 'action' - of the Transtheoretical Model (TTM) of behaviour proposed by Prochaska and DiClemente (1983) and updated by Prochaska, DiClemente and Norcross (1992), as shown in figure 2 below.

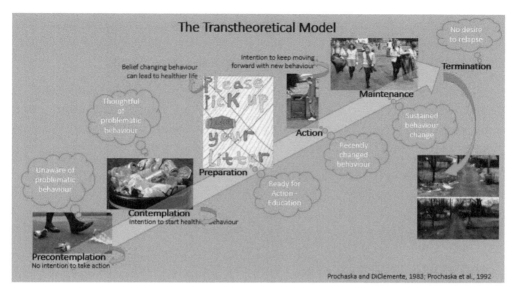

Figure 2: The Transtheoretical Model (TTM) after Prochaska *et al.* (1992).

Whether this process will enable true change is open to debate. It is argued by Adams and White (2004) that despite progressing through the various stages relating to TTM, a behavioural change may not necessarily be the result.

I was invited to speak at my son's Primary School about my research interests and community activism about littering. The school itself has approximately 60 pupils and is in a rural setting. My intervention was relayed to the children through a mix of PowerPoint slides, figure 3, visual props and discussion. The visual props were two large bags of rubbish that had been collected in the local area over the previous two days, along with the equipment used to pick up the rubbish. When discussing the tangible results of removing litter I asked the children what their world may look like in years to come if litter continued to be incorrectly disposed of. I used this tactic to move the children through to the contemplation stage (stage 2) of the TTM by championing the benefit of change. It was hoped that the discussion would last around ten minutes and that the audience would share their experiences. Such was the children's enthusiasm for the subject the presentation overran with several children happy to share their experiences in front of their peers.

Once the presentation concluded the children moved on to their morning break. Some children, having collected their morning snack, approached me to further share their experiences and, most importantly showed a high locus of control and self-efficacy in wanting to address the littering issue. Of the children addressed it is assumed there will be some who remained at the first stage of the TTM, 'precontemplation'. However, it would appear from talking to the children there were some who were contemplating (stage 2) or preparing (stage 3) to act. The discussion with the children also followed a simple model proposed by Cooper (1998) which considers awareness, empowerment and commitment.

The outcomes of the discussion suggested a need for the children to act, it gave them knowledge on how to act concerning the littering issue and as stated above some were willing to act. Indeed, some have acted by getting involved with the local volunteer group and regularly picking up litter with their parents.

Figure 3: Talking Rubbish – a presentation about littering and behaviour change to children at a primary School (Welch, 2023).

Slide 1

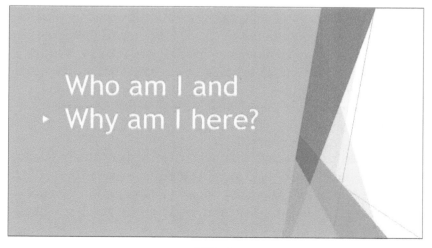

Slide 2

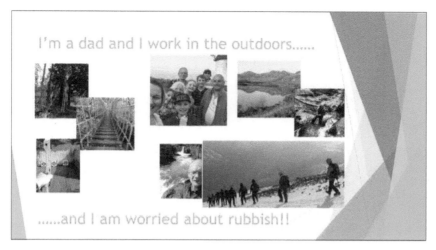

Slide 3

Slide 4

Slide 5

Slide 6

Slide 7

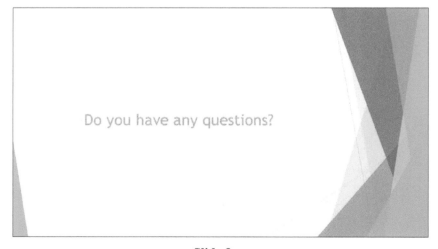

Slide 8

As an adult addressing children, I appreciate that I was in a position of influence. Ethically, it is important that such a position is not abused. (NB: see ethics declaration at the end of the paper). I was aware that my son was a member of the audience, and I was careful to treat the audience equally. Prior to the presentation consideration was given to how the message was to be conveyed, especially when discussing who is responsible for dropping litter. Care was given not to accuse the members of audience. The aim of the presentation was to raise the young people's awareness of how much littering was occurring in their local community, with a view to changing their attitude and possible future behaviour. I was also careful to share with the children the potential health risks associated with picking up litter and showed them the correct equipment to litter pick safely.

Conclusion

Aside from promoting change with the children I believe that during this process I have also undergone a change. After my first litter pick, I was surprised and disappointed with the amount of litter on the streets. Those feelings remain in place. At subsequent litter-picking 'interventions' as part of my field research, these feelings are joined with anger and depression –emotional responses highlighted by Coward (2018). However, having started this process of awareness raising, which I intend to continue through other schools and associations, I also feel a degree of optimism. The feedback received, coupled with my efforts, indicate that there is an appetite for individuals to change their behaviours and attitudes towards litter.

The reason for speaking with the school children was to make them aware of the problem and through using visual aids, the scale of the problem. During the discussion, their engagement was good, they appeared to be interested. I am mindful that generally children have an altruistic approach, something Tomasello, Skyrms, Spelke and Chasman (2009) also propose. Therefore, perhaps the level of interest was just the children being polite, indeed, is a 20-minute chat enough to spark a change or to ignite a passion when each stage of TTM can take months to move through? Ideally, follow-up sessions could be held with the children to ensure that the topic remains fresh. The future sessions could be a vehicle for the young people to further share their experiences, celebrate their successes and provide motivation to develop, enhance esteem and show belonging as proposed by Maslow (1943) in his hierarchy of needs. From the action taken it is difficult to make a judgement on whether a changed has occurred, it is certainly very difficult at this stage to measure success. However, since the initial presentation I have been approached by parents who have said that their child has become more aware of littering and indeed have taken it upon themselves to independently pick up pieces of litter when out in their community. This feedback indicates that stage 4 of the TTM has been achieved. Perhaps therefore, a real change, albeit small, has occurred.

References

Asch, S.E. (1951) Effects of group pressure upon the modification and distortion of judgment (57-72). In, Guetzkow, H. (Ed.) *Groups, Leadership and Men*. Carnegie Press, Pittsburgh (PA) USA.

Adams, J. and White, M. (2004) Why don't stage-based activity promotion interventions work? *Health Education Research*, 20, 2, 237-243.

Bandura, A. (1977) *Social Learning Theory*. Prentice Hall, Englewood Cliffs (NJ) USA.

Bandura, A. (1986) *Social foundations of thought and action: A social cognitive theory*. Prentice Hall, Englewood Cliffs (NJ) USA.

Campbell, F. (2007) *People Who Litter*. Environmental Campaigns Ltd (ENCAMS), Wigan, UK.

Clean Neighbourhoods and Environment Act 2005. [online]. Available at: https://legislation.gov.uk/ukpga/2005/16/contents (Accessed on 31st December 2020).

Cooper, G. (1998) *Outdoors with young people: a leader's guide to outdoor activities, the environment and sustainability*. Russell House, Lyme Regis.

Coward, R. (2018) *Telling litterers to change is a waste of time. Here's another solution*. The Guardian posted 29th March [online]. Available at: https://www.theguardian.com/commentisfree/2018/mar/29/litterers-wont-change-litter-zero-waste-national-strategy (Accessed 3rd January 2020).

Department for Environment, Food and Rural Affairs (2006) *Code of Practice on Litter and Refuse*. DEFRA Publications, London.

Department of the Environment (1991) Environmental Protection Act 1990: Code of Practice on Litter and Refuse. HMSO, London.

Environmental Protection Act 1990. [online]. Available at: https://legislation.gov.uk/ukpga/1990/43/contents (Accessed 31st December 2022).

Geller, E.S. (1995) Actively caring for the environment: an integration of behaviourism and humanism. *Environment and Behaviour*, 27, 2, 184-195.

Gray, L. (2010) *Bill Bryson warns litter is 'trashing' Britain*. The Telegraph posted on 24th March [online]. Available at: https://www.telegraph.co.uk/news/earth/environment/climatechange/7506107/Bill-Bryson-warns-litter-is-trashing-Britain.html (Accessed 5th January 2022).

Jarratt, D. (2015) Sense of place at a British coastal resort: Exploring 'seasideness' in Morecambe. *Tourism: An International Interdisciplinary Journal*, 63, 3, 351-363.

Madhani, J.T., Dawes, L.A. and Brown, R.J. (2009) A perspective of littering attitudes in Australia. *The Environmental Engineer*, 9, 4, 13-20.

Martin, B., Breunig, M., Wagstaff, M. and Goldenberg, M. (2017) *Outdoor Leadership Theory and Practice* (2nd ed.). Human Kinetics, Champaign (IL) USA.

Maslow, A.H. (1943) A theory of human motivation. *Psychological Review*. 50, 4, 370-96.

Maynard, L. and Stuart, K. (2018) *Promoting young people's wellbeing through empowerment and agency: a critical framework for practice*. Routledge, Abingdon.

Our Blue Planet. Blue Planet II. British Broadcasting Corporation. London. 10th December 2017.

Prasetio, Y.L., Rambito, S., Yudhistira, A., Aulia, S.F. and Chowanda, A. (2018) Teaching social critique to adults with a desktop horror myth game. *Procedia Computer Science*, 135, 624-631.

Prochaska, J.O., DiClemente, C.C. (1983) Stages and processes of self-change of smoking: toward an integrative model of change. *Journal of Consulting and Clinical Psychology*, 51, 3, 390-395.

Prochaska, J.O., DiClemente, C.C. and Norcross J.C. (1992) In search of how people change: applications to the addictive behaviors. *American Psychologist*, 47, 1102-1114.

Priest, S. and Gass, M. (2018) *Effective Leadership in Adventure Programming* (3rd ed.). Human Kinetics, Champaign (IL), USA.

Roper, S. and Parker, C. (2008) The rubbish of marketing. *Journal of Marketing Management*, 24, 9-10, 881-892.

Shook, J. (2010) *How to change a culture: lessons from NUMMI*. MIT Sloan Management Review, 51, 2, 63-68.

Tomasello, M., Skyrms, B., Spelke, E.S. and Chasman, D. (2009) *Why We Cooperate*. MIT Press, Cambridge (MA) USA.

Williams, E., Curnow, R. and Streker, P. (1997) *Understanding littering behaviour in Australia: A community change consultants report prepared for the Beverage Industry Environment Council*. Beverage Industry Environment Council, Sydney, NSW (Australia).

Ethics statement: This research was conducted with ethical approval from the University of Central Lancashire.

JQRSS Author Profiles

Jez Welch[1] graduated in 2020 with BA (Hons) in Outdoor Adventure Leadership and currently works at the University of Central Lancashire where he is an Outdoor Instructor supporting the BA Outdoor Adventure Leadership programme. In 2021 he commenced to postgraduate studies on a PhD registered at UCLan. His research aims to investigate the socio-cultural phenomenon of littering with regard to social responsibility, citizenship, environmental impacts and care, generating an understanding about littering habits and attitude for positive behaviour change. Email: jjwelch@uclan.ac.uk

Clive Palmer[2] is a research supervisor in the School of Sport and Health and a doctoral education lead in the Graduate Research School for the University of Central Lancashire. https://orcid.org/0000-0001-9925-2811 Email: capalmer@uclan.ac.uk

Joe Pryle[3] is an Academic Coach within the School of Sport and Health Sciences. His PhD completed in 2020, was on the socio-cultural phenomena of cricket in California, USA.

Carmen Byrne[4] completed her PhD in 2019 specialising in narrative research promoting co-productive working to inform changes to systems and services linked to health and wellbeing.

Reviewer Comments

While closely examining the issues of littering, what comes through in this paper is genuine concern for the issue, and that it is not simply an academic exercise for the lead author. As a teacher, what I found commendable was that he highlights the issue of littering and seeks to influence change. He does this by becoming personally involved and leading the group of children by example. He helped the children understand that there was a need to act and through the presentation and discussion he equipped them with knowledge on how to act. If we are to support children into environmental stewardship, the need to be connected to the planet and then understanding ways to correct it, is essential. His thoughtful analysis of what the litter included, where it was and when it was occurring to fully understand 'who' was actually littering, was comprehensive and persuasive. To analyse why the littering was occurring, the wide reading undertaken and the use of social media to garner opinion seems to set the scene and lead the reader into the space the author has created to base his further research around primary data. The author's final comment about change strongly resonated with me. After several decades in teaching, real positive change, however small, should always be celebrated.

Jez Welch (2023) *Litter: an impact study into this socio-cultural phenomenon and environmental problem –imperatives for outdoor educators.* IOL Northwest conference: Institute of Outdoor Learning, University of Cumbria, Ambleside, Friday 27th January.

Stringer, J. and Owen, A. (2023) Young gym goers experiences of online fitspiration:
a thematic analysis. *Journal of Qualitative Research in Sports Studies*, 17, 1, 15-26

Young gym goers experiences of online fitspiration: a thematic analysis

Jordana Stringer and Alison Owen

(Staffordshire University)

Keywords: *fitness, gym, social media, appearance, qualitative, interviews*

Abstract

The aim of this research was to look at people's first-hand experiences with Fitspiration, a social media movement started to encourage fitness, and for people to share and create fitness related content. Five participants (three male and two female) who identified as regular gym goers, were interviewed about their individual experiences with the gym and Fitspiration. Thematic analysis was used to fully gain insight into the responses given. Overall, the findings of this research concluded that Fitspiration does have many positives, including motivating people to improve their fitness, and providing them with learning advice, alongside some more negative and risky impacts, such as making participants feel pressured or more negative about their appearance or fitness progress. The implications of this research highlight that Fitspiration can have both positive and negative impacts on gym goers, but further research is needed to investigate how Fitspiration can impact other groups of people, for example older adults.

Introduction

The term Fitspiration has been developed over recent years (Carrotte *et al.,* 2017), with its main premise being to encourage fitness, and for people to share and create fitness related content (DiBisceglie and Arigo, 2021). Overall, Fitspiration promotes health and well-being through the promotion of healthy eating, exercise and self-care, and the overall philosophy is one which emphasises strength and empowerment (Tiggemann and Zaccardo, 2018). Tiggemann and Zaccardo (2015) suggest that Fitspiration has been put forward as a healthy antidote to another Internet-based trend known as 'Thinspiration', a trend which consists of social media content of emaciated people and accompanying text designed to inspire viewers to lose weight and promote an eating disorder lifestyle. Over recent years Fitspiration has become increasingly popular, with anyone being able to post fitness related content on social media, including people who may not have any relevant experience in the area (Easton *et al.,* 2018).

Tiggemann and Zagardo (2018) carried out a content analysis of Fitspiration imagery on the social networking site Instagram. The site was searched for any

JQRSS Article No: 2/9-17-1-2023-UG[41]-163
ISSN: 1754-2375 [print] ISSN: 2755-5240 [online]
Web: https://uclan.academia.edu/ClivePalmer/Journal-of-Qualitative-Research-in-Sports-Studies

image marked with the 'Fitspiration' hashtag, and the authors coded the first 600 images identified in their search, for body type, activity, objectification and textual elements. The authors found that the majority of images were of people (63.7%), followed by food (19.0%), and other (17.3%). Of the food images, most (91.2%) were of healthy food items, such as fruit smoothies or protein shakes. Images categorized as 'other' were mostly backgrounds (plain or patterned) for quotations (41.4%), followed by statistics (14.4%), and pictures of gym equipment (11.5%) or exercise clothing (8.7%). The authors found that in the photos of people, the majority of images were of women (67.3%). They found that the majority of women featured in the Fitspiration posts were thin (75.2%) and had a visible level of muscle tone (56.2%). For men, the majority were of an average build (98.6%) and most had a high level of muscularity (60.0%).

There have been a number of pieces of research conducted that have looked at Fitspiration content and its impact on people. Prichard *et al.,* (2020) carried out a study with 108 women, aged 17–25 years, who were randomly assigned to view either Fitspiration images or images of travel. They found that exposure to the Fitspiration images led to significantly higher negative mood and body dissatisfaction, compared to the participants who had viewed the travel images. They found there was no difference in actual exercise behaviour according to image type, however, participants who had exercised following exposure to the Fitspiration images, were significantly more likely to report higher subjective exertion ratings. Fioravantina *et al.,* (2021) carried out a similar design, with 442 female undergraduate students, who were randomly exposed to view either Fitspiration or travel Instagram images and found that viewing Fitspiration models on Instagram was more likely to lower self-perceived sexual attractiveness among the participants than if they had viewed the travel images.

In terms of qualitative research that has explored Fitspiration, a piece of work was carried out by Easton *et al.,* (2018). The researchers carried out interviews and focus groups with 20 young adults who declared themselves to be Fitspiration followers. They found that following Fitspirational posts on social media can provide young people with knowledge and motivation that may support healthy lifestyle behaviours. However, they also reported that a range of harms also appeared to arise from viewing Fitspiration, ranging from minor annoyances and frustrations, to deeper negative effects on peoples' psychological and physical health. The authors advised that further research should be carried out to confirm the scale and intensity of positive and negative effects of Fitspiration.

There has been a mixture of reports as to whether the impact of Fitspiration is positive or negative, with some identifying the beneficial aspects, but others reporting on the negative impacts on viewers overall wellbeing (Raggatt *et al.,* 2018).

The aim of this project was to look further at peoples' experiences, understanding and interactions with Fitspiration. It was decided to focus on a specific group of people, in this case young gym goers, so we could focus on the experiences of one particular group, and how they talked about and felt about Fitspiration. With previous research indicating a range of both and positive negative impacts around Fitspiration, the aim of this research was to help understand more about how people feel about Fitspiration.

Method

Participants: Five university student participants (two female, three male) aged 19-23 were recruited. Participants were chosen based on their experiences with Fitspiration on social media and how active they were at the gym. Due to the potentially sensitive nature of the research, there were some exclusion criteria set in place for potential participants. These included issues regarding mental health in relation to body image, including previous diagnosis of body dysmorphia and previous or current eating disorders.

Procedure: Before the research was conducted, ethical approval was gained from the University Ethics committee. All participants were recruited through word of mouth, and got in contact with the researcher prior to the session, to arrange a time suitable for the interview to take place. Once a time had been organised, the participants were sent an information sheet and consent form via email, to read through and sign before the interview took place, informing them of the inclusion and exclusion criteria of the study, for example ensuring they were regular gym goers, and that they did not have issues with body image.

Four of the interviews took place in person, on the University campus, and one was conducted through Microsoft teams. When conducting the interview, the researcher made sure the interviewee was comfortable and ready to begin, and had read and filled out all the relevant documentation. The sessions were recorded on a recording device. The researcher had their questions set in front of them as a guide for the semi-structured interview. The interview schedule was designed to ensure participants were able to open up fully about their experiences of Fitspiration and included questions such as 'Have you heard of Fitspiration?', 'What does the term mean to you?' and 'Do you follow or look at things considered under the Fitspiration category on social media?'. Once all of the questions had been answered, each interviewee was given the chance to add anything else that they did not feel had been covered in the rest of the interview, and once the interview concluded, the recording was stopped. A debrief form was then emailed over to the participant to read through, which included any helplines they could potentially contact if needed regarding body image and mental health issues.

Analysis

The data were analysed using inductive thematic analysis, which is a method for identifying, analysing and reporting patterns within data, using the guidelines of Braun and Clarke (2006, 2013, 2021). A realist theoretical approach was taken for analysis, with the researcher treating participants responses as a reflection of reality in terms of their knowledge and awareness of the topic. Four main themes were identified from the transcripts. These were: Why Fitspiration? Positive Aspects of Fitspiration, Negative Aspects of Fitspiration and Managing Content. Each of these themes are discussed below, with quotes to help understand the participants thoughts and feelings.

Theme 1: 'It gives me a reason, a goal to hit': why fitspiration?

Participants all reported using Fitspiration and viewing content aimed at inspiring fitness. Participants reported a number of varied reasons as to why they viewed Fitspiration, with one of the major reasons being for motivation:

I use it mainly for like motivation. (Ellie)

Seeing somebody that's bigger than you...it's not a jealousy thing, it's motivation. (Daniel)

It gives me a reason, a goal to hit, gives me motivation to go to the gym in the first place. (Aaron)

As seen above, the participants explicitly reported that seeing Fitspiration content helped with motivation, and giving them a push to go to the gym, or work towards particular goals. Participants also reported viewing Fitspiration so that they could see content from professionals, for example personal trainers or nutritionists, who they felt had good knowledge and scientific background in their content:

He posts videos...er- that have got scientific research behind them, and he shows all the research on...building bigger biceps or like certain body parts and how you should plan your week out erm...in the gym. (Daniel)

I prefer the professionals because you've got actual...scientific in- like study behind it to prove that what they're saying isn't just a load of rubbish. (Daniel)

The use of 'scientific research' or 'scientific study' in posts gave reassurance to these participants as there is a clear explanation as to where the information has come from, as opposed to laypeople without training, who are just posting their personal thoughts and experiences.

All of the participants expressed that another reason they used Fitspiration was that they felt that viewing content could help them in improving their fitness, in terms of teaching them things they did not know before. One of the factors participants discussed was that content was useful in showing them how to do things at the gym, for example using machines, how to avoid injury etc.

You see videos of injuries, for example, but then it's saying how to avoid these so then again, injuries are still a positive outlook because then it's telling you what not to do as well. (Daniel)

It's more just how to do exercises properly, rather than – so you don't hurt yourself or anything like that. (Ben)

The posting of injuries could be a source of deterrence for some viewers, however, it appears that the explanation of how to avoid them offers a sense of reassurance and learning for those viewing it, which enhances the positive role Fitspiration can play in the development of fitness. For Cora, not only did Fitspiration help her learn what to do at the gym, it also helped her create a more positive mindset of her progress:

You can look at the things that can help you get there online, rather than things that are saying where you should be. (Cora)

For the participants, there were a variety of different reasons that they viewed Fitspiration content on social media platforms, including for motivation, and for teaching them about fitness and equipment. The next theme talks about what positives people felt that they got from viewing Fitspiration.

Theme 2: 'It allows me to see that everybody's different': positive aspects of fitspiration

As seen in the previous theme, participants did feel that Fitspiration was something that motivated them and taught them things to help in their fitness journey. This theme covered how participants felt that Fitspiration was something that was positive, and made them feel good about their body image, as well as helping them set realistic goals. Participants discussed that a lot of the Fitspiration content that they viewed was from 'realistic' content creators, who were showing people in realistic poses and lighting, as opposed to the more professional photos you might see in fitness magazines, for example:

A lot of the accounts I follow show like, realistic poses and what people actually look like when they're at the gym as opposed to...under professional lighting ... I prefer to look at the content I would deem to be more authentic. (Ellie)

This suggests that for these participants, 'realistic' and 'authentic' images were preferable, as they were able to see the positives and negatives of a gym experience, rather than place an idea that everything needs to be perfect. Cora also talked about this, and touched upon how viewing Fitspiration posted by people with 'natural bodies' helped with her motivation and inspiration:

The truer side of the gym or like a lot of body positive ... erm ... videos and stuff like that ... the natural bodies, for example, like or like the rolls... and the cellulite ... but they're going to the gym anyways ... showing that it's okay to go to the gym and be a bigger girl. (Cora)

Again, Ellie talked about how seeing content showing peoples imperfections helped her body image, helping her to see that everyone's bodies were different:

It allows me to see that everybody's different and everybody actually ... has their flaws and er imperfections because it shows the more er imperfections because it shows the more erm like real side ... so yeah I suppose it's had a good impact on me. (Ellie)

Cora also commented on the honesty posted about lifestyles surrounding the gym, as well as what can be done in the gym:

Majority of people don't wake up at 6am ... they wake up at 12 o clock and they feel like crap ... but they bring themselves to the gym anyway and come out of it feeling better ... to me that's the positive, the social media aspect of it ... I've seen the other side of it, which is more realistic, which related to me. (Cora)

These mentions of the more 'lifestyle' themed Fitspiration posts, still highlighted the need for a more realistic element of social media, bringing in the more human side for viewers, for example, understanding people's mental health issues but still showing them ways to keep active.

Theme 3: 'Why don't I look like that?': negative aspects of fitspiration

Despite the participants talking about the positives of Fitspiration, for example feeling inspired and motivated to get fitter, and learning how to use equipment correctly, there were also a number of negatives, which could be a cause for concern. One of the negative results of viewing Fitspiration revealed within this research was the participants comparing themselves to what they see online and how this could negatively impact mental health. For example, Aaron said:

It might... sort of tarnish how you feel about yourself a little bit...just because... I don't look like that yet. (Aaron)

From comments such as this, it can be inferred that even though positive comparisons help aid in the motivation to work out more, there are also negative consequences, in which comparisons may go too far and can counteract the beneficial information received. This particular aspect of comparisons was noted again by Aaron who said:

Let's say I look better than somebody, but he can lift more than me ... I'll probably be sat there thinking ... why? Like why is he stronger than me when he's been going for less time? (Aaron)

For Aaron, it can be understood that as his fitness journey continued, and his goals may change, his mentality was to still find things that can be comparable, and question why he is not achieving the same results as other people. The participants all expressed feelings of comparisons to the Fitspiration images that they saw online of people, leading to doubts about their own fitness journey or appearance.

Another more worrying aspect of online Fitspiration that was discussed by the participants was the use of steroids, with all participants mentioning the use of steroids.

I don't wanna ever go on steroids I-I don't plan to I don't think I ever will. (Aaron)

I don't take creatine and stuff like that because, m-mostly because I'm ... not knowledgeable of how it works or what it does or the side effects, so I don't bother. (Ben)

Participants talked about seeing Fitspiration posts where people were visibly using steroids, for example:

There's definitely been times where I've look at it too much and I've seen images of women who are, clearly, on steroids ... and it's err it is I-it's uncomfortable because you don't know ... whether they are whether they aren't so ... to you it's creating a false image like 'aw why don't I look like that? (Ellie)

You have to mitigate the problematic side of it, that, you know, like I've said the steroids, you know, not giving the whole picture just tr-posting a transformation like it happened overnight. (Ellie)

It is good that participants such as Ellie, were able to look at an image and acknowledge that even if a person has not openly reported using steroids, it is possible that they may have done, rather than just looking at the images and presuming that people had got there through diet and exercise alone, but obviously it could be that not all viewers of these Fitspiration images would make this association. The participants talked about the negative impacts of social media and Fitspiration content on body image, both their own and other peoples, for example Cora discussed body dysmorphia, a mental health condition where a person spends a lot of time worrying about flaws in their appearance (NHS, 2023):

I think a lot of people I- evidently struggle, like I mean like... I think especially on the internet and because of social media, like body dysmorphia, mental health, like eating disorders. (Cora)

A lot of body dysmorphia ... a lot of ... feeling like I wasn't good enough, in like I could never get there, like even if I did lose weight and even if I did gain muscle, it was never gonna be enough. (Cora)

Interestingly, despite all of the participants reporting that Fitspiration content helped motivate them towards achieving their fitness goals, there was also a sense of the opposite happening at times. For example, Ellie talked about self-doubt, and feeling demotivated at times:

So ... to you it's like creating this false image like 'aw, why don't I look like that?'... so you start questioning yourself and yeah you can get down about it, you can get demotivated about it. (Ellie)

The aim of Fitspiration posts is mainly to help motivate and encourage people to keep up with fit and healthy lifestyles, so for the participants to report that at times they feel demotivated and 'down' about viewing images online, is definitely something negative, that is not helping people in their fitness journeys.

Theme 4: Managing content

As seen above, alongside the positives of viewing Fitspiration content, the participants also reported negatives. Fortunately, alongside the negatives, participants also reported having methods of dealing with viewing content, to help with possible negative interactions. One way that participants reported dealing with viewing their content was by limiting their exposure to it, and acknowledging when it is time to stop, for example:

I think it's more of a matter of how ... good you feel about yourself and like your ability to like stop your exposure to that content when you know ... it's a ... necessary ... for like your own mental health' ... 'Now I'm just very careful of what I look at and how long I look at social media for. (Ellie)

Another way that all of the participants mentioned was the filtering out of content that they did not want to see, for example Ben talked about filtering out the more negative content that he viewed on social media:

I actively filter out the bad things. (Ben)

Aaron talked about social media filtering out steroid users on his homepage on the social media platform TikTok, so that he only sees 'naturals', i.e., those who do not use performance enhancing drugs:

'I think that social medias' narrowed it down a bit so all of the naturals are on my For You Page sort of thing, you know what I mean' (Aaron)

All participants talked about how after many months or even years of viewing Fitspiration content, they had managed to formulate posts that they prefer to see. Cora talked about how filtering the posts to seeing ones that she wanted to, had helped her:

Social media's definitely affected me, like obviously I have my own mindset and my own struggles within myself, but s- on my off days or even on my good days, seeing some things on social media before I really started filtering it down to what I wanted to see, with like the algorithms and stuff I- it impacted me. (Cora)

The participants all seemed to have an understanding of the negative impact that some social media posts could have on them and had actively taken their time to understand this and look at methods of reducing that negative impact. It appeared that for these participants, the filtering out of more negative Fitspiration is what allowed them to have a more enjoyable and motivating experience when viewing the content.

Discussion

The main aim of this research was to understand young gym goers' experiences of Fitspiration, and their thoughts and feelings about the topic. Overall, it seems that for these participants, there were both positive and negative impacts around Fitspiration. Fitspiration allowed them to feel motivated, as well as teaching them things about health and fitness, for example the correct ways of using gym equipment. However, the participants also reported feeling more negative impacts from Fitspiration content, for example in terms of social comparisons, and feeling demotivated after comparing themselves to other people, and seeing slower progress.

In terms of the positive findings from this research, the participants' feelings about how Fitspiration provided them with a good deal of motivation and knowledge, the findings back up those by Easton *et al.,* (2018) who found that following Fitspirational posts on social media can provide young people with knowledge and motivation that may support healthy lifestyle behaviours. These findings do suggest that Fitspiration may be a useful tool, if used correctly and with appropriate experts, to teach people about different health and fitness routines, as well as teaching them more practical lessons such as how to correctly use equipment in gyms and sports venues.

One of the things participants talked about was that they enjoyed Fitspiration content because it used 'realistic' and 'authentic' images, and they were able to see the positives and negatives of a gym experience, rather than have an idea that everything needed to be 'perfect'. A previous study conducted by Steen (2022) found that there was no correlation between body dissatisfaction and edited or realistic photos. This differs from the findings in this current study as the use of realistic images, in relation to Fitspiration, was preferred by participants, as it allowed them to feel more included and accepted regardless of their body image and gym skills.

In terms of the negatives of viewing Fitspiration images, participants reported that viewing other people could lead them to feeling demotivated, as they were comparing themselves to other people, and felt down about not looking like they did. Body image has been researched greatly in relation to Social Comparison theory, which was conceptualized by Festinger (1958) and attempts to explain that comparisons to others form part of everyday life and people's opinions of themselves are evaluated from this. Previous research backs up the findings related to comparisons in the current study. Fardouly and Diedrichs (2020) looked at societal demands regarding body image and the presentation of bodies online that many people are witnessing, comparing themselves to and internalizing these unrealistic standards on beauty, and suggest that these ultimately cause low mood and low body image. This is further recognised within the research of Pryde and Prichard (2022) who found that viewing 'fitspiration' on TikTok contributes to negative moods and comparisons of appearance.

The participants also discussed viewing steroids on Fitspiration posts, both openly, alongside people who did not explicitly report using steroids to gain their physique, but that the participants felt possibly were using them. Previous research has found that those who lack knowledge on the subject of steroids, usually younger people, are much more affected by the images of anabolic androgenic steroids that are posted on social media (Cox *et al.,* 2023). This is worrying, as it was something that the participants were encountering fairly often and is something that needs to be looked into in the future, for example by the social media regulators and platforms. The fact that on posts, it is not made clear whether someone is on steroids or not, and there is no necessity for them to be open about this, and could lie about how they've gained their physique, is definitely a criticism of social media posts about fitness, however a positive does seem to be that for these participants, they were able to look at an image and acknowledge that even if a person has not openly reported using steroids, it is possible that they have done.

One good thing to hear from the participants is that they all reported actively managing both the time they spent viewing Fitspiration content, and the posts that they saw, by filtering outposts that did not appeal to them, or made them feel negative about themselves or their bodies, for example through the filtering out of posts where people were using performance enhancing drugs. There has been some research on systems that filter posts according to a responders' patterns (Athira and Thampi, 2018), but it is good to see that some viewers of Fitspiration content do take steps to actively filter out the posts themselves, alongside managing the time spent viewing content.

Limitations and suggestions for future research

This study looked at the views of five participants, in a limited age range. It would be useful in future to carry out work in different groups of people, for example older gymgoers and sportspeople, and how they use Fitspiration, and how they feel it impacts them. Further research would also be interesting to look at the differences between those that have just started their gym training and are beginning to see Fitspiration posts, and other gym content online, and those that have been active for a long time, and see how they speak about Fitspiration and how it motivates them. All participants had experience in viewing content related to steroid use online. Further research could investigate the impact steroid users have on viewers when they witness it online, whether it can lead to more steroid use or deter people from using them.

Conclusion

In conclusion, the findings of this research suggest that used as a tool for motivating and educating, Fitspiration can be something that is used by gym goers to help them on their health and fitness journeys. It is a tool that can be used to help peoples' body image, for example through viewing images of people with 'realistic' bodies, as opposed to the more airbrushed and perfected images they see in fitness magazines. However, there are some possible negatives to viewing Fitspiration content online, for example in terms of questioning why they are not getting the same results as other people they are viewing online. Further research needs to be carried out to explore the impact of Fitspiration further, for example in different age groups, and in people at different levels of sport and fitness.

References

Braun, V. and Clarke, V. (2013) *Successful Qualitative Research: A Practical Guide for Beginners.* London: Sage.

Braun, V. and Clarke, V. (2021) *Thematic Analysis: A Practical Guide.* Sage, London.

Braun, V. and Clarke, V. (2006) Using thematic analysis in psychology. *Qualitative Research in Psychology*, 3, 1, 77–101.

Carrotte, E., Prichard, I., Megan, and Lim, S. (2017) 'Fitspiration' on social media: a content analysis of gendered images. *Journal of Medical Internet Research*, 19, 3, March.

Cox, L., Gibbs, N. and Turnock, L.A. (2023) Emerging anabolic androgenic steroid markets; the prominence of social media. *Drugs: Education, Prevention and Policy*, 1-14.

DiBisceglie, S. and Arigo, D. (2019) Perceptions of #Fitspiration activity on Instagram: Patterns of use, response, and preferences among fitstagrammers and followers. *Journal of Health Psychology*, 26, 8, 1206-1220.

Easton, S., Morton, K., Tappy, Z., Francis, D. and Dennison, L. (2018) Young people's experiences of viewing the fitspiration social media trend: qualitative study. *Journal of Medical Internet Research*, 20, 6, e219.

Fardouly, J., Kakar, V. and Diedrichs, P.C. (2020) Body image and global media (Chapter 10, pp:146-170). In, Goins, M.N., McAlister, J.F. and Alexander, B.K. (Eds.) *The Routledge Handbook of Gender and Communication*. Routledge, Abingdon.

Fioravanti, G., Tonioni, C. *and* Casale, S. (2021) Fitspiration on Instagram: The effects of fitness-related images on women's self-perceived sexual attractiveness. *Scandinavian Journal of Psychology*, 62, 5, 746-751.

Katebi, V. M. (2022) *Understanding how message features of fitspiration posts affect body image perceptions and exercise intentions* (PhD Thesis, University of Georgia).

Kirvesmäki, I. (2021) *The elements of health and fitness influencers' credibility on social media* Doctoral Thesis, Aalto University, Finland [online]. Available at: https://aaltodoc.aalto.fi/handle/123456789/111686 (accessed 15.07.2023)

NHS (2023) *Body dysmorphic disorder* (BDD) NHS [online]. Available at: https://www.nhs.uk/mental-health/conditions/body-dysmorphia/ (accessed 15.07.2023).

Prichard, I., Kavanagh, E., Mulgrew, K.E., Lim, M.S.C. and Tiggemann, M. (2020) The effect of Instagram #fitspiration images on young women's mood, body image, and exercise behaviour. *Body Image*, 33, 1–6.

Pryde, S. *and* Prichard, I. (2022) TikTok on the clock but the #fitspo don't stop: The impact of TikTok Fitspiration videos on women's body image concerns. *Body Image*, 43, 244–252.

Raggatt, M., Wright, C.J.C., Carrotte, E., Jenkinson, R., Mulgrew, K., Prichard, I. and Lim, M.S.C. (2018) 'I aspire to look and feel healthy like the posts convey': engagement with fitness inspiration on social media and perceptions of its influence on health and wellbeing. *BMC Public Health*, 18, #1002,

Schlegel, P., Křehký, A. and Dostálová, R. (2021) Social media fitness challenge: risks and benefits. *Acta Facultatis Educationis Physicae Universitatis Comenianae*, 61, 2, 238-248.

Steen, V. (2022) *Keeping it fit on the gram: fitfluencers and fitspiration (edited vs realistic) on instagram (post vs story) and their influence on men's body dissatisfaction, mediated by the self-objectification theory* [online]. Available at: http://arno.uvt.nl/show.cgi?fid=157573 (15.7.2023)

Tiggemann, *and* Zaccardo, M. (2015) Exercise to be fit, not skinny: The effect of fitspiration imagery on women's body image. *Body Image*, 15, 61–67.

Ethics statement: This research was conducted with ethical approval from Staffordshire University

JQRSS Author Profiles

Jordana Stringer[1]: has a BSc (Hons) in Psychology and Criminology, awarded from Staffordshire University, UK. Her research interest lies in the psychology around gym goers, as well as how this links to criminology, for example the use of performance enhancing drugs.

Alison Owen[2] is a Lecturer in Health Psychology at Staffordshire University, UK. Her main research interests are health promotion and body image. E:alison.owen@staffs.ac.uk https://orcid.org/0000-0002-4436-4055

Reviewer Comments

This paper provides an interesting, practical research account which explores young gymgoers experiences with the social media movement of 'Fitspiration', and its influence upon their wellbeing and fitness engagement. Exercise and a healthy lifestyle have both short, and long-term benefits, not only upon the individual who partakes, but also the pervasive demands faced by National Health Service. Thus, this exploratory research is both timely and imperative. Utilising a 'lived experience' approach, the authors present several positive 'themes', with participants' raw data comments (within the text) providing authenticity as to the benefits of engaging with 'Fitspiration'. However, a cautionary tale is also presented as to the potential pitfalls of such engagement. This paper provides a great insight into the social media movement of 'Fitspiration' and the suggestions for future must be seen as positive step in the promotion of physical and mental wellbeing.

Pywell, S., Palmer, C. and Roddam, H. (2023) Traversing reflexivity in palliative care research: interpreting stress and anxiety. *Journal of Qualitative Research in Sports Studies*, 17, 1, 27-44

Traversing reflexivity in palliative care research: interpreting stress and anxiety

Samantha Pywell, Clive Palmer and Hazel Roddam

(University of Central Lancashire)

Keywords: *Reflexivity, occupational therapy, anxiety, stress, palliative care*

Abstract

This article explains how reflexivity was used in research by an Occupational Therapist (OT) with clinical experience of working with individuals in palliative care. Profession-specific reflections and interpretations of anxiety and stress are explored. An applied example of using 'reflexive triggers' from participants' data is set out, alongside diary entries that navigate the researcher forwards through the project. By means of honest accounting of 'lessons learned' to collect her data, light is shed upon some common concerns by qualitative researchers; such as about contaminating the data, or leading and influencing the participants, or whether sufficient depth of insight is gained by, in this instance, the use of telephone interviews versus (face-to-face) focus groups. The tensions between the OT in palliative care and the academic interests of the doctoral researcher are discussed in this clinical context. The article concludes that there has been a significant shift in interpretation and meaning of language surrounding the practice of OTs with a recommendation that clients' interpretations of anxiety and stress are to be valued.

Introduction

Different understandings of reflexivity

Reflexivity is essential within qualitative research to evidence validity, methodical process and conceptual reasoning, particularly within interpretivist research (Finlay and Gough, 2003; Darawsheh, 2014). Reflexivity is also critical to the audit trail within research, which Lincoln and Guba (1985, cited in Nowell *et al.,* 2017), and Finlay and Gough (2003:ix), defined as, 'being reflexive is to bend back upon oneself' complementing Etherington's (2004:19) interpretation of reflexivity:

> To be reflexive we need to be aware of our personal responses and to be able to make choices about how to use them. We also need to be aware of the personal, social and cultural contexts in which we live and work and to understand how these impact on the ways we interpret the world.

Etherington (2004:32), whose background was also a community OT (similar to my own time as a clinician in the NHS), goes on to explain how researcher reflexivity 'closes the illusory gap between the researcher and researched by viewing

JQRSS Article No: 3/9-17-1-2023-PG[107]-164
ISSN: 1754-2375 [print] ISSN: 2755-5240 [online] Copyright ©: CC-BY-NC-ND
Web: https://uclan.academia.edu/ClivePalmer/Journal-of-Qualitative-Research-in-Sports-Studies

our relationship with participants as one of consultancy and collaboration', which is described as a 'bridge between research and practice that is essential to the argument' (Etherington, 2004:31). Although the broad use of reflexivity is well documented, the styles differ between Etherington (2004) and Finlay and Gough (2003). In Finlay and Gough's work (2003) they separate reflexivity into core tasks, one of which is to explore the reflexive triggers which influence one's research. It is these triggers I experimented with in my research, to demonstrate the connections between the transparency of the researcher (in terms of my influence and actions), and how this shaped my doctoral research with my supervisors acting as critical friends (Pywell, Roddam, Milston, Archer, 2017).

The researcher's journey can be framed in a variety of ways. Smith (2006:209) recommends use of both the 'realist' and 'confessional' approaches specific to OTs to maximise reflexivity and not unnecessarily expose, but constructively account for the researcher's decisions and choices throughout their research. Both approaches are valid, as only utilising a realist approach could be considered reductionist which limits the potential for reflexivity to excavate deeper understanding when used to its full potential (Conneeley, 2002:187). It was through 'bracketing', as described by Finlay (2011:23) that I was able to start 'pushing aside our habitual ways of perceiving the world'. In my doctoral research on anxiety and stress in the context of meaningful activities (occupations) and palliative care, I felt this was needed, but it was important to record how I did this and why, to embrace reflexivity and acknowledge potential biases, including cognitive biases, along this research path.

Specific to rigour, Smith (2006:210) argues that reflexivity can 'make the process more auditable, enhancing transparency of informal discussion, to make the research process more visible'. Smith (2006:214) goes on to contextualise researcher reflexivity as being essential to improve the 'quality of qualitative research in health and social care'. Lambert, Jomeen and McSherry (2010) argued the importance of using reflexivity for validation based on their extensive literature review of reflexivity in qualitative research for Midwifery. Unlike Lambert *et al.* (2010), Conneeley (2002) rejects validity within reflexivity as only having a place within quantitative research. However, while opinions are divided, validity is still called for in qualitative research (Taylor, 2017) so evidencing reflexivity, therefore, becomes a critical process within the research journey.

A reflexive journal, as described by Ballinger (2004:542) was used as a method to check for rigour or trustworthiness in qualitative research (Taylor, 2017). Smith (2006:210) successfully argued the purpose of reflexivity is to 'enhance future practice', but also warns us of not *just* walking through the steps of reflexivity, but to be effective with it. The reflexive strategy I used in my research was to complete a reflexive diary, filled with scribbles, drawing, colour and scraps of information I gathered to connect my thoughts on the research and my emotions. This was my interpretivism in action, looking to understand the meaning within (Crotty, 2011). This scrapbook style could be likened to Smith's (2006:212) 'reflective log' and Conneeley's (2002:187) 'field diary'. It was primarily through these notes as diaries that I explored the research, being reflexive about the original reasons for choices and actions I made. This began with reflections on the clients I had worked with who had anxiety and stress, and my 'clinical self', wanting to be a better clinician.

Within clinical practice in the NHS, it was the experience of working with one individual in the community that had greatest impact on me, following a palliative prognosis of Motor Neurone Disease (Bulbar Palsy, a nasty, fast-progressing condition). They had declined speech aids from the speech and language therapist which fuelled part of this research. Their preference was to communicate issues and feelings through email, as speech and writing became physically tiring as the disease progressed. I can understand now that there is an aspect of increased privacy with these forms of communication. Emails have more characters than texting on phones or social media messages but still lack subtle cues and the opportunity to ask questions in a timely manner, unless the OT can respond immediately via a virtual conversation. I reflected upon the words that were used by this client and have wondered over the years if this form of communication was a familiar comfort zone for them, as perhaps used by work, and the communication of emotion was therefore done as if 'in work' format: very punctual, formal and to the point.

My reflections since were on what words were used and what I heard at the time. It is these reflections, complexities and challenges that the OT must rise to in order to facilitate best practice in communication. With clinical reflection, research and reflexivity, I continue to hear and learn more.

Research reflexivity versus clinical reflection

Part of being an effective researcher is to grasp the differences between researcher reflexivity and clinical reflection, and where each has positively contributed to or influenced the other (Finlay and Gough, 2003). Both have a place in research. Etherington (2004) explores the differences between reflection and reflexivity, particularly in Occupational Therapy and counselling, as mere professional reflection may not encompass the many facets of researcher reflexivity. This raw perspective within reflexivity allowed me as a researcher to reflect on my part within the research, to take ownership and perhaps to identify why, if repeated, different researchers doing the same or similar research may have different perspectives. This article is therefore not merely a reflection but an in-depth reflexive stance on my research where I take full responsibility for the consequences of my decisions and actions as they have both added to and helped to develop the research to this level.

From my reflections as a clinical practitioner, anxiety and stress are experienced by many patients, but each experience, and articulation of it, is personal to the patient in the context of their occupations. Anxiety and stress do not restrict themselves solely to the diagnosed. They affect a person's occupations and are rife within palliative care. Anxiety and stress are immensely important to address and require advanced communication skills by the OT to do so. They are complex issues, often intertwined with facets of social, physical, mental and environmental concern and require the OT to look holistically at situations to address these complex and changing problems as the palliative condition progresses. Acknowledging that my clinical experience directly influenced my choice of research topic was an aspect of my reflexivity, for transparency, alongside accounting for my decisions and actions during the research. For instance, another researcher, one without any clinical experience, would likely approach this topic completely differently to me, and they would create their own reflexive account of research activity. Reflexivity, therefore, is the mirror - and the mirror's mirror.

Reflexive triggers

Reflexive triggers, as described by Finlay and Gough (2003), were used to demonstrate validity of the data and transparency of this research process (see figure 1) which contains a selection of participants' responses and researcher's reflexive thoughts. This formed part of the 'audit trail for trustworthiness' (Nowell *et al.*, 2017:3). Reflexive triggers were captured under 'notes' within MAXQDA (software for thematic analysis of transcripts) during coding. Other reflexive triggers were captured within my research diaries. In essence, reflexivity, nebulous by nature, never stops and is only restricted by the researcher's project timeline.

Figure 1. Reflexive triggers: anonymised participant identifiers are P1, P2 etc.

Reflexive trigger	My thoughts
P1: 'I wouldn't directly ask a patient if they were anxious. I would perhaps say, you know, do you think perhaps there is something, you're a little bit frightened about or worried about rather than directly using the word anxious or stressed, because I feel that may limit the response.'	*This was fascinating. The first interview captured in the participants' words, that they wouldn't use the words anxiety or stress and reason why.* *Not every participant framed their reasons in this way but wow, this was a brilliant start.* *The dialogue flowed and at this point. it was where I had some regrets about not being able to ask them more, not having a conversation, but I was at that point of being so fearful of contaminating the data and really wanted to step back and try to be as removed from this as possible and not be seen as asking leading questions or influencing this.* *I could feel my confidence growing as a researcher.*

Reflexive trigger	My thoughts
P2: 'I think everybody has their own version of what they mean by anxiety and stress.'	*This was very clear that common discourses are personal.* *Some of the participant statements were very, very clear on the point of individual interpretation.* *It was these nuances, these bits of information that when you collect them together, like bits of confetti, they become something beautiful.* *It was beautiful to start to see this, and to come back and see the clarified statements by participants.* *It made me proud to be an OT.* *They all communicated this passion for the individual's perspective and the individual's point of view and back to the other interview where they used 'their words'....* *Coming back to this and connecting the dots again I can see this common thread of the strength and value and importance of individual interpretation.* *Additionally, the need to prepare OTs to navigate this and not see the potential interpretations as a negative thing, for there is potential to shy away from this.*
Reflexive trigger	**My thoughts**
P3: 'I think sometimes as healthcare professionals we fall into this trap of erm, er being, of having to deal with other quite highly qualified, well, sort of, highly experienced professionals, and it's quite hard to then sort of come back down to this more sort of, erm, easy to understand language.'	*It made me think of not only how communication changes from being a newly qualified OT, to when you hit ten years in a workplace, to reflecting on what assumptions are made in conversations of emotion and what are the more 'easy to understand' terms and why.* *When I read more, I get a sense that this is connected to aspects of Fricker (2003) and social injustice...* *e.g. where it might, just might, be possible for a type of social injustice to exist.* *That is, where professionals intentionally or unintentionally use language or specific words around anxiety and stress, which did not connect, resonate with the patient and might even have an adverse effect.*

Reflexive trigger	My thoughts
P4: 'I've seen lots of patients experiencing anxiety and stress and that can be related to their breathlessness or coming to terms with the different stages of their palliative illness journey.'	*This was from a Macmillan specialist, again what I heard during and just after the interview was the clinical experience of seeing lots of patients with anxiety and stress was common.*
	They connected this to breathlessness and points in time, or the 'stages of the palliative illness journey'.
	The journey. Not a neat start and finish, but rather an individual journey is still a personal journey. Was I hearing exactly what they said?
	I felt a connection to the participant through the clinical experiences they reported. It felt like I was listening to a colleague in my team.
	Then I pulled back – was I supposed to 'like' some responses and not others in the research?
	How could I remain impartial and without judgement?
	Going back to these thoughts on the research helped connect the pathways of how I got from a to z, resulting in a greater transparency and trustworthiness.
	But was the reality I heard, the actual reality?
	Was I giving true justice to the participants (and the people they had worked with) through this exploration?
	I found myself being less clear than at the start.
Reflexive trigger	**My thoughts**
P5: 'It's kind of a hidden subject, a taboo subject, and many people think of it, you know, if you say anxiety it's a trendy word...'	*I thought this was brilliant. I found this interview really rewarding to listen to.*
	This participant provided many examples of how the meaning and interpretation of anxiety and stress could be different, and they were all things I could relate to.
	I wondered if more people saw and heard these things. Delving into the phrase 'hidden subject' made me look at the theme of invisibility and see multiple phrases across interviews applying to invisibility (the understanding of anxiety and stress as being invisible and the process of connecting meaning being invisible also). This became challenging during the iterations of coding as I built an argument in my head for nearly the entire code structure to fall within invisibility.
	Yet, on reflection, not all the codes fell comfortably within invisibility, and I added more justification and reasoning as to why within coding software.

Reflexive trigger	My thoughts
P6: 'I think worry is again very much a layman's term that people would just think if a patient's worried that's very normal, but when you're getting into the realm of anxiety that's when it's becoming more of a clinical condition.'	*This section of the interview really stuck with me.* *I couldn't believe how clearly the participant had separated the terms. This participant acknowledged working currently in the NHS and I couldn't help but connect my clinical experiences with this. Was there something in the way these terms are used within different health and social care systems? Do they mean different things to different professionals?* *Why is 'worry' not seen by some as an issue?* *From experience this can be how some articulate their emotional connection to the problem, but the problem still really affects their life hence the need to be seen by occupational therapy to unpick these reasons.* *But what is this? Is this my belief changing and affecting my interpretation of this research?* *(Looking back at the end of the research I felt at this point the need to embrace, tackle and go with the potential for political influencers of language, and for that to include the potential use of language within systems.* *This was also the trigger for considering Foucault (2002) and Fairclough's (1989) work, and my experiences from clinical practice.*

Participants and their expectations of contributing to research

Within these diaries and utilising reflexive triggers, I saw other parts of the research differently. To begin with, the basic practicalities of doing, constructing, reporting and analysing the research can be viewed with a wider gaze thanks to reflexivity. Participant consent initially appeared as a very straightforward construct, yet now I see other things, particularly after reading Cohn and Lyons (2003). I was quite emotionally detached from the consent process and did not view it as a problem or with having problems, as I had not observed anyone sign the consent form, these were done on trust. It had not occurred to me until much later that participants knowing I was an OT, and also a postgraduate research 'student' conducting doctoral research, may have put them off consenting or altered their responses.

This is in line with the pragmatics of power and language imbalance (see Grice's principles 1975, in Archer *et al.*, 2012:47) where a speaker may expect a certain kind of response from a listener. As research participants, therefore, they may have assumed professional language was expected from them throughout their responses, as if in a test situation, and this may have altered the language they used - or could have put them off completely from responding. As I was an OT and a researcher, both positions of relative power, I thought being 'detached' (not *leading*) was a good thing (the interviews being conducted by telephone), but I now acknowledge there was a lack of an emotional connection with the participants at the time, which might have otherwise brought about more candid and open responses if conducted face to face. As Wenger (2002:5) discusses in his *Communities of Practice*, 'having a genuine voice can be viewed as something that participants appreciate as it may promote openness in exchanges without necessarily losing professional language'.

The participant role as described in Cohn and Lyons (2003) indicates a symbiotic relationship whereby they may change their responses based on who they think the researcher is and what they think the researcher expects from them. This is a kind of Hawthorne Effect, a sense of 'giving the researcher what they want' attitude from the participant (Sedgwick and Greenwood, 2015). The only expectation I had was to encourage the participants to talk, so I guess when they were unable to answer questions in depth, I felt frustrated as I wanted the content of what they said to analyse. But my frustration was hidden as they couldn't see my facial expressions due telephone interviews. Reflexivity helped me to see the value of focus groups that came later in my research and not being afraid to be among participants and listening to the richness of discussion and debate.

The lone researcher

The 'lone researcher' phenomenon is discussed by authors Etherington (2004) and Creswell (2018) from which I could see positive and negative perspectives of critique about my own research. For example, there are benefits to being part of a larger research team to collect data in different forms to shed light on an issue or topic such as 'patient experience', where employing those with different research specialisms in qualitative and quantitative techniques can be of great benefit. Conversely, as lone researcher, I managed the research design myself and took responsibility for data collection and its interpretation, but all the time accepting the limitations of it being solely my perspective on the data which in turn directed the research as a whole. For these reasons the practice of reflexivity by the researcher is very important, as it is for any research project (however methodologically aligned), helping the researcher to make discoveries from their data, direct their research, supporting their learning and ultimately in this health context, improve the quality of care and provision as a health professional.

'Lone-ness' as a doctoral researcher is a widely acknowledged concept (Tan, 2022; Sibai, Figueiredo and Ferreira, 2019; Cantor, 2020) which, in my case, was more to do with independence to lead my research (Gower, 2021), as I was not alone, and nor did I ever feel alone due to my generous research supervision. Interestingly, Conneeley (2002), although explicit about her reflexivity never wrote in her journal article about being or feeling alone, perhaps as she was also working and researching in the same location. Therefore the idea of the 'lone researcher' could be considered just another interpretation of being involved with self-directed research. Smith and Palmer's (2015; 2021) research discusses being alone or being a lone entity on a mission to explore, which is not the same as loneliness, or being solitary (reclusive), and nor it is not the same as 'seeking solitude' which can often usefully lead to heightened sensory awareness and deeper critical moments in reflection.

Uncomfortable questions on stress and anxiety

Reflexivity techniques helped me to explore the unexplored depths of the data from participants and my responses, given that my reflexivity notes became part of the overall stock of data for the whole project. An uncomfortable question for my professional reflection was, *'How might OTs make their clients' anxiety and stress worse?* In response, Participant 1 indicated that anxiety can be made worse by using the words 'anxiety' and/or 'stress', so I tried to stay clear of using both of those terms when I was with clients. To acknowledge this 'elephant in the room' was uncomfortable, yet, reflection on this perspective was needed to meet their needs.

No single definition of anxiety and stress is all-encompassing for the OT engaged in therapeutic communication with their client. Acknowledgement of this may prevent the assumption that everything is known within a conversation of anxiety and stress. OTs therefore need to reflect upon what may happen and what they need to be mindful of to navigate these interpretations in communication. This reinforces the idea that an individual's interpretation of anxiety and stress is significantly challenging for them as it relates to meaningful activity in palliative care. It is not possible to know how another person will define anxiety and stress or use these words until you ask them, so anything up to that point is an assumption. They may use and define anxiety and stress the same way you do, they may not. Just because you share one interpretation (e.g. anxiety with breathlessness) does not mean all other uses when framed with occupations and palliative care are the same.

When crossing this threshold of understanding, each term, every discussion about 'anxiety' and 'stress' and 'meaningful activity' becomes eye-opening within clinical reflection. Listening to the individual and understanding their meaning and interpretation of anxiety and stress is important to many types of clinical reasoning including narrative storytelling (Gunaratnam and Oliviere, 2009) and pragmatic clinical reasoning (Duncan, 2011). Despite the best of intentions, the semantic interpretation of anxiety and stress can be incorrect through assumptions which lead to misunderstandings (Archer *et al.*, 2012). Added to that, the individual may not stick to a definition either intentionally or unintentionally, depending upon their understanding of the terms. There is, therefore, potential for no single all-encompassing definition of anxiety and stress that suits every individual. This is a paradoxical phenomenon of communicating about anxiety and stress in palliative care for the OT.

By being open to this potential for semantic misunderstanding, OTs may analyse and articulate these nuanced meanings through advanced communication skills (Wilkinson *et al.,* 2008; Turner, Payne and O'Brien, 2011; Brighton and Bristowe, 2016). By asking ourselves what we may have done, or what might have increased a patient's anxiety and/or stress, and what we would do differently are questions to change aspects of our practice, this being a critical piece of the puzzle within reflection by the OT. Thanks to the participants in this research, they have highlighted the potential for multiple interpretations of stress and anxiety which really do matter in clinical practice. It is the voices of experienced OTs connected with the evidence base from participants that confirms Etherington's (2004:32) conclusion that, 'When we enable other people (and ourselves) to give voice to our experience, those voices create a sense of power and authority'.

The transparent (but not invisible) researcher

Absolute transparency of the researcher is said to enhance the reflexivity process (Etherington, 2004). Therefore, to 'contextualise myself' further as Etherington (2004:19) suggests, is to expose my emotions and unmask the researcher. As the researcher who never physically met any of the participants, I was initially invisible to them. However, in this article I hope to demonstrate my transparency as the researcher who was evolving, becoming visible and present in my research through reflexivity. Etherington (2004), although in anecdotal expert voice, has a pervasive argument about the use of 'I' when talking about one's reflexivity. In order to be transparent, but not invisible, I, am therefore going to use I throughout this section to add weight, volume and clarity to my thoughts. This section was surprisingly difficult to write, yet I have asked so many patients to talk about anxiety and stress without ever really considering it a difficult or onerous task in clinical practice. To put myself into this research I wondered how I would answer the questions. 'I', the OT, the researcher, the individual now and the future potential patient are separate individuals, separated by time, space and perspective, individuals who use different terminology. For instance, 'I' the OT would never swear as this would be unprofessional, yet 'I' as a person, a human being when anxious or stressed uses some swear words which I cannot bring myself to type in this article. Such a separation in language demarcates the patient and the professional 'I'.

I used terms included neither in clinical guidance nor in lists of medical definitions. To be honest, there are days where having studied this remit extensively, I still cannot clearly separate my personal definition(s) and use of anxiety and stress in my head – they are too complicated. Retrospective description of emotion is more useful to me, but as time has passed the emotional intensity seems to dilute which I am never quite sure if I can truly capture and explain. This is one example of cognitive bias, fading effect bias, where negative emotions are forgotten more easily than positive ones. Surely, we need to reflect that in some ways, the expectations to clearly define emotional connections to occupation and their impact (when stressed or anxious) could be asking too much at the wrong moment? When, therefore, is the right moment to ask and get the answer? Thanks to this research, I am energised by the thought of 'what is their interpretation?', and 'why didn't they use the term anxiety or stress?' When the term is present, it centres my mind on the client's language preferences in communication of meaningful activities (occupations).

This researcher dilemma, I recorded in my diaries as personal preconceptions and assumptions of anxiety and stress, as Conneeley (2002:185) pointed out, 'before putting pen to paper, I did not realise this [issue] existed'. Without reflexivity I would not have been able to write this. Yet still there is the gap, the gap we know to be between the demand for person-centred care and the realities of working in clinical practice. What anxiety and stress mean for each of us is personal, and at times very private. Mind this gap! The gap is whether we need to experience anxiety and / or stress to feel empathy and communicate successfully with our patients to help them through their journey, or is training enough? Initially within this research, and whilst I was in clinical practice doing this research, I thought the main reason for common discourses and different interpretations around anxiety and stress was negative. I thought this would require quite a straightforward approach to tackle it, which I realise now was mistaken. By using reflexivity, it is very clear now that this research is not the end, it is the beginning of a more sophisticated and complex understanding.

Acknowledging my 'emotional involvement' and how it 'influences the research' (Conneeley, 2002:187) is significant as my roles within the research required demonstrably separate perspectives on emotional constructs. My personal emotional opinion of anxiety and stress is separate to my professional emotional opinion as I can separate the two. Compartmentalisation of these emotions has been essential for me to practice in this context. The emotional opinion I have as a researcher is different again, and in my reflexive notes I explored my feelings about remaining 'detached' and not getting involved with a patient as a community OT would do. Rather, as researcher I was taking a step back to reflect on clinical practice; my experiences and from other qualified OTs, but also I was recognising my ethical role, boundaries and limitations … protecting myself, them and the data.

Cognitive biases (Haselton *et al.,* 2015) align well with reflexivity here, for this is also about my own emotional journey and how this has affected my research. By doing telephone interviews it was possible to maintain a distance from the participants. Conneeley (2002), an OT who used similar data collection methods such as interviews and phenomenology, was explicit about how she used reflexivity to improve transparency of her research, and therefore its trustworthiness and rigour. However, Conneeley (2002) was exposed in her role as the researcher as she worked in the same environment as the participants received treatment and conducted her research, something I had tried to avoid. I have in effect tried to stay somewhat hidden and separate, again through fear of influencing the results too much. Ironically, this behaviour still influences the research. Reflexivity ensures nothing escapes, and observations from all perspectives are identified and pursued.

Concern: data contamination in focus groups

My main concern and reason for not doing focus groups initially was the risk of inadvertently affecting or influencing the language participants used either by my presence or the language I might use. Darawsheh (2014:562) refers to this as 'contamination'. I initially saw this variable as having a negative impact including:

1. Would the group share and use a certain style of language because of their professional peers?

2. Would participants volunteer from a similar employer?

An alternative scenario is where I could have used focus groups, and been a part of the discussion, and revealed my own experiences as I am doing in this article, with the group. Smith (2006:213) describes how, as part of the reflexive process:

> Revealing these tantalising snippets of selected personal information, all one was doing was encouraging the participants to reveal more of themselves and their thoughts.

This is a strong benefit I had not considered about my participation as a researcher in a focus group. I was worried I would influence or 'contaminate' the data through conversation and by my presence, or by accidentally asking leading questions. Perhaps my own voice, as the researcher asking questions over the phone was impersonal somehow, maybe a face-to-face interview with a cup of tea and biscuits may have elicited a different response? The benefits of doing focus groups are now clearer to me, as is being a part of them, revealing some of my thoughts and experiences about my background, or clinical experiences, can add positively to the quality of the research. My voice is both as a researcher and a qualified OT colleague. Through my reflexivity, I now understand my voice too has strength and weight within this research, although some may argue I cannot be my own participant, but I can be present and heard.

Telephone interviews allowed a positive space for participants to articulate their language use without immediate influence from others within a conversation, other than the researcher asking the questions. There are so many variables that would have influenced the participant's use of language leading up to the telephone interview. These include culture, family, religion, spirituality, mood (and affect) to name but a few. Another scenario is where, if repeated, the interviewer could be a different person to the researcher, i.e. there would perhaps be another level of separation between the participant and the researcher. Perception of the influence of an interviewer may have influenced results, as Cohn and Lyons (2003:42 citing Foucault, 1980) point out:

> A 'power reflexive stance' takes reflexivity one step further by asking researchers to consider not only themselves as individuals but to consider the vector of power in all research interactions.

Power dynamics have impacted on this research, as with all research, and are weighty within this topic area as Smith (2006:213) has described, 'the webs of power that circulate within the research process'. This resonates with Conneeley (2002:185) who gave explicit examples of power in research including 'the way the respondents placed me in the research, the information that they chose to give and my subsequent interpretation of the data'. Cohn and Lyons (2003:42) in exploring power in interpretive research for OTs, reiterated the dangers of this power as 'the potential to oppress others, reproduce inequality, or minimise the perspective of others'. Acknowledging these impacts would increase the transparency of the research, particularly with regards to its interpretive nature and its results being derived from a relatively limited number of participants. These insights into power and influence I considered at the start of the research with Fairclough (1989) and Foucault (2002) informing my decisions in relation to the language participants used, that was instigated by me as researcher.

It could be argued that by stating the researcher was an OT in the participant information sheet initiated a power dynamic. Cohn and Lyons (2003) connected this as being a decision about the power a researcher has. However, conversely Smith (2006:214) has suggested that 'confessional tales may expose the nature of the relationship the researcher has with the participant, which may help redress the power balance between the two'. These researcher relationships and power dynamics are influential in communication during interpretive research and therefore require consideration through the phenomenon of reflexivity.

Prioritising interpretations of anxiety and stress: a fault in the system

The different interpretations of anxiety and stress were all important to my research, however, prioritising their importance was a challenge impacting my data analysis i.e. the decisions I had to make about words and phrases to promote or relegate their importance in the research process. Placing these interpretations in a linear scale did not do justice to their inferred meaning simply from the perspective that anxiety and stress may be defined by the individual and their relationship with emotion and occupation at that point in time. To look at an individual's meaning, interpretation and occupational use of the words anxiety and stress is significantly time-consuming to do in detail, which were facets of how demanding the research experience was, captured in my diary entries at the time. However, comprehending the potential impact stemming from insights to different interpretations of anxiety and stress were these strengthening notions of social power. This reflects research on power and ambiguous discourse within macro-systems discussed by Fairclough (1989), Foucault (2002) and Fricker (2003). For example, as a product of Western attitudes to medicine and health care, Benjamin (2012:337) argued that the prevailing medical model was constricting the potential of mental health care:

> The system puts people in boxes, treats them as 'problems to be fixed' and 'ticked from the list'… that is, from a more positivist, objectivist viewpoint, that a Western medicalised model / system adopts.

For individuals not meeting the criteria for support or care, that is, through the assessment of their symptoms they are deemed to be 'stressed' but not 'anxious', or vice versa, is a diagnostic fault within the assessment system where misinterpretations can occur. Fundamentally, the client's need remains: their need to receive Occupational Therapy when they are struggling with emotional challenges impacting their occupations (Cooper, 2013).

Using the term 'patient', 'service user', 'client', or 'individual' is a power discourse within itself (Greenhalgh, 2017). An individual may use different words to describe an event of anxiety and stress at one point in time, within one occupation, using their understanding of the construct of anxiety and stress in their world, which is not incorrect, it is the individual's interpretation and holds value. Deconstructing organisational or formal system definitions of anxiety and stress can create realignment possibilities where the problem is not the individual and the language they use, it's the system, or part of it, which cannot accommodate the individual and their language discourse around anxiety and stress. It is this tension which may be the fault within the system. Formal service criteria terms, official definitions, may be limiting who 'fits the criteria' for care or treatment. If you guide individuals to plan their own care, you empower them. If you remove judgement within the system that anxiety is worse than stress or worry, or vice versa then there is refocus on occupations that are meaningful, promoting open conversations about what is happening, what is important and why. The supportive aim is 'we are going on the therapeutic journey together', led by the individual, not a fault in the system.

Acknowledging the potential existence for different interpretations around anxiety and stress could empower the OT's and the clients' communication by accepting real-world communication that includes individual interpretations and some ambiguous discourses. Yanow and Ybema (2009:39) argued that 'what you see depends on where you stand: perspective is all when it comes to knowing and knowledge'. The reality is that systems are imperfect, and we hold imperfect understandings of our own and others' constructs of anxiety and stress that can be difficult for individuals requiring absolute and definite answers. This imperfect reality also contributes to the potential of ambiguities in communicating about anxiety and stress. Within formal systems, one can argue imperfections in definitions and understandings of anxiety and stress are in themselves, flaws. Therefore, interpretations of anxiety and stress in the context of occupations are not imperfections, but rather individual understandings and perspectives to be valued.

In recent years, communication challenges were exacerbated by the impacts of the COVID-19 pandemic on professional practice, and especially since this research was completed, suffice to say that the clinical world changed significantly due to the pandemic. With face masks hiding spoken and unspoken words, and periods of telehealth (video-calling clients) primarily due to national lockdowns, OTs continued to address client needs around anxiety, stress and occupations in palliative care (Pywell, 2021a). Clinicians anecdotally reported in a workshop at the Royal College of Occupational Therapists (Pywell, 2021b) that conversations had changed due to the increased worries of the pandemic. This made me reflect again on how much had changed during this research, and on what has potential to be a significant 'meaning shift' in communication (Le Fevre, Matheny and Kolt, 2010:726). This meaning shift will have inevitably altered clients' descriptions, interpretations and understandings of their anxiety and stress, indicating that further, ongoing research is a constant necessity.

Conclusion

Through the theory and application of reflexivity contextualised in this research, interpretations of anxiety and stress in palliative care have been explored through an OT's lens. This experimentation with reflexivity has brought to the surface some valuable findings around researcher biases and impacts in this clinical context, especially the accounts of power imbalances and language use or interpretation, that are ever present in socio-cultural research.

The accounts and reflections offered in this article are beacons of how reflexivity can be conducted to guide the researcher through complex situations, focussing in on characteristics of social interaction and researcher decision making, and analysing their influences. We commend that a researcher's qualitative data will be similarly enriched for the consciousness to become reflexive about comparable or related phenomena as they will be rewarded for the effort to observe, record and reflect upon their observations. Finally, we have emphasised the methodological importance of reflexivity in the clinical research process, for the benefit of the researcher, research findings, and ideally an improvement in the patients' experience of receiving care.

References

Archer, D., Wichmann A., Aijmer K. (Eds.) (2012) *Pragmatics: An advanced resource book for students.* Routledge, London.

Ballinger, C. (2004) Writing up rigour: Representing and evaluating good scholarship in qualitative research. *The British Journal of Occupational Therapy*, 67, 12, 540-546.

Benjamin, E. (2012) Humanistic psychology and the mental health worker. *International Journal of Psychology Research*, 7, 5, 337-368.

Brighton, L.J. and Bristowe, K. (2016) Communication in palliative care: talking about the end of life, before the end of life. *Postgraduate Medical Journal*, 92, 1090, 466-470.

Cantor, G. (2020) The loneliness of the long-distance (PhD) researcher. *Psychodynamic Practice*, 26, 1, 56-67.

Cohn, E.S. and Lyons, K.D. (2003) The perils of power in interpretive research. *American Journal of Occupational Therapy*, 57, 1, 40-48.

Cooper, J. (Ed.) (2013) *Occupational therapy in oncology and palliative care.* (2nd ed.). Wiley, England.

Conneeley, A.L. (2002) Methodological issues in qualitative research for the researcher / practitioner. *British Journal of Occupational Therapy*, 65, 4, 185-190.

Crotty, M. (2011) *The foundations of social research: Meaning and perspective in the research process.* Sage, London.

Creswell, J.W. and Creswell J.D. (2018) *Research Design: Qualitative, Quantitative and Mixed Methods Approaches* (5th ed.). Sage, Los Angeles.

Darawsheh, W. (2014) Reflexivity in research: Promoting rigour, reliability and validity in qualitative research. *International Journal of Therapy and Rehabilitation*, 21, 12, 560-568.

Duncan, E.A. (ed.) (2011) *Foundations for Practice in Occupational Therapy.* E-BOOK. Elsevier Health Sciences.

Etherington, K. (2004) *Becoming a reflexive researcher - using ourselves in research.* Jessica Kingsley Publishers, United Kingdom.

Fairclough, N. (1989) *Language and Power.* Longman, London.

Finlay, L. and Gough, B. (2003) *Reflexivity: a practical guide for researchers in health and social sciences.* Oxford: Blackwell Science.

Finlay, L. (2011) *Phenomenology for Therapists: Researching the Lived World.* John Wiley and Sons Inc., West Sussex, England.

Foucault, M. (2002) *The Archaeology of Knowledge.* Routledge, London.

Foucault, M. (1980) cited in Cohn, E.S. and Lyons, K.D. (2003) The perils of power in interpretive research. *American Journal of Occupational Therapy*, 57, 1, 40-48.

Fricker, M. (2003) Epistemic justice and a role for virtue in the politics of knowing. *Metaphilosophy*, 34, 1-2, 154-173.

Gower, O. (2021) *The hidden curriculum in doctoral education* [online]. Available at: https://drhiddencurriculum.wordpress.com/2021/10/28/the-hidden-meanings-of-independent-researcher/ (Accessed 3.11.2023)

Greenhalgh, T. (2017) Citizens (chapter 6 (pp. 99-117). In, Greenhalgh, T. (Ed.) *How to implement evidence-based healthcare.* John Wiley and Sons, West Sussex, England.

Grice, H.P. (1975) Grice's cooperative principle and the conversational maxims (pp.51-66). In, Archer, D., Aijmer K. and Wichmann A. (Eds.) (2012) *Pragmatics: An Advanced Resource Book for Students.* Routledge, Oxon.

Gunaratnam, Y. and Oliviere, D. (2009) *Narrative and stories in health care: illness, dying and bereavement.* Oxford University Press, Oxford, UK.

Habermas, J. (1984) *Theory of communicative action (vol. 1) reason and the rationalization of society.* Beacon Press, Boston, MA.

Haselton, M.G., Nettle, D. and Murray, D.R. (2015) *The evolution of cognitive bias. Part vii. Interfaces with traditional psychology disciplines*. John Wiley and Sons, West Sussex, England.

Lambert, C., Jomeen, J. and McSherry, W. (2010) Reflexivity: A review of the literature in the context of midwifery research. *British Journal of Midwifery,* 18, 5, 321-326.

Le Fevre, M., Matheny, J. and Kolt, G.S. (2003) Eustress, distress, and interpretation in occupational stress. *Journal of Managerial Psychology*, 18, 7, 726-744.

Lincoln, Y. and Guba, E.G. (1985) *Naturalistic Inquiry.* Sage. Newbury Park, CA, USA.

Nowell, L., Norris, J., White, D. and Moules, N. (2017). Thematic analysis: striving to meet trustworthiness criteria. *International Journal of Qualitative Methods*, 16, 1-13.

Pywell, S., Roddam, H., Milston, A. and Archer, D. (2017) Anxiety and stress: Exploration of common discourses influencing occupational therapy practices in palliative care [Abstract]. *British Journal of Occupational Therapy*, 80, 47-47.

Pywell, S. (2021a) *#OTalk. Anxiety and Stress: What words matter to clients?* [online]. Available at: https://otalk.co.uk/2021/01/20/otalk-26th-january-2021-anxiety-and-stress-what-words-matter-to-clients/ (Accessed 26th January 2021).

Pywell, S. (2021b) *Interpretations of anxiety and stress in palliative care*. Presentation to RCOT Royal College of Occupational Therapists Major Health Conditions specialist section, 15th May.

Sedgwick, P. and Greenwood, N. (2015) Understanding the Hawthorne effect. *British Medical Journal,* 351: h4672

Sibai, O., Figueiredo, B. and Ferreira, M.C. (2019) The loneliness of the long-suffering researcher. *Social Science Space* posted 30th January [online]. Available at: https://www.socialsciencespace.com/2019/01/the-loneliness-of-the-long-suffering-researcher/#:~:text=Social%20isolation%20is%20particularly%20common,fulfilling%20experience%20of%20being%20alone. (Accessed 3.11.2023)

Smith, S. (2006) Encouraging the use of reflexivity in the writing up of qualitative research. *International Journal of Therapy and Rehabilitation,* 13, 5, 209-214.

Smith, H. and Palmer, C. (2015) Alone: a study of solo expedition experiences. *Journal of Qualitative Research in Sports Studies*, 9, 1, 21-54.

Smith, H. and Palmer, C. (2021) Self-discovery through the senses (Chapter 19: pp.134-143). In, Palmer, C. (Ed.) *Arts-Based Education in Outdoor Learning*. Sport and Wellbeing Press, Preston, UK.

Tan, J. (2022) *Feeling lonely in research? You're not alone - Opening up about my feelings during my PhD was powerful and cathartic.* Nature: Career column posted 1st September [online]. Available at: https://www.nature.com/articles/d41586-022-02801-w (Accessed 3.11.2023)

Taylor, R.R. (2017) *Kielhofner's Research in Occupational Therapy: Methods of Inquiry for Enhancing Practice*. FA Davis Company, Philadelphia, PA.

Turner, M., Payne, S. and O'Brien, T. (2011) Mandatory communication skills training for cancer and palliative care: Does one size fit all? *European Journal of Oncology Nursing*, 15, 5, 398-403.

Wenger, E. (2002) in McDermott R.A., McDermott, R. and Snyder, W. (Eds.) *Cultivating Communities of Practice: A Guide to Managing Knowledge*. Harvard Business School Press. Boston, Mass.

Wilkinson, S., Perry, R., Blanchard, K. and Linsell, L. (2008) Effectiveness of a three-day communication skills course in changing nurses' communication skills with cancer/palliative care patients: a randomised controlled trial. *Palliative Medicine*, 22, 4, 365-375.

Yanow, D. and Ybema, S. (2009) Interpretivism in Organizational Research: on elephants and blind researchers (chapter 3: pp.39-60). In Buchanan, D. and Bryman, A. (Eds.) *The Sage Handbook of Organizational Research Methods*. Sage, London.

Ethics statement: This research was conducted with ethical approval from the University of Central Lancashire.

JQRSS Author Profiles

Samantha Pywell[1] trained as an Occupational Therapist and has over 18 years' experience across the NHS, social care, Care Quality Commission (CQC) and now in academia. Sam has taught on pre-registration Occupational Therapy courses and is currently the Social Prescribing Unit co-ordinator at the University of Central Lancashire, Preston, UK.

Clive Palmer[2] is a research supervisor in the School of Sport and Health and a Doctoral Education Lead in the Graduate Research School for the University of Central Lancashire. ORCID-ID https://orcid.org/0000-0001-9925-2811 Email: capalmer@uclan.ac.uk

Hazel Roddam[3] is a Speech and Language Therapist (SLT) with 25 years of experience as a clinician and service manager in NHS and Local Authority organizations, prior to joining the Allied Health research unit at University of Central Lancashire in September 2006.

Acknowledgements: Professor Dawn Archer, Dr Anne Milston, Professor Louise Connell, and Dr Heather Stewart.

Reviewer Comments

Reviewer 1: This article, through a structured plan for reflexivity in research, exposes the tension between professional and research roles. It acknowledges and highlights the emotional complexity of working in the palliative care setting, and the weight that one carries both as a professional operating in this space, and even more so as a researcher. Navigating the responsibilities of both roles is explored without shying away from the difficult questions such as the immersion of the researcher, and conversely how visible the researcher is to others. The approach taken by the authors into the reflexive domain are valuable, particularly the discussion about the lone researcher which is sensitively unpacked, something that many would find comfort in and derive value from. Exposing personal thoughts about stress and anxiety in the public domain takes a moral courage that many researchers could also take note from, and for which the authors should be applauded.

Reviewer 2: This paper made me reflect on my own reflexivity and my work's impact on those whom it intends to help. The link of practitioners' use of language to social injustice really hit home as did many of the other points raised in this insightful paper. For example, divisions revealed through the use of common language; 'stress' and 'anxiety', as they may relate to the layman/patient versus the clinical professional, resonated with me greatly. The study made me appreciate the different perspectives these terms have for colleagues in my realm of sport; coaches, athletes, parents and administrators, and the loaded nature of these terms and labels. The use of the Reflexive Triggers framework provided a valuable and coordinated plan for reflexivity, demonstrating good qualitative rigor in the research process. A key part of this reflexivity was to become 'visible and present' in the research, and to acknowledge the 'power imbalances' in the conduct of research with participants. Although unpacked in this instance in the clinical setting of palliate care, the messages here are clear and easily generalisable to many other research contexts.

An inquiry into the influence of nature on young adolescent learners

Gail Keech[1] and Paul Gray[2]

[1] International School of Luxembourg,
[2] University of Central Lancashire, UK.

Keywords: *mainstream schools, environment, nature, learning, engagement, pedagogy*

Abstract

This educational research seeks to understand the impact of embedding nature experiences into the curriculum, through a bespoke programme called Nature Based Learning (NBL). The research was conducted at an international school in Luxembourg, but the practices reported here are felt to be applicable in many similar urban, mainstream school settings. A qualitative methodology was applied through a learner-centred engagement to collect data through observation, photo-elicitation and reflexivity of the researcher, co-observers and the participants. Major themes revealed that the influence of nature on young adolescent learners is: i. an appreciation and connection with nature; ii. inspiration for hands-on inquiry learning, iii. develops a positive relation with risk, iv. feelings of calm and freedom, v. encourages physical challenge in the environment, and vi. facilitates positive social interactions. While the NBL programme was experimental in design and implementation, the positive outcomes for learners were so influential that a new whole-school approach has been developed to support NBL across the curriculum.

Introduction

Context: Our school is an established, private, not for profit, well resourced, high achieving international school in a wealthy European capital city. We have over fifty nationalities within the student body and over twenty nationalities within the staff. The school has excellent facilities with two libraries, multiple gymnasia, 50m and 25m swimming pools, synthetic running track, science laboratories, two auditoriums, technology spaces and kitchens. We cater for students from early years to high school graduation, successfully preparing them for some of the world's top universities. We have had many students continue their education at Oxford, Cambridge, Edinburgh, Harvard, Princeton, M.I.T. and Stanford to name just a few. We do not, however, expect all learners to find a linear academic route to their chosen life path. Our school website states that:

We recognise that students differ as learners in terms of background, culture, language, gender, interests, readiness to learn, modes of learning, speed of learning, support

JQRSS Article No: 4/9-17-1-2023-PG[108]-165
ISSN: 1754-2375 [print] ISSN: 2755-5240 [online] Copyright ©: CC-BY-NC-ND
Web: https://uclan.academia.edu/ClivePalmer/Journal-of-Qualitative-Research-in-Sports-Studies

systems for learning, self-awareness as a learner, confidence as a learner and independence as a learner. These differences profoundly impact how students learn and the support they will need at various points in the learning process. Teachers create flexible, rich learning environments and construct learning experiences based on what they know about each of their learners in order for each student to continue to develop further. (https://www.islux.lu/)

To that end, we have a particularly robust multi-tiered support system. We have a highly qualified staff including a large team of counsellors, a team of learning support staff and an even bigger team of teachers for English as an additional language as well as medical nurses. Simply put, if students need support in a specific area to make progress, then they receive it. However, those students for whom the school environment may be part of their challenge are currently not catered for. If they have a problem, they talk to a counsellor - in a room. If they have a discipline issue, they are talked to by an administrator - in a room. If they need academic support, they are given individual or small group instruction - in a room. If they have a medical issue, they consult with a nurse - in a room. All windows look out onto buildings or roads and when students go out for recess time, it is to an artificial turf pitch or a concrete playground. It seems that the schoolyards are designed for easy maintenance rather than for any kind of stimulation. Apparently, we are not alone in this; one study suggested that many school grounds are more like car parks than invigorating learning environments (White, 2004). However, ecological theory suggests that contact with nature is important for students as it promotes cognitive and intellectual development and enhances social relationships (Heerwagen and Orians, 2002; Kellert, 2005, 2008). Therefore, an area of support that is missing from our multi-tiered support system is a change of environment, that being *learning in nature*. The students are surrounded by human-made structures and materials which they interact with in all our indoor and outdoor spaces. The fabulous facilities of the school are all *human made*. Students' interactions with nature are almost non-existent - as can be seen from the photographs below: figure 1.

Figure 1: Concrete and glass structures - the school environment

In addition, we are now into our third year of disruption, confinement, compliance, and contagion following the Covid-19 pandemic. It would appear that some students no longer know how to be together inside school. This is especially noticeable in the hormonal middle years. In our school, the upswing in the need for counselling and the increase in disengagement, melancholy and behaviours deemed disruptive is staggering. These phenomena are apparently not peculiar to our school. In the last year, there has been discussion of the widespread erosion of joyfulness as witnessed by many schools and educational institutions (Hough, 2022).

Avoiding romanticism

My own experiences in nature are always positive. It is where I go to energise and also to unwind. I chose to wild camp for my honeymoon! During the last decade my husband and I have experienced the deaths of eight family members and two good friends, several major traumatic events and like everyone else, a global pandemic. Due to this, time in nature has become even more influential and more necessary for us. It is my 'happy place', and as such I have often been guilty of romantic framing and having a romantic approach (North, 2015). Due to my romanticism and in order to attempt to avoid any confirmation bias, I completed a case study before beginning this research. I chose a relatively disaffected eleven-

47

year-old for several reasons. He is a student at my school and my friend's son and so access and permissions were no problem, and he is a sporty student who loves to play outside. I thought that it might be enough for him to simply run around and get fresh air in order to be supported in his experience at our school. I thought that perhaps the novelty, feeling of freedom and increase in sensory stimulation outside may be enough for a positive response. I was wrong. There was a huge difference in the level of joy, curiosity and the attitude that he displayed in the two environments. The natural environment was more effective for learning provocation and holistic support. From the student's perspective (and using his grading scale) the outdoor experiences scored an average of 4 and the nature experiences scored an average of 9. From my perspective, the student was happier, less introspective, more engaged, more curious, self-directed and more physically active in his natural experiences.

Figure 2: Case study subject in natural environments

Consequently, considering the impact on my case study, the overall positive impact of nature on children's development (Louv, 2008), their stress levels (Van den Berg and Custers, 2011), and their ability to deal with adversity (Wells and Evans, 2003), my research was an inquiry into the influence that nature had on young adolescent learners. Could it viably be used as part of the multi-tiered support system that we have in place at our school?

Methods

Philosophical approach

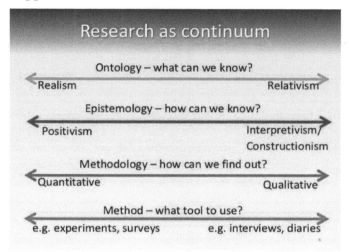

Constructivism refers to the idea that learners construct knowledge for themselves, each learner individually and socially constructs meaning as they learn. Therefore, constructivism is a theory of learning that likens the acquisition of knowledge to a process of building. Each learner should actively participate in the learning processes as everyone builds their own knowledge (Hein, 2001).

I have been an educator for 35 years. I have worked with students from 3 to 18 years old using US, UK, and international curriculums. I have worked in nine schools on three continents in seven very different cultures. I have a background in Physical Education and a Sports Therapy qualification plus a Postgraduate qualification in primary education and certificate in advanced international teaching. I have a love of all things active, the outdoors, and have run the DofE International Award for more than a decade. As a learner, I have a firm preference for bodily/kinaesthetic activities (Gardner, 1983). I think that my two hours of swimming training before and after school with (depending on the season) an hour of hockey or track + field practice at lunch time were the only reasons that I managed to tolerate my own school years. This need to move, explore and discover has affected my own style as an educator. As such, I have four constructivists as my driving force for supporting and understanding students' (and my own) learning; Bruner's 'discovery learning', Dewey's 'learning by doing', Vygotsky's 'zone of proximal development' and Piaget's 'adding on to existing knowledge' (Lutz and Huitt, 2004) steer me as a learner and facilitator of learning. I fall very much on the right-hand side of the above continuum.

The purpose of my research was to seek understanding and an insight into the experiences of the students. It should therefore come as no surprise that my research took a constructivist view with an inductive approach (Thomas, 2006) to the thematic analysis of the data (Braun and Clarke, 2012). The flexibility and organic approach to theme development allowed me to identify patterns in relation to the participants' lived experience and helped me understand what the participants thought, felt and did (Terry *et al.,* 2017). I therefore fully acknowledge my own voice in this research because my beliefs and experiences shape the questions, methods and analysis.

As a constructivist, American philosopher and educator, John Dewey suggested that education is not telling and being told but an active process. Consequently, in order to foster student agency and have them be active in the construction of their learning, the students involved in the research, led the exploration of the natural environment. I would argue that many learning opportunities are approached from the adults' perspective, as, with the best intentions, or due to directives, culture or external pressures, teachers tend to guide or direct their students' learning (Pakarinen *et al.,* 2023). However, hands-on experience and exploration of the natural world in order to discover its secrets is more appealing to students than an instructional approach (Ballantyne and Packer, 2009). Therefore, if as a result of this research, I am to find new ways to genuinely support and not lead the learning in nature, I have to take my lead from the students. Consequently, the research participants had to be able to take ownership of the direction their learning took. I needed to investigate nature-based learning from their perspective, so I needed to examine their perception of their learning (Struyven *et al.,* 2008) in the natural environment.

Attempting to impart knowledge before students have developed curiosity or an emotional bond with something is, in my experience, futile. In my own learning and the learning I witness in students, authoritarian, autocratic teaching creates a culture of conformity (or disaffection) and pockets of disconnected knowledge (Kaplan *et al.*, 2002). If we ask ourselves about student needs and how we best meet their needs it builds a learning community (Kohn, 2006). We are then in a position to facilitate learning through student-led experiences that create a richer array of pedagogical responses and a more open relationship where mutually constructed ways of thinking develop. Finding a way to ensure that education is part of, rather than separate from, life is the goal (Gardner, 1991). This meant that in the study I needed to carefully examine what the students were engaging with (Taylor and Parsons, 2011) while they were out in nature and take note of questions asked, so that these elements could be explored together at a later date.

In addition, the association between liking and learning is strong (Blunsdon *et al.,* 2003). The more enjoyable an educational experience, the more the students perceive it is increasing their learning. Students think they have learned more, think they can apply it, and will engage in further learning if they have enjoyed it (Hagenauer and Hascher, 2014). This highlights the need for the study to ascertain the learning enjoyment that the students were experiencing while they were investigating their natural surroundings.

Therefore, for this study, I delved into the young adolescents' world and explored the influence that nature had on them. It is suggested that the study of 'Nature Based Learning' has two main strands that converge. One is interested in the influence of experiences in nature on learning. That is, learning in nature to enhance knowledge, skills and personal development. The other which is interested in the influence of natural settings on conditions for learning. That is, using nature to increase well-being and the capacity to learn efficiently (Jordan and Chawla, 2019). In this study, I touched on both strands to see what influences nature had on the student learners.

In summary, this research investigated the influence of nature on young adolescent learners through the following objectives:

1. Explore students' perceptions of nature-based learning
2. Investigate students' engagement with nature-based learning
3. Examine students' enjoyment of nature-based learning

Ethics
Approval was granted by the University of Central Lancashire and also by the Director of the school and the two section Principals at the International School in Luxembourg. I presented the research idea to the administration team from the section of the school that I work in, and they gave permission for me to present to teachers. Benefits to well-being (Louv, 2016), cognitive health (Kellert and Wilson, 1995), neurodevelopment and social, emotional skills (Kuo, 2003) were highlighted as potential gains for the students. I used purposive sampling for the participants and as such, advice from counsellors, learning support teachers, classroom/subject specific teachers and administration was sought, as to who might benefit from this nature intervention (Capaldi *et al.,* 2015; Gray, 2018). The students themselves, once invited also had the choice to opt-in or opt-out of the study.

As part of the referral process, a form was sent to teachers outlining possible reasons for the Nature Based Learning Referral. See figure 3 below.

The students who scored highest on the benefit and urgency scale were chosen for the study.

Figure 3: Nature Based Learning Referral process: online questionnaire.

To participate, students needed to respond to their invitation with written assent and their guardians needed to provide written consent. Information detailing the study aims was provided to participants, parents and teachers and the opportunity to ask questions about the research project was available. Participants, parents and teachers were made aware that participants could withdraw or be withdrawn from the study at any time they wished. Any paper-based data was stored in locked storage and electronic data was collected on school devices and stored in a password protected secure school server. All data was anonymised and all participants, observers, locations and institutions remain anonymous. Pseudonyms are used for the participants with appropriate cultural connections for the names chosen (Hoeber, 2023). All permissions have been granted for the use of photographs in this paper.

Observers

The observers that were used are adults already connected to the school. Both observers are retired, this was important to ensure that they were available each week for the six weeks of the study. One, R, is female and was a teaching colleague, the other, C, is male, a parent of one of my previous students, a Learning Assistance Programme volunteer with a background in a variety of businesses. Both have experience in an educational field. Rightly or wrongly, I thought this would perhaps ensure their data was useful and relevant. I also thought their personalities would suit the diverse profiles of the students. They are both empathetic but able to be 'hands off' and can enjoy and embrace a mixed group of students. Both had current police checks. This was obviously important, as they were to be in contact with minors. They both have a positive relationship with nature, which proved crucial on moody, wet, cold, windy days.

Participants

The study used critical case (Rai and Thapa, 2015), a type of purposive sampling (Campbell *et al.*, 2020) technique, with the goal of the study being an in depth understanding with the richest evidence possible for the situation (Patton, 2002). Participants in this study were early adolescents, from the 10 - 14 years of age range. The reason for targeting this age group was because this is where we, as educators, see the most need for intervention - for something 'different' (Farmer *et al.*, 2013). Even before the post Covid challenges and behaviours mentioned earlier, traditional school instruction methods did not in general seem to work as well with this age group (Beamon, 2001). Worldwide, learning engagement at school within this age range appears to be the lowest of all school age students. The dip (Galton *et al.* 2003) has been well documented. Exploring a different approach to learning for some students of this age is a priority at the international school where the study took place.

There were seven students, all from the 10 - 12 age range. They were chosen based on the teachers' perceptions of the level of benefit they might gain from the experience and the level of urgency to try something different with them. None were seen as 'thriving' in the school environment. Meet the participants:

One student, we will call Kaya. She has Japanese as a home language and, despite more than two years in our school, spent time with only those students who spoke the same home language. She was seen as lacking confidence and had very limited English language acquisition.

One student, we will call Louise. She is a Francophone with a self-confessed love of nature. She was seen as: having low self-esteem, oppositional, unwilling to conform and had regular conflicts with peers and teachers.

One student, we will call Hela. She has French, Italian and English as home languages. She had a recent ADHD (Attention Deficit Hyperactivity Disorder) diagnosis, was seen as disruptive and was struggling to focus and thrive in the classroom environment.

One student, we will call Seb. He has English as his home language, had attended the international school from preschool. He was physically much more mature than others in the same age range, struggled to control impulses and seemed confined by the school buildings.

One student, we will call Matt. He has Polish and German as his home languages, was seen as depressed and had completely withdrawn from learning activities and the other students in his class.

One student, we will call Mo. He has English as his home language, was brand new to the country and school and was struggling to settle. He was seen to be anxious, have a 'fixed mindset' and a fear of failure.

One student, we will call Rob. His parents are English and New Zealander and he has English as his home language. He had been in the country for several years but was new to the school. He was seen to be 'dark', unhappy, disorganised and passive in his learning.

Methods

The first priority in the inquiry into the influence of nature on the young adolescent learners was obviously to change the learning environment. Each Friday for six weeks, we spent the whole day out of school. We changed from the classrooms and the synthetic outdoor spaces that students usually had, to environments that enabled the students to have direct and spontaneous contact with nature.

We explored a diversity of spaces where the children were exposed to natural stimuli and there was room to roam and explore so that nature's influence could be examined. The country where the study was based is small and predominantly rural with a free public transport system and a wealth of nature destinations, therefore access to natural spaces was not a huge challenge. We explored a deciduous forest, a steep sided river valley, a UNESCO Global Geopark (an area of bizarre sandstone rock formations) and a lake. I deliberately returned to the deciduous forest as I thought that was the most 'boring'. I wanted to see if novelty had any effect on the response of the students.

Week 1 - Deciduous Forest	Week 2 - UNESCO Geopark (North)	Week 3 - Lake
Week 4 – Steep sided river valley	Week 5 - UNESCO Geopark (South)	Week 6 - Deciduous Forest

Figure 4: Participants' photographs of the six locations.

In an attempt to understand the social world through the participants', observers' and researcher's perspective, data was collected from the students at three time points: pre-activity, during activity and post activity. Data was collected from the observers during the activity. As the researcher, I kept a reflexive journal of the process to identify and analyse thoughts, influences and findings. In situ conversations (if student initiated) were used to allow for a deeper exploration of participants' views and perceptions.

Participants' data

Pre-activity notes were written onto specific coloured Post It notes, figure 5, which were a different colour each collection period (although I used pink twice by mistake). The Post It notes were small and colourful to ensure they were child friendly and not overwhelming with the amount of space to 'fill'. We use many of these notes during the Harvard, Project Zero, Thinking Routines that we use in school and so it is a very familiar method for the students to make their 'thinking visible' (Ritchhart, Church and Morrison, 2011).

Data collection cycle at all 6 locations

Participants	Pre-activity What do you want from this experience? (Written: Post It notes)
	During activity What are you interested in? How are you feeling? (self-generated data using iPods to collect photos/videos/voice memos)
	Post activity PANAS scale questionnaire (+ optional written reflection)
Observers	During activity Action/interaction observations In situ conversations (if students-initiated engagement)
Researcher	Reflexive journal

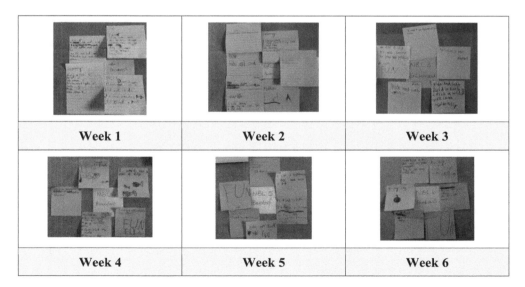

Week 1	**Week 2**	**Week 3**
Week 4	**Week 5**	**Week 6**

Figure 5: Completed Post It notes (pre-activity data)

The use of the Post It notes ensured the wishes, goals and expectations of the students were recorded and collected. I could not hope to be responsive or support motivation and self-efficacy (Schunk and Miller, 2002), without acknowledging and recording students' aims. The colour coding was to ensure that changes over time could be easily monitored.

During the activities, students had individual school owned iPods to collect their data (figure 6). To support safety and security, the iPods were connected to the school password protected system. The iPods were only distributed for the study activities. The collection of visual images from the participants themselves rather than from the researcher or observer (Ziller, 1990; Zaltman, 1996), was in order to empower the students, and capture, authentically, their lived experience. They were able to capture their own evidence with photographs, videos or voice memos. Two open-ended questions were the only prompts for their collection. 'What are you interested in? How are you feeling?' The breadth of possibilities with these two questions was to facilitate a deeper insight into the engagement and enjoyment of their experience, to gain a viewpoint of the recipients. To create a useful and successful short-term learning intervention in nature, the students' voice and student engagement will have to be a driving force (McKellar, 2020).

Figure 6: Participants recording using school iPods

The post activity data collection was via the Positive and Negative Affect Schedule (PANAS questionnaires, see figure 7). This is a self-report questionnaire that consists of two 10-item scales to measure both the positive and negative emotions experienced during the 'intervention'. The participants decide to what extent they have felt the described way during the experience. This scale was chosen due to its simplicity and its longevity of use. It is tried and tested. Any extra written comments reflecting on the students' experience were able to be captured on the back of the PANAS questionnaire. This was the only quantitative data that I collected and despite some doubts and misgivings due to the approach I was taking, I went ahead with it. I felt that this was a simple, speedy way of discovering the students' perception of the nature-based experience.

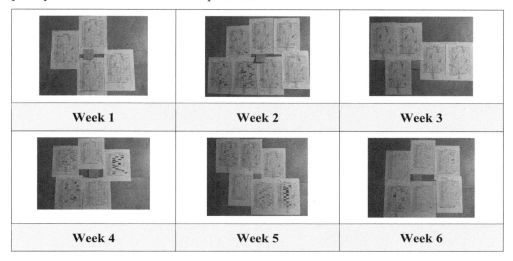

| Week 1 | Week 2 | Week 3 |
| Week 4 | Week 5 | Week 6 |

Figure 7: Completed PANAS Questionnaires.

Observers' data

Observers also used individual school owned iPods. Using theoretical social roles for fieldwork, the adult chaperones, as far as possible, took the role of 'observer as participant' (Atkinson and Hammersley, 1998). In order to dissuade the students from any change in action or interaction observers, as unobtrusively as possible, took note of student reactions to each other; the stimuli around them and the choices they made. Observers like the students, recorded data through the use of voice memos, photographs and videos. The first data collection was taking note of anything they found noteworthy in the students' actions or interactions.

Figure 8: Two observers and lead researcher 'on location'.

The data from the first activity informed later observations. This was to allow for different layers of meaning to be revealed (Feilzer, 2010) and a more complete picture of the students' learning to emerge. Data collection became more focused or specific depending on what surfaced. If the students initiated conversations then the observers responded appropriately and conversed on the topics the students selected, taking note of any interactions they felt were of interest in furthering the study. Having two observers plus a researcher (figure 8), was to ensure multiple perspectives and hopefully minimise the possibility of our failure to note maybe trivial but perhaps crucial data (Silverman, 2021).

Researcher's data

I kept a reflexive journal throughout the research period. I recorded my thought processes through any decision-making and attempted to acknowledge and analyse any assumptions and beliefs that I brought to the research. This critical introspection (Meyer and Willis, 2019) was to support me unveiling the way the findings of the study were reached. For example, short excerpts from researcher's reflexive journal:

30.09.22 - NBL 1 Deciduous Forest
Data
I have WAY TOO MUCH data! It took me 4 hours yesterday just to transfer the photos, videos and voice memos to the central iPad. 88 photos and 114 videos + 5 voice memos are too much to analyse carefully. I expected to have too much but the reality is much 'worse' than I thought.

Technology
I created my whole research around capturing with the iPods and their batteries are not holding their charge. This was discussed before the summer but I found out when I returned that there was not the budget to replace them.

My back up plan of using the iPad from the HS is not perfect as they are so big and bulky. I only gave them to the observers this time but it was not ideal. I think it will be even worse when the weather is cold and rainy. One idea is to take a portable charger with us. Also, perhaps I can limit the student data collection to just two iPods rather than them having one each - the others could then be spares? More thought required.

4.11.22 - NBL 3 Lake
Interpersonal
I am not sure whether I was unconsciously looking for this due to my experience with Zee in the non-natural setting in my case study. However, it seemed to me that the students were more focussed on each other rather than their surroundings this time. I also noticed that two of the students did not record anything that they were interested in or how they were feeling. Again, I don't know whether this was because they knew from my interactions and reactions that this situation that they were in was not what had been planned. This could mean that they were not as motivated to collect data. On the other hand, perhaps they genuinely did not find anything that they were interested in.

> To further consider...maybe next data collection cycle?
> Have I adequately considered the relationship between me and participants and/or R+C and participants?
> Have I adequately described the participants' characteristics?

18.11.22 - NBL 5 UNESCO Geopark (2)
Situation
The caves in both week 4 and 5 seemed to influence the data collected. After the students spent time together in the caves they seemed to become more focussed on each other rather than their surroundings. Was this due to the dark and close proximity that they had experienced? As young adolescents did the cave bring about feelings that they were not sure what to do with but could not let go?

25.11.22 - NBL 6 Deciduous Forest
Interpersonal and Situation
There were a couple of things that I felt may have influenced the data collected this week.
1. It is the only time we have returned to a previously visited location.
2. It was the last time we would all be together on one of these trips.

This week only three students took iPods when we first got to the location. This is the first time this has happened. Normally they have enjoyed taking photos and videos of things they have been interested in. I am not sure why. Perhaps the repetition of a location. Mo took an iPod later as he was totally intrigued by a luminous yellow substance on a fallen tree. It is the first time he has taken a photo of anything.

This week there was MUCH more socialising. When we first went down to the pond area, they had their snack and then just sat around in the hut chatting. It is the first time they have done that. I tried not to influence them, but I did wonder whether it was because it was a man-made shelter, so I moved them away for a game of predator. The boys did not engage with the game and disappeared into the dark pine tree location and laid on the floor and chatted. - Was this due to the repetition of the location? Maybe they thought there was nothing new to explore and discover? R said that she thought they had now created their own 'tribe' and so the surroundings were not as important to them as the people. Maybe the fact that this was their final trip meant that they concentrated on each other rather than what was around them?

Academic rigour

As a naive researcher, a concern that I had was academic rigour in my study. The non-numerical, subjective approach made me a little uncomfortable to begin with, so I did a lot of reading around this. I found that Daniel's (2019) TACT framework broke the qualitative research process down into four sections, Trustworthiness, Auditability, Credibility, and Transferability, with guiding questions for each section to demonstrate academic rigour. These questions became a significant part of my research process. Reproduced in figure 9 for reference:

	Research Problem	Methods	Data Analysis	Findings
Trustworthiness	- Is the research problem framed within the context of related literature? - Does the researcher clearly describe their background? - Does the researcher's background have any degree of familiarity with the phenomenon and the setting under the proposed study?	- Are the methods used for data collection appropriate for the type of research problem? - Was the recruitment strategy appropriate to the aims of the research?	- Has the relationship between the researcher and the participants been adequately considered? - Can it be verified that data presented reflect the views of the participants? - How was data analysed (codes, themes, theory etc)? - Are the themes extracted from data match-examples of the quotation? - Is the analysis based on an established and relevant method?	- Are the outcomes of the research dependable? - Does the conclusion drawn from the data adequately relate to the research problem? - Does the conclusion recognise that multiple realities exist? - Do the researchers' outline personal experiences and viewpoints that may have resulted in methodological bias? - Do the findings clearly and accurately present participants perspectives?
Auditability	- Is the research problem clearly described?	- was the data collection process transparent?	- Is the data analysis process systematic? - Are the questions made during data analysis fully described?	- Are the findings verified against the stated research problem? - Doers the researcher clearly describe how data was collected, where, when, how, and how the analysis was undertaken? - Can another researcher follow the decision trail used by the investigator in the study?

	Research Problem	Methods	Data Analysis	Findings
Credibility	- is the research problem adequately justified?	- Can data be triangulated? - Are the methods used for data collection appropriate?	- Is the method(s) of data analysis theoretically grounded? - Does the study lend itself to a multidisciplinary approach, likely to be investigated from a number of different theoretical perspectives?	- Can findings be theoretically verified? - Can the accuracy of the findings be established? - Is there any congruence between findings with assumptions? - Do the findings contribute to any new knowledge? - Can a degree of neutrality in the research study's findings be established?
Transferability	- Is the research problem clearly described? - Is there a detailed description of the study context, times and phenomenon?	- Are the methods of data collection clearly described? - Are participants characteristics clearly described?	- Is the approach for data collection clearly described?	- Are multiple realities acknowledged? - is the currency of findings and applicability transferable to similar contexts?

Figure 9: TACT framework - principles of rigour in qualitative research (Daniel, 2019).

Excerpt from Reflexive Journal Week 4 - referring to the TACT framework

The trustworthiness question, which relates to methods, that I thought about this week was, 'Are the methods used for data collection appropriate for the type of research problem proposed?' The question I am examining is the influence of nature on young adolescent learners, focussing on engagement and enjoyment. I think that each data collection method I am using gives me something towards that area. I have not made any deep or well thought through judgements yet as to which methods are the most useful, but I do feel that they all give me 'something'. No doubt when I begin to analyse the data closely, some of the methods will emerge as being more helpful / dependable / applicable...

Analysis

Thematic analysis

Thematic analysis is a process of generating patterns or themes within qualitative data. It is suggested that it should be the first qualitative method that is learned as it includes core skills that can be built upon for other kinds of analysis (Braun and Clarke, 2006). It is a flexible method which is an advantage in the diversity of work in learning and teaching (Maguire and Delahunt, 2017). Consequently, as a first-time researcher and in my role as an educator, I used thematic analysis for the data generated for this study.

Step one of the process is to familiarise oneself with the data. Therefore, I spent two to three weeks skimming through the data; written responses, photographs, videos and voice memos. I then summarised all voice memos and labelled all photographs and videos with an appropriate title to describe and summarise their contents in a simple way. Unfortunately, the number of data points generated was overwhelming to begin with. I did not count all, but for illustrative purposes here, I counted all from trip number 4. Two of the students were absent, but even so, there were:

> ➤ 5 Post It notes including 12 phrases
> ➤ 65 voice memos
> ➤ 190 photographs/videos
> ➤ 5 PANAS questionnaires including 100 entries

It was all a little much to begin with but I needed to begin somewhere, so I started the analysis with the PANAS. It was the only data collection that I had been directly involved with, and so it was more familiar to me right from the first week. It was a manageable 33 sheets of paper with only 20 points on each paper and I was not particularly hopeful that it would generate much of any specific interest, so it was a good place to practise analysis and not be too worried that I would miss anything significant. The PANAS scale includes 20 emotions, 10 negative and 10 positive. Participants tick the appropriate box to highlight whether they have felt that particular emotion that day, from very slightly to extremely. The boxes are allocated a sliding scale of points 1 to 5. 1 for 'slightly' - 5 for 'extremely'. For example:

#	Emotion To what extent did you feel this way today?	Very slightly or not at all	A little	Moderately	Quite a bit	Extremely
1.	Interested					
2.	Distressed					

Due to the concerns I had about this being the only quantitative method, I originally thought that I might abandon this PANAS questionnaire after the first couple of cycles. However, it became useful as vocabulary acquisition and part of the structure of the day, and so it was maintained for the whole research period. During the first week, the participants, observers and I met at a table with bench seats in the reception area of the school. Here, we worked through the practicalities for the day. We ended the day in that same place where we collected equipment and completed the PANAS questionnaire. We spent time that first week, translating the vocabulary into home languages and finding synonyms and antonyms to ensure the students understood the emotions, before analysing to what extent they had felt that way during the day.

Excerpt from Reflexive Journal Week 1 - Related to PANAS

I know that there are some questions over using the PANAS scale but the students seemed to enjoy it as a reflection on their feelings about the day. I feel that it is worth persevering with for a while longer. Some issues with language of the descriptors. Not all vocabulary was understood fully. Words are quite nuanced for students who are not native English speakers.

During the second week we met at the same table to begin our day. When we returned to school, the students were already sitting at the table with their pencils and translation tools ready when I had finished signing us back in. The whole study was supposed to be attempting to capture student voice and choice and so I felt obliged to take my lead from the participants. It felt almost churlish not to complete the questionnaire when they were ready and waiting, and so it became part of the structure of our day. Thinking as a teacher rather than researcher, it was an excellent tool to not only increase vocabulary but also to refocus and calm the students on our return to the building. The analysis of the questionnaire did not, however, seem to be particularly helpful in furthering my understanding of the research question. I did find, see figure 10 below, that numerically the emotions reported in response to nature-based learning were overwhelmingly positive.

NBL week 4

Louise	Seb	Kaya	Hela
N = 25 / P = 43	Absent	N = 15 / P = 33	N = 15 / P = 41
Mo	Rob	Matt	
N = 14 / P = 40	Absent	N = 13 / P = 32	

NBL week 6

Louise	Seb	Kaya	Hela
N = 20 / P = 38	N = 10 / P = 50	N = 12 / P = 37	N = 12 / P = 38
Mo	Rob	Matt	
N = 13 / P = 36	N = 10 / P = 38	Absent	

Figure 10: Results of PANAS Scale Questionnaire (N: Negative P: Positive) weeks 4 and 6

When the data was transferred into graph form, (using google sheets, figures 11, 12 and 13) I could see more clearly that there was just one participant, Matt, who scored only one of the trips below 20 in the positive scale. In addition, there were just two participants, Louise and Mo, who scored two trips above 20 in the negative scale. This graph representation was another way to see that in general the students were feeling hugely positive about their time in nature.

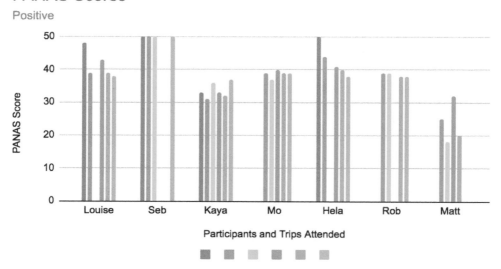

Figure 11: PANAS scores: POSITIVE

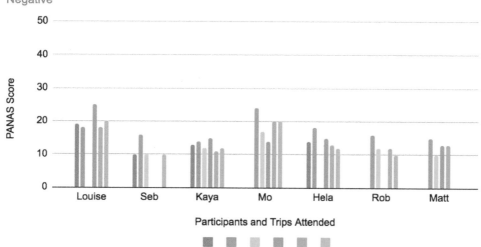

Figure 12: PANAS scores: NEGATIVE

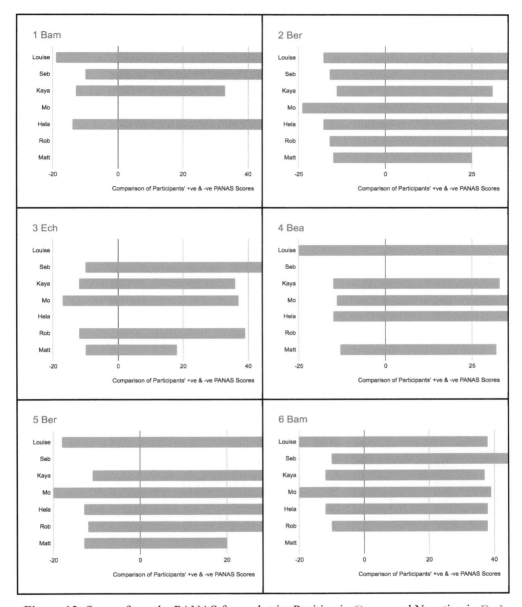

Figure 13: Scores from the PANAS for each trip. Positive in Green and Negative in Red

After a more thorough examination, a few things that did capture my attention from analysing the PANAS scores were:

- Matt's positive scores were generally lower than the other participants. As a teacher, this concerned me as he had been put forward as a participant for the study as he was seen as depressed. Perhaps, this data reflected that. As a researcher, however, it did not help me move forward in my understanding of the research focus.

- An area that did interest me as a researcher was that Kaya was the only participant whose positive scores became more positive as the study progressed. Was this perhaps an indication that more time in nature was helping her feel more positive?

- Hela became less positive as the study progressed but she also became less negative too. With ADHD as part of her profile, perhaps less volatile swings in her emotions were an indication of more 'calm' and therefore a helpful influence that nature was having on her.

- Rob had been described as being dark and it was rewarding to see that he maintained a steady positive score but a downward trajectory in his negative scores. Hopefully this was an indication that he was beginning to feel less 'dark'.

- Mo's negative score from trip two was his highest. However, this trip was his first and probably the 'scariest' due to the exploration of the high sandstone stacks of the Geopark (figure 14). In this instance, the emotions of being nervous and scared are not actually negative. This trip was an introduction to more risk taking for Mo as you should be able to see from the photographs below.

Figure 14: Photographs from the location of trip 2 – Geopark

Excerpt from Reflexive Journal Week 2 - Related to PANAS

Scared, nervous, afraid scored high on the negative on some occasions. They are actually not negative in this context as we want the students to feel those things when they are risk taking.

- Louise's score on trip 4 was the highest negative score but she had said that this was her favourite trip, so I found that interesting. I even noted in my journal that this one had been particularly enjoyable for Louise. She was able to find time to be alone and quiet. Maybe the time that she had carved out to be alone in nature had been a risk-taking activity and therefore a little scary for her.

> **Excerpt from Reflexive Journal Week 4 - Alone Time**
>
> *One of the students, L, has said they crave calm and quiet and highlights the sounds and smells of nature as one of the things they want out of their experience. Another one of the students, H, has ADHD as part of their profile and enjoys the space and freedom, when we are out, to be a little 'wild'. This week the 'calm' student found many situations where they were able to manipulate space and time to be alone. I have not noticed this before and I wonder whether their previous experiences, where they have been in closer proximity to the 'wild' student, were as enjoyable as this one.*

However while my analytical thought processes had begun, there was not much in the numerical data alone that genuinely helped me understand the influence of nature on the participants.

After deciding that the numerical data did not help me significantly further my understanding of the research questions, I wondered if I could somehow make more of the descriptive vocabulary that we had worked so hard to ensure the students understood. I chose the only trip that all participants had attended, which was trip number 2. Instead of giving each emotion for each participant a score out of 5, I typed each word the equivalent number of times into a word cloud generator. A word cloud generator pulls out the words that appear most frequently and makes them larger and dominant. I used WordArt.com, figure 15 as it was free, recommended by the tech coach and could cope with chunks of text rather than individual words typed in one at a time, as some of these tools require. I thought this might at least give me a visual understanding and more importantly a visual description of the emotions that the students were feeling most often, rather than just the positive/negative labels.

Figure 15: The emotions that the participants felt during week 2

When I did that, the image above was the result and was much more helpful in moving me forward in my exploration of the students' perceptions of their experiences. Bearing in mind that the participants in the study are from our most disaffected age range, this visual representation of their responses was pleasing to see. As a researcher, I felt it was useful in my general understanding of the participants' emotions. As a teacher, I felt it would be useful for the school community as persuasion or justification for a nature-based learning programme as it is such a simple yet impactful presentation of the students' emotions in response to nature-based learning.

Through the use of the word cloud generator, the PANAS data in its slightly underwhelming numerical form came to life and was more specific and useful. As a result, I decided to also use the word cloud generator for the summaries I had created of the voice memos. I hoped that this would help me make sense of the observations.

Example of a selection of voice memo summaries from observer R - Week 5

> *R off on an alternative path followed by Mo*
> *Cheese throwing*
> *More daring*
> *H found sand repelling the water*
> *H in sand pit in small cave, R on his device*
> *H found another sand pit and is back in water with sand*
> *H helping R to get up ravine*
> *Ma and H in a cave*
> *Ma created musical instrument with stick*
> *Ma up a ravine, talking to himself*
> *Mo following group up the valley*
> *Waterfall entices exploration*
> *R did not make it to waterfall - pushing Mo*
> *Mo and R trying to push each other into the stream*
> *R kicked water to try to get a reaction*

I first eliminated pronouns, (she, him, they...) articles, (an, this, the...) and conjunctions, (and, but, because...) because I did not feel that these parts of speech would further my understanding. I then decided to eliminate prepositions (beside, through, against...). I did not feel that these words were significant enough to help me understand the influence that nature had on the participants. This left me with around five hundred words, mainly verbs and nouns with some adjectives and/or adverbs. I thought that this would be the significant vocabulary that would help me see what and how the participants were engaging with nature. I did not use any kind of digital tool to help me with this process. As part of the quest to develop trustworthiness and authenticity, (Daniel, 2019) I engaged in persistent, repetitive, interaction with the data (Coleman, 2014). I read and re-read in the hope that by going over the words multiple times it would help me see patterns, categories and identify themes. All the words that were left after the filtering process, were in different tenses and forms. I am not sure whether this was significant but whatever the reasons, I did not find the word cloud that was generated from the voice memos at all helpful in furthering my understanding of the research focus. It did however, create a pleasing image that we may well be able to use as a logo for a nature-based learning programme: figure 16.

Figure 16: What and how participants were interacting with nature

The next data I analysed were the Post It notes. This was because this data was easily manageable. The information I had obtained from the voice memos, with this first attempt at analysing it, had not yielded anything that I had found particularly compelling and had been incredibly time consuming and frustrating. I needed to feel like I was moving forward in my understanding of the research focus and needed something that felt a little less overwhelming. There were only 33 Post It notes with an average of 3 aims for the day: figure 17.

Figure 17: Post It notes completed by participants

The first stage of analysis was to collate the Post It note comments onto a Nature Based Learning table to generate an overview of comments per week of the programme. Figure 18 is an example of collating Post It comments from week 2.

NBL 2

Louise Having fun Seeing animals	Seb A shelter/fort A cold comforting cave A wild Ma Cool animals Cool/weird parts of nature	Kaya I want see reafs (leaves?)	Hela Fort
Mo I would like a whole day of fun	Rob Hide and Seek	Matt A wild S To find a cool rock A cold cave	

Figure 18: Analysis i: collating Post It comments from week 2.

After collation, I began a process of reading and scanning to find any repeated words/phrases/concepts and highlighting them to see if there were any emerging patterns or themes of interest that caught my attention, see figure 19 below.

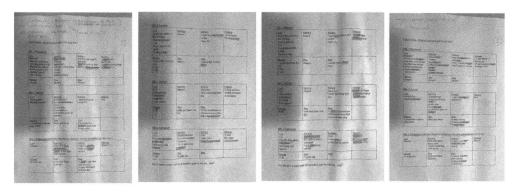

Figure 19: Analysis ii: grouping and theming of Post It comments from week 2.

When I did the highlighting, the first thing that struck me was the increase in the number of times that fun/happy were mentioned as an aim for the day. In week 1, only one student mentioned fun. By week 5, five students had written fun/happy as one of their aims for the day. As a teacher, this made me happy to see because the disaffection in learning for many students in this age group was the stimulus for this whole study. As a researcher, I felt that this was somehow significant, but was not sure why, to begin with. To verify what I thought I was seeing, I again used a word cloud generator and typed into it the aims from the Post It notes: figure 20.

Figure 20: Representing significant responses from the Post It note responses

The word cloud simply confirmed what I had noticed that fun became a particularly significant aim for the group. On closer inspection, I noticed that the student, Kaya, went from no 'fun' mentioned at all until week 4 when it first appeared at the bottom of her list. In week 5, 'Have fun' was the first thing on the list. In week 6, 'Fun!' was the first thing on her list: figure 21.

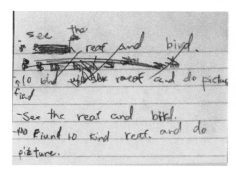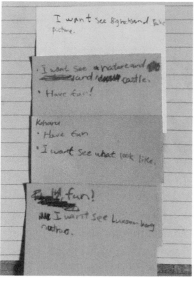

Figure 21: Kara's data track towards fun in learning through the NBL programme.

Two reflexive journal comments seemed to add more substance to my initial thoughts of fun and enjoyment and also a possible link to confidence. For example, excerpts from my reflexive journal for weeks 3 and 5 show Kaya opening up.

Reflexive journal, Week 3, Kaya opening up.

C observed Kaya and said that he thought the data collection had been more successful this time because K was more familiar with him and he felt she was opening up to him.

Reflexive Journal Week 5 - Kaya Interacting.

K is now interacting with the group and is louder and seems to smile and laugh more. I wonder if her data will now include more pictures and clips of the others in the group? She even spent time in the cave with the 'noisy' students at lunch time.

Kaya was a participant in the study because she was struggling to learn English and would only interact with other students who spoke the same home language. My judgements about her improved learning engagement from the Nature based learning Programme are based on the increase in positive scores on the PANAS that I had noticed, the increase in the importance of fun in the aims that she had written on the Post It notes, and progressive observations noted in my reflexive journal comments.

It seemed, that as the weeks were progressing, Kaya was having more fun, opening up, interacting more successfully and developing confidence. I chatted to her homeroom teacher who also felt that she was gaining confidence and was, 'interacting with her peers in different ways'.

This felt like forward momentum in the study and somehow significant in my quest to understand the research focus; the influence that nature was having on students, Kaya in this instance. I decided that to help me understand her experience from her perspective, I would follow Kaya more closely through the rest of the data. To do this I used a generic inductive approach to allow significant themes inherent in raw data to be identified and summarised without the restrictions of structured methodologies (Thomas, 2006). I studied the videos, photographs and voice memos systematically and repeatedly to consider how they fitted with my developing categories. If new categories emerged, then the data was restudied with the new lens.

Once nothing new was emerging for Kaya, I switched to a more deductive approach of coding as I studied the data of the other participants using Kaya's thematic lens. This blended approach (Graebner *et al.,* 2012) was to ensure relevance, and to make sure that the findings were transferable and applicable to the research focus of 'young adolescent learners' and not just one individual (applying TACT: figure 9 after Daniel, 2019).

When deciding how to present the theme that had been identified, I felt that to transfer and synthesis the vibrant data of video, photograph and voice down into words on paper, which would also be a less impactful means of communicating than capturing them in their original form. I felt that, as in teaching, too much telling and too little showing would lower the quality, so showing the data would illustrate more effectively how I had reached the theme (Pratt, 2009). I again sought the advice, expertise and patience of the technology coach at school who supported me in learning how to use a video editor tool called 'WeVideo'. I was able to use this tool to collate and display all the forms of data that had been identified as evidence of the theme. I practised using the tool by using the study data to create a video for the teachers to share what we had been doing with the research, and obtain names for the second group of Nature Based Learners.

 **Click on the link: NBL for Teachers (4:21)**

As you will have noticed, there were a few glitches in this video. Dark spaces, long transitions and background music that became somewhat irritating! Despite the hours of practice, I was not very competent using the tool. I practised again by using the study data to create a video for the parents of prospective Nature Based Learning students, to help them understand what the benefits for their children might be.

Click on the link: **NBL for Parents (1:56)**

This one was great for the audience it was intended for but a little too simplistic for this study, in that it had no video or voice memos included. However, by this time, I had learned enough to use the tool to collate all types of data into a narrative.

This video is the result of following Kaya through the data.

Click on the link: **Kaya (2:28)**

Following Kaya through the data in this way genuinely helped me to build a picture and construct my understanding of the influence that nature was having on this young adolescent learner. She did have fun, there was an increase in her learning enjoyment, she did gain an enormous amount of confidence, it did help her language acquisition, she did interact more openly, frequently and successfully with others and her gains were transferred into the classroom setting.

Using a generic inductive approach and following an individual participant had been the most successful process to help move me forward in my understanding of the research focus. In addition, the gathering of data in order to practise using the 'WeVideo' tool had helped me become incredibly familiar with the photographs, videos and voice memos that had been gathered. Therefore, I decided to use this inductive format as a structure for the rest of the analysis. I needed to know the influence that nature was having on the wide variety of learning profiles of the participants, so I decided to follow each student through the data. This would ensure that the themes were driven by student voice with a personal approach for each one. Hopefully the students' world would be revealed and help me understand how each participant was interpreting their own experience. I would see how nature was influencing each one of the young adolescent learners.

Matt

Matt was part of this research group as he had completely withdrawn from learning and any interactions with the students in his class. He spent all his time, with his hood up, drawing, in a corner of the classroom. He was having regular counselling and support from outside agencies had been sought. His teachers were worried. He was anxious about joining the group and to begin with spent a lot of time finding reasons not to join. He did not attend the first week.

This video is representative of following Matt through the data.

Click on the link: Matt (3:22)

Even before my close analysis of the data after week six, Matt's developing enjoyment, immersion in, and appreciation for, the nature he was surrounded by, was becoming more evident. This was captured in an excerpt from my Reflexive Journal for week 5 - Matt Sharing Discoveries

Reflexive Journal Week 5 - Matt Sharing Discoveries

M was happiest alone with his stick this trip. He did not interact much with the others. He talked to others briefly then dipped out again. He gathered more data about what aspects of nature he was interested in this time - he enjoyed sharing his photographs and videos when he had taken something. He also enjoyed taking the adults in the group to the things he had discovered. I notice he constantly makes noises and self-talks - is this some kind of self-soothing mechanism?

Following Matt through the data in this way, again helped me to build a picture and construct my understanding of the influence that nature was having on this young adolescent learner. He did immerse himself in nature. It did interest and engage him. It did generate curiosity and seem to establish appreciation. He did gradually interact with his peers and the adults around him more positively. The gains from his time in nature were transferred to the classroom setting. It seems that directing his interests outwards into nature, also supported the change in his own focus from withdrawn and introspective to more sociable and outward looking. In the long term, we can also hope that his genuine appreciation of the nature around him will develop into environmental stewardship.

Hela

In all participants of the study, curiosity about the natural world around them was clearly evident. Coupled with a recent ADHD diagnosis and a seemingly unending supply of energy, Hela thoroughly explored and investigated all elements of the environments visited. This video is representative of following Hela through the data.

 Click on the link: <u>Hela</u> (2:45)

The hands-on, multi-sensory, self-directed, problem solving style of inquiry was highly motivating for Hela. She could roam freely and the more she explored, the more she discovered, the more curious she became, and the more hands-on inquiry she undertook. This style of learning is something that we should be encouraging in all our students. To be able to stay ahead of the curve in our rapidly changing world, the critical, creative and innovative thinkers that we can help develop with this style of learning are essential. We need to support students in finding their own way through an increasingly complex and volatile world (Schleicher, 2018). Hela's sense of awe and wonder about the natural world coupled with a penchant for hands-on inquiry is a combination that I feel we should be strongly encouraging for a sustainable future.

Mo

Mo was a participant in the study as he was new to the country and the school. He had come from a very different learning environment and was struggling to settle into his new situation. His classroom teacher felt he was risk averse due to a fear of failure and had a fixed mindset (Dweck, 2006). This video is representative of following Mo through the data.

 Click on the link: <u>Mo</u> (2:34)

Mo's increase in confidence and more positive relationship with risk were evident even before my close analysis of the data after completion of the six-week period. This was captured in an excerpt from my Reflexive Journal for Week 5 - Positive Risk Taking.

> *Reflexive Journal for Week 5 - Positive Risk Taking*
>
> *Mo seems to enjoy spending time with C and likes to share ideas and thoughts with him. He seems to enjoy challenging himself now. Whatever is there he tries some kind of challenge. Climbing to the top of a mound, exploring a cave...*

Not only did the development of a positive relationship with risk during his nature-based learning have a positive effect on his classroom behaviours, but also in his everyday life. A panoramic elevator and funicular tram, figure 22, are part of the transport system around an area through which Mo travels regularly. Due to his fears, when travelling as a family, alternatives had to be found.

Figure 22: Problematic forms of transport for Mo, with a fear of heights.

After week five, his mum came to see me and declared that I had performed a miracle. He had travelled on the funicular and down in the elevator with no problems, and when questioned about his less fearful attitude, he had attributed it to his nature-based learning experiences!

Louise

The similarities between Matt and Louise were evident from the beginnings of the study. The behaviours observed in school were opposite in that Matt was withdrawn and uncommunicative and Louise was oppositional and argumentative. However, the restorative benefits of nature and their quest for calm and solitude were common factors, as excerpts from my reflexive journal for weeks 4 and 5 illustrates:

Reflexive Journal Week 4 - Time Alone

We used purposive sampling for selection of students for this study. They are wide ranging in their learning profile and personalities. During the last data cycle, I wondered if I had adequately considered the relationship between me/observers and participants and whether this had any bearing on any of the data being collected. However, a couple of incidents this week made me question the relationship among the students and whether this had any influence on the enjoyment or engagement in their experience.

L often spends time alone but it seemed more this week. I wonder if L and/or M's enjoyment and engagement were affected because of the interactions rather than anything to do with nature?

> *Reflexive Journal Week 5 - Sounds of Nature*
>
> *L seemed to enjoy time alone again. C actually described her as a trailblazer. She sat with R and I for lunch as the cave group were too noisy and she said they were spoiling the sounds of nature. M joined us too. I wonder would they spend as much time alone if their 'good' friends were on the trips?*

The sounds and sights of nature and solitude had a calming effect on Louise. With Matt, the nature-based learning experiences encouraged him to look outward, to be more aware of his surroundings and the environment, and also to be more communicative. With Louise, the experiences seemed to allow her to feel less negative and pessimistic when she looked inwards. It seemed to help her feel more positive, feel less constrained and restricted so that she was more comfortable with herself, saying 'I feel good, feel happy, feel wild/free'. This video is representative of following Louise through the data.

 **Click on the link: Louise (1:43)**

In school we have what we call W.I.N. time (What I Need) and for Louise these nature-based learning experiences were exactly what she needed. Louise said… 'I can cope with Monday to Thursday if Fridays are going to be like this'. Louise's comment to me after only week one which seems to echo the 'biophilia hypothesis' (Kellert and Wilson, 1995) and the 'stress reduction theory' (Ulrich, 1984). These theories describe how spending time in nature might influence emotions and reduce stress because of humans' innate connection to the natural world.

I also had a brief conversation with Louise's older sister during a school function. She reiterated what benefits there were for Louise in the nature-based learning experiences and how positive she was beginning to feel. The sister also expressed disappointment that she could not attend something similar as she said she did not feel like the learning environment at school was always positive for her either. Louise's sister said to me,

'I feel like I have a head full of colourful balloons and I have to come to work in a black and white factory'.

As a researcher this made me happy as it confirmed my rationale for exploring the idea of nature as support for learning. As a teacher, in the school the sister attends, it broke my heart a little.

And finally... Seb and Rob

The themes that I identified for the final two participants, Seb and Rob, were the physical challenge and positive social interactions that their time in nature brought. Seb is mature and much bigger than the other students of his age. The focus on physical challenges for him was evident from the first trip; 'Mrs Keech, I feel like throwing stuff!' Physical challenge through exposure to small and large loose parts play and exploration is essential for the physical development of children (Nicholson, 1971). The development of fine and gross motor skills, the firing of mobiliser and stabiliser muscles and the improvement in balance and coordination as well as endurance are all physical benefits that we want our students to obtain. As an antidote to screen time and the idleness of modern life, physical challenge in natural surroundings is more important than ever for the health and well-being of our 21ˢᵗ Century learners (Calogiuri, 2016). Figure 23: Seb seeking physical challenges:

Figure 23: Seb seeking physical challenges in the woods on the NBL programme

Rob's reflective comments about his nature-based learning experiences, highlighted what was important to him, '...to know new people and know people in a new way'. As a new student to school these positive social interactions were a hugely positive part of his time in nature. The experiences helped him settle into the school and develop a sense of belonging. An excerpt from my Reflexive Journal in week 5 – captured something of Rob's desire for social interaction, and figure 24.

Reflexive Journal week 5 – Rob's Desire for Social Interaction Evident

Rob seems to want interaction all the time. When he was not interacting with the others in the group. He was interacting with his iPod, taking selfies and editing photos and videos. For him there now seems to be more of a desire to interact with the other students in the group rather than aspects of nature. His desire to have the attention of Hela consumes much of his time. This focus on this relationship seemed to stop him looking at aspects of nature that were engaging him earlier in the research... Could this mean that people have more of an influence on his enjoyment and engagement than nature does?

The positive social and emotional skills that our students develop will help bring happiness (Holder and Coleman, 2009), support them in building strong relationships and hopefully thrive in their chosen life path (Mygind *et al.*, 2019).

Figure 24: Rob Seeking Social Interactions, outdoors on the NBL programme

I feel that these final two themes have been explored sufficiently in this study. Physical development and positive social interactions are admittedly incredibly important, and the identification of these two themes will be shared with the wider school community as a benefit of nature-based learning. However, I feel that these themes can also be addressed in other areas of our school curriculum. They can be gained from experiences other than nature-based learning. The purpose of this study was to try to establish what influence the addition of nature experiences could bring to our young adolescent learners. The benefits of physical challenge and positive social interactions are certainly influences that we need to consider, but I do not feel that they are unique to nature-based learning experiences, preserving, or prompting scope for further study on this topic.

Discussion
- Strengths of this research
- Limitations of this research

Participants
The number of participants and their reasons for inclusion, the purposive sampling, was a strength of this study. The masses of reading I had done on the potential benefits of nature-based learning meant that I could give informed advice on the kinds of students who may profit from time in natural surroundings. Seeking input from a variety of sources in school meant that, it was felt from multiple perspectives, that there was a genuine need to try something different with the students who were chosen. The students had a chance to experience something new and this meant that even though they might not be particularly happy in the school environment, they were enthusiastic and positive about participating in the study. The number and wide variety of profiles of the participants was also a strength. It gave varied perspectives, and they collected varied data but the group size was small

enough so that the 'nature' experiences could remain so, and did not become human experiences. The number was also small enough for me to manage so that the experiences could remain relaxed and participant focused. I noted these things in my reflexive journal in week 5:

Reflexive Journal Week 5 - Differing Profiles of Participants Evident

Seb was missing due to ill health. The group were more fractured and seemed more niggly without him there this week.

Rob seems to want interaction all the time. When he was not interacting with the others in the group. He was interacting with his iPod.

Matt was happiest alone with his stick this trip.

Louise seemed to enjoy time alone again.

Kaya is now interacting with the group and is louder and seems to smile and laugh more.

Hela seems to find someone to yell at and 'fight' with each week.

⤵ Observers

The use of the observers was also a strength of the study. The personalities, skills, willingness and availability of the observers was carefully thought through before invitation. They were different from each other and different from me and so offered alternative perspectives. They were adults and unknown to the participants to begin with, which meant that their role as 'participant as observer' (Atkinson and Hammersley, 1998) while friendly, never became too intimate or lost the researchers' focus. Giving them a choice of three methods to document the actions and interactions of the participants and a free choice of who and how many to observe were also strengths. It meant that they could be as unobtrusive as they felt necessary and flexible in their choice of what, who and how to observe depending on their preferences and what materialised. My reflexive journal for week 4 notes:

Excerpt from Reflexive Journal Week 4 - Freedom for Observers

Giving C and R the freedom to choose who and how many students they observed this week, seemed to be a positive one. R felt able to change her mind about collecting from two students and moved to just one, relatively early in the day. C decided on two as he felt that observing just one was a little intrusive and perhaps 'intense' for the student.

Using observers to gather data meant that I did not influence what was collected. This was important from a safety / risk assessment point of view because during the trips my role was mainly that of teacher and facilitator running the trip.

⤵ Locations

The locations chosen were a strength of the study. They were familiar to me and had been thoroughly risk assessed so I felt comfortable with the students safely exploring relatively independently. They each had a different aspect of nature at their core so their appeal to the participants could be noted. For example:

83

> *Excerpt from Reflexive Journal Week 3 - 'Plan C' - Lake*
>
> *The lake that we ended up at during trip number three is a beautiful although man made area. The concrete paths are beautifully maintained and so accessible for wheelchairs, baby buggies and little bikes. The 'activities' around the edge are created with mainly natural materials and are positioned so that they do not detract too much from the forest around. And yet, it feels to me, too 'coiffured' and tidy. If the students are like me, and like Zee in my case study then they will not have responded the same way to this more man-made location, as they do to the more natural surroundings. It may be evident when I compare the data that they collect.*

There was always an element of novelty with the locations so that participants' interest was piqued, which meant that activities could remain student-led without the need for any teacher intervention. This meant that the data collected was wide ranging and genuinely dependent on the participants' interests. It also gave me time as the researcher to observe and think. For example,

> *Excerpt from Reflexive Journal Week 4 - Near Home*
>
> *I felt more relaxed this week as I knew exactly how long each section of the planned day would take. Having the minibus (so no bus times to stick to) meant that I felt I could be more responsive. I know the area very well indeed and the two areas that we based ourselves worked really well. The students could explore easily and the observers could monitor from close and from afar, whichever was most appropriate. Even though I was the only teacher in charge of the students this week as SR was absent, any insecurities and nervousness I have had being in charge of students out in nature was gone. I am not sure whether this could have had any bearing on the data collected. However, I explored the idea of my anxiety and frustration at the location having some bearing last week so it makes sense to acknowledge that my calm, confidence in this location could have had some influence.*

In addition, locations were never further than an hour away from school so that boredom with the journey did not become a factor for the participants.

✦ Keeping a reflexive journal

The use of the structured reflexive journal was a strength. It meant that I thought deeply about every aspect of the research process. Its presence and my commitment to making comprehensive entries after each trip meant that I remained focussed on the research even while acting as a teacher during the trips. Observations that I may well have forgotten or missed without it, were noted and were analysed carefully when following the students through the data. My Reflexive Journal comments were used as evidence to support and enhance themes and categories as they were being identified. For example, one entry alludes to the impact of journalling my progress:

> *Excerpt from Reflexive Journal Week 2 - Structuring Entries*
>
> *After reading the 'practical guide to reflexivity in qualitative research' journal article, I am attempting a more structured entry into my journal rather than random thoughts.*
> ➢ *Personal - how are my unique perspectives influencing the research?*

> ➤ Interpersonal - what relationships exist and how are they influencing the research and people involved?
>
> ➤ Methods - how are we making methodological decisions and what are the implications?
>
> ➤ Situational/Contextual - how are aspects of the context influencing the research and people?

⊹ Subjectivity

One of the strengths of this study was that I learned not to apologise for any bias that I brought to it. I have lived with the context in which the study was set for more than a decade and have several other contexts with which to compare. My two favourite places to work were on an island in Malaysia in Southeast Asia, and in Uganda in East Africa. In both places the grounds of the schools were in fabulous locations and as exotic and beautiful as botanical gardens. In fact, on my first day working in Uganda, I watched an African Harrier Hawk swoop down into a huge Mvule tree on the campus, pick up an unsuspecting small bird and then proceed to eat it, sitting on the terrace outside my classroom. It was gruesome and such a privilege all at the same time. When I was swimming front crawl while training in the pool on the campus in Penang, Malaysia, I used to breathe to the right on the way up the pool and to the left on the way back. This was so that I could watch the waves lapping onto the beach, on the edge of the school grounds, at the same time as swimming. The grey, concrete human made environment of the school where I work at the moment, does not inspire me. I have a sense of dread, disappointment and anxiety every time I enter the campus. I know that it does not work for me, therefore I predicted that there were also at least some students for whom the campus did not work either. The whole study was devised around my distaste and discomfort with the campus and my love of and reaction to nature. Adopting reflexive thematic analysis meant that my subjectivity was always in the foreground. Hopefully this transparency will lend credibility to the findings and lessons learned. Excerpts in my reflexive journal from weeks 2 and 3 indicate my thoughts to explore subjectivity and about my growing awareness as a researcher:

Excerpt from Reflexive Journal Week 2 - Realising I had to Explore Subjectivity.
Q - How do you think the research is going so far?

I feel that perhaps I am focussing on the teaching and learning more than the research. I can see massive benefits in terms of the students' learning. The feedback from students, parents and teachers is incredibly positive. Because this is my job and I want these students to feel good, be engaged and have fun, perhaps I am thinking too much about that and not enough about the actual research. I want this new element to my role to be successful and I want to do more of it so I think I am biased and do not think I can claim any objectivity at all. It may be the sports science side of me but I feel that a lack of objectivity is a problem. I read that I should embrace subjectivity but how then do I ensure the rigour in the research? I need to explore the idea of embracing subjectivity...

> *Excerpt from Reflexive Journal Entry Week 3 - Growing Awareness*
> *Personal*
>
> *I have been trying not to influence the students or the observers during the data collection, but after some reading on embracing subjectivity in qualitative research I think I am making a mistake. I don't think there is any way that I can be impartial or objective or completely uninfluential, so I need to embrace my influence and ensure I am disclosing my 'position' (life history, experiences, relationships...) as an integral part of the data. I shall try to do that in this journal entry...*

Integrity

Another strength of the study is the integrity with which it has been carried out. At each stage of the process I have paused and reflected using guiding questions and checks. This was noted in my reflexive journal at weeks 3 and 4:

> *Excerpt from Reflexive Journal Week 3 - Rigour*
>
> *I have been struggling with the idea of academic rigour in qualitative research so I have been reading a number of articles to do with this. I found one which outlines the TACT framework, (Daniel, 2019) Trustworthiness, Auditability, Credibility and Transferability. There are some guiding questions for each of these areas, for each phase of the research. I found these particularly helpful and will try to use some of them in these journal entries.*
>
> *Excerpt from Reflexive Journal Week 4 - Credibility*
>
> *I also talked to C and R, the observers, about the credibility question this week. To ensure credibility at the analysis stage, C and R have agreed to look over whatever themes emerge to ensure that they agree with what's been said.*
>
> *I will also share themes and ideas for learning engagements that emerge with the students. They will no doubt be brutally honest in their verification of my findings! This is apparently called 'member checking' (Loh, 2013).*

A significant time of reflection was when I first identified the seven themes. To test whether the findings were robust enough to move forward with, I assessed them in terms of transferability. The guiding question I used *from* Daniel (2019) was:

'Is the currency of findings transferable to similar contexts?'

At school, we were already into the final week of the second group of Nature Based Learners. Therefore, in order to answer the question, I analysed the photographs taken of the second group to find evidence that matched the themes found in this study. I found multiple examples of each theme. Figure 24 are the display boards that I created with the photographs from my second group, where the transferability of the themes is clearly evident. In addition, I shared a summary of my findings with the two observers to see if they agreed with what I had highlighted... they appear to have agreed, one, Observer C, indicating this in an email response, in figure 25:

Figure 24: Experiences on the Nature Based Learning programme shared on school display boards

---

Sent: 15 May 2023 09:05
Subject: Your research themes

Hi Gail,

I'm on my way back from Sydney where I attended a reunion at my old rugby club and have just had the opportunity to look at the video. It brought back terrific memories of some fabulous days out in nature with great kids and adults. There is nothing I see in the presentation that I would disagree with and the way you have articulated the themes. It is fascinating to see a structure developing from the learnings of our time with the kids.

It was a highly enjoyable activity for me and I can't wait to hear of further developments in your project.

Thanks again for keeping me up to date.

Best, Name

Figure 25: Data verification, email confirmation from Observer C.

⌁ Participants' voices

I feel that the use of participants' and observers' voices was another strength of the study. While acknowledging the subjectivity of the work, but avoiding my personal confirmation bias, their voices ensured authenticity and rigour. Presenting the data with videos meant that the participants' perspective of nature-based learning experiences was faithfully seen and heard. For example, as I noted in my journal:

Excerpt from Reflexive Journal Week 2 - Trying to Eliminate my 'Voice'

Even though I am not collecting any data so that I can avoid any bias confirmation, I have already found myself deleting photographs and videos. I feel that this is a judgemental and subjective action. I realised after I had done it, that I deleted a couple of selfies that the kids took because I presumed that they were just 'messing about' with the cameras. When I thought about it afterwards, they could have been trying to capture how they were feeling...

I need to collate everything and see where it takes me. I can't make any kind of judgement or assessment of anything, yet.

Following each student through the data meant that there was no attempt to generalise but live the experience through each participant. Understanding the influence of nature on each one of the diverse profiles of the participants was important to be able to answer the research focus and feed back to the school.

⊹ Flexibility and variety

You don't just learn knowledge; you have to create it. Get in the driver's seat, don't just be a passenger. You have to contribute to it or you don't understand it.

Attributed to Dr W. Edwards-Deming

My flexibility and willingness to try many different data collection techniques and data analysis strategies to construct my understanding of the research focus was a strength of the study. I was not simply going through the motions to obtain a further qualification. I genuinely wanted to be in the driver's seat and understand the research process and I genuinely wanted to understand the research focus. Entries in my reflexive journal bear out my intrinsic quest for understanding:

Excerpt from Reflexive Journal Week 4 - Quest for Understanding

The trustworthiness question, which relates to methods, that I thought about this week was, 'Are the methods used for data collection appropriate for the type of research problem proposed?' The question I am examining is the influence of nature on young adolescent learners, focussing on engagement and enjoyment. I think that each data collection strategy I am using gives me something towards that area. I have not made any deep or well thought through judgements yet as to which methods are the most useful, but I do feel that they all give me 'something'. No doubt when I begin to analyse the data closely, some of the methods will emerge as being more helpful / dependable / applicable...

Excerpt from Reflexive Journal Entry - Continued Quest for Understanding
15th December 2022

I think I will analyse the voice memos first. As I am looking for engagement and enjoyment and I asked the observers to do action observation and interaction observation, my first focus will be on verbs. Perhaps if I hear a particular verb x 10, take a note of it? Is the number 10 just arbitrary though? Maybe I have to listen carefully to a couple of entries and then plan in more detail.

The acknowledged messiness of the repeated manual manipulation of the data in a variety of ways, supported the shaping and reshaping of my thinking. In addition, I was willing to be reactive and add data collection methods that were not in the proposal, but helpful to further my understanding of the research focus. You will notice from the videos that I sought the perspective of the participants' homeroom teachers to ascertain if there had been any benefits transferred to the classroom setting. This additional data was not necessary to answer the research questions relating to interests and engagement, but it did help me further understand the reach of the influence that nature had on the participants.

I am claiming the variety and flexibility as a strength as I feel that this was, in part, why the research questions were well answered. To ensure that the 'messiness' can be seen as a strength, I have tried to make sure there is enough detail and reasoning about the approach and methods so that the reader can appropriately evaluate it (Caelli *et al.*, 2003). Entries in my reflexive journal allude to my coming to terms with the messiness of the research process:

Excerpt from Reflexive Journal Entry - 180 degrees of Messiness!

5th February 2023
I think I have decided to abandon the student data. I think it needs too much work to ensure it is valid and useful.

25th February 2023
After reflection, I have decided the exact opposite of the above comment. I think the student voice is the most important voice in all this and so I am going to base everything around their voices and have them as the driving force.

As I go through the data, an idea that I seem to be formulating is that I can answer the inquiry question, using one student for each data method. This means that I should get the breadth of influence that nature has on a student group with widely differing profiles, while ensuring a reasonable depth of analysis. I will use the data gathered from them with back up from the observers.

However, the flexibility and variety in the study also developed from and led to a lack of coherence which point to a series of limitations in the research.

❖ Limitations of this research

❖ Technology

My first issue with the research was the technology aspect. I should have more comprehensively tested the systems I had set up before I began. I had several meetings with the technology support team and several coaching sessions with the technology coach at the school, and I thought the systems I had devised were effective. However, they were not adequate for the amount of data that the students and observers collected. The first two weeks were particularly stressful. I worked every evening and all weekend uploading, downloading and organising the data. Some data may have been 'lost' or labelled incorrectly during this time, which is obviously a significant limitation. I had several more sessions with the technology coach and by week three I had a manageable system in place and the collation of the data was organised well and only took a few hours each week.

The second issue was the actual technology, the hardware. I had several meetings with the technology department and I thought I had everything organised before the summer break. Unfortunately, the school iPods did not hold charge for long enough to collect all the data that the participants and observers wanted. I tried using school iPads but they were too big, heavy and obtrusive to be feasible. I bought a couple of small chargers to be used as needed but they were not enough. Finally, I found two school iPhones that the observers could use which meant that they were happy and could collect everything that they wanted using voice, video or photograph. Observers using phones meant that we now had two spare iPods and the chargers as back up too. However, this had taken until week 3 so maybe something significant in week 1 or 2 could have been missed. I also think the situation with the iPods created a little distrust and frustration for the participants and perhaps that influenced the data they collected. An entry into my reflexive journal for week 2 shows how my frustration with technology was showing through:

Excerpt from Reflexive Journal Week 2 - Frustration with Technology Evident!
Context Q - how do you feel the situation is influencing your research?

The technology tools and processes that I am using are influencing data collection and collation way more than I had anticipated. At this early stage, I have spent more time working out how best to make the technology do what I want it to, than on any other element. The tech is supposed to be a tool to find out what I need to, however, the tool and process have become the focus instead. The dying batteries on the iPods have caused so many issues. I will be going out for the third trip this week and this will be the third iteration of the tech tools and process of collection. To be perfectly honest, I have not thought about much else regarding the research apart from the collection tools and collation procedures. This means I may be missing key moments or situations in the data collection/collation. It is particularly frustrating as the small iPods are exactly right for the job at hand - if their batteries had held out!

I was so overwhelmed with my perception of the difficulty of the situation after the last trip that I took a whole week off, to enable me to go without thinking about anything to do with the research. This has had a knock-on effect of making me feel that I am 'behind'.

The iPods are the perfect tool for the students and the observers and although I have not noticed the students voice much frustration, the observers certainly have. As well as all the other negative feelings resulting from the technology, I feel responsible and guilty for causing the observers any problems.

Finally, on this latest trip the students were reluctant to capture anything that they were interested in or engaged with. This was because they either had to carry the big bulky iPad with them or find one of us collect the device and then go back to whatever they wanted to capture. This meant that often the moment was lost and not captured.

❖ Dwindling data

Even with a technology system that seemed to be working, the data collected by the students dwindled as the weeks progressed. I am not sure whether it was the lack of trust in the iPods holding their charge, or the novelty of using the iPods wearing off, but the participants did not gather as much data towards the end of the six weeks. I did not have a conversation about it with the participants as they did not bring it up (also a limitation of the study - discussed later) so maybe it was neither of the two. Perhaps a little less data towards the end of the sessions had a more positive reason:

> ➤ Perhaps participants became more discerning in their choice of data to collect?

> ➤ Maybe participants were weaned away from screens by their exposure to the sights and sounds of nature?

> ➤ As they became more confident spending time in the natural environments, perhaps they needed the device as a security crutch less than they had?

> ➤ Another alternative could be that participants were perhaps spending less time capturing data as a result of becoming more familiar with each other. Maybe they were spending more time bonding with each other and interacting among them rather than interacting with their devices?

As a teacher, the dwindling data collected on the iPods made me happy. I was watching the students engaging with nature, each other and the adults in the group. Any time young adolescents are away from screens I see it as a positive development. As a researcher however, a lack of data could have been a major challenge. Fortunately, because the observers were also collecting data and there had been so much collected in the previous weeks, I was not at all concerned that I would not have enough to answer the research questions. This situation did make me feel more content about the number of different methods of data collection that I had used as I always had a 'back up'.

❖ PANAS problems

The PANAS (Positive and Negative Affect Scale) questionnaire was the only quantitative method that was employed in the study. As such, in a qualitative study with a constructivist's view, it seemed not to fit. However, I decided to forge ahead with its use for several reasons. Two of the research questions were about exploring the students' perceptions and examining their enjoyment of nature-based learning. Considering the age, the home languages and the language acquisition stage of the participants in the study, I felt that the students would need some support in order to describe these relatively abstract concepts. This was one of the many places where I embraced my role as researcher and teacher and used the questionnaire as a research tool and a learning opportunity for the participants, to support an increase in their vocabulary. In addition, the audience for my research was the university, but also the international school community where I work. Therefore, if I was to have the participants' voices as the driving force of the study, and in order to appeal to the wider community in our academic community setting, I felt I would need more than fun, good, bad, cold or even more problematic for the audience 'slay' and 'sick' as the only descriptors for perception and enjoyment. Although the use of the PANAS was not assigned any kind of dominant status whatsoever (Johnson *et al.*, 2007), my thinking was that the survey would still be useful to allow the participants to think more deeply and expose them to ways of describing their feelings that they may have not known before. As such, the justification for this method was that it taught as it learned (Romm, 2013). In the end, as a researcher, I did not obtain much from this method, apart from a few initial thoughts and a persuasive visual, so I could possibly have done without it.

❖ Conversations not questionnaires

To help the participants think more deeply, rather than the PANAS questionnaire, I could have engaged them in conversation. Sitting young adolescents down and trying to talk to them about a prescribed topic at a certain time is never particularly fruitful. However, I had several hours in the locations where less intimidating side by side walking conversations could have been possible. In addition, the bus rides were an opportunity where the students were a 'captive audience' and so that time could have been used for follow up questions. When planning the research, I had wanted to stay out of the data collection as much as possible in an attempt to create more objectivity. I had deliberately included conversations with the participants only when they initiated them. On reflection, I think it was actually a limitation of the study and I think that I actually missed an opportunity.

❖ Methods cancelling each other out

Another issue that I did not foresee was that two of the data collection methods that I chose actually cancelled each other out for Mo. His main aim that he wrote on the Post It note for each trip was 'fun', figure 26. After week 4, I realised that Mo had not gathered any data at all on the iPads. During the trip on week 5, I asked him

about his lack of data. He said that his aim for each trip was to have fun and taking photographs and videos and recording voice memos was not fun for him, so he was not doing it. I am not sure whether eliminating the Post It notes specifying student aims for the day would have meant that he did collect what he was interested in via photographs or videos. However, I do know that he used one of the methods I had employed to justify his desire to cancel out another method. I feel that this alone means that the combination of these two methods was a limitation of the study. I noted my concerns in my reflexive journal on week 5.

Figure 26: Mo's aims for each trip on the NBL programme

Excerpt from Reflexive Journal Week 5
Methods

There were two things that happened this week which made me think that the characteristics of the students may well be influential in the data collected and so I thought I better describe them clearly.

Mo (new to school and country, quirky, ASD? OCD?) - on the Post It that I have been using to get the students to record their aims for the day, he wrote that his aim for the day was fun. When I asked him why he had not collected any data during any of the trips he said that his aim for the day was fun and taking photographs and videos was not fun. (!!!) So that made me wonder whether the inclusion of the post it notes negatively influenced the other data? Perhaps the inclusion of the Post Its was a mistake as the photos and videos may well be more useful data to collect to answer the engagement and enjoyment question.

❖ Tool used as a toy

Using technology as a tool in any situation with young adolescents is a challenge. In school, the pull of gaming and social media is often too strong for them to focus solely on the learning task at hand. As educators we have to be very aware of the movement of the students' hands over the keyboard, the tabs that they have open and their eye movements, as they are all tell-tale signs of distraction. Helping students learn to manage these distractions is part of our job and as such is always a factor in situations where technology is used. I did not want the focus of the study to become the management of the technology tool and for this reason, I removed everything from the iPods apart from the camera functions and voice memos. However, despite the preparation, I think that use of the technology tool did affect the data collected. I noticed that in week 4 and 5 some of the students spent time in caves and used their iPods for flashlights and then spent time recording echoes and sounds to try to scare themselves and others. Time in the caves was not unexpected as young adolescents enjoy finding or creating spaces away from adults. They are also sensation seekers, as can be seen by their enjoyment of roller coaster rides, horror fiction and extreme sports (Duell and Steinberg, 2020). What did surprise me was that after the time spent in the caves using their devices, two students then collected nothing at all about the natural surroundings but spent time editing video clips and photographs of the other participants in the group, figure 27.

Figure 27: Photographs Collected in and after the Caves on the NBL programme

Does this mean that the method I used to collect the data did not support or enhance the quality of it? Did it actually distract the participants from the focus of the study and detract from the quality of the data collected?

> *Excerpt from Reflexive Journal Week 5*
> *Methods (cont.)*
>
> *The use of technology tools as a collection device may well have influenced the data collected. Two students, R and Matt seemed particularly influenced by their interactions with the other members of the group. Their mood changed and their behaviours changed depending on the nature of the interactions. In Beau last week and Berd this week, the difference in data collected before the cave and after the cave was quite startling to me. Matt in Beau and R in Berd stopped collecting anything from their surroundings and concentrated solely on editing pictures and clips of people after their time spent in the cave with the iPods. Does this mean that because I used technology tools to collect data, the tools actually distracted the students away from nature?*

❖ Researcher versus teacher

Another of the limitations of this study was my dual role of teacher and researcher. I was aware of these identities at every stage of the research. Sometimes my role as a teacher enhanced the study. For example, the amount of research and time spent on the selection of participants. As a teacher, I worked hard to ensure that the students who I felt would benefit the most would have the opportunity to participate. As a result of the careful choice of participants the study obtained rich, vibrant, diverse data. Sometimes however the role of teacher inhibited my role as researcher. For example, I committed to my reflexive journal:

> *Excerpt from Reflexive Journal - Teacher v Researcher*
> *12th March 2023*
>
> *Much thinking done this week about the themes that I have identified. I need to make sure that the themes are powerful and possibly unique to ensure that the writing is persuasive and the school board are convinced that NBL has a significant role in the future of the school.*

The above journal entry clearly shows that I was thinking as a teacher with the school board as an audience for my findings, rather than a researcher with a university as the audience for my findings. As a researcher, perhaps I could have gone 'deeper' in my analysis with a focus on just two participants. The similarities and differences between Matt and Louise, for example, could have made a complete study. Following their nature-based learning experiences, he developed an ability to look outwards and she developed an acceptance when looking inwards. There was enough data to examine this connection in meticulous detail. This detailed focus on just two students would not however, have been as powerful or persuasive for the school community as the wider focus on all seven participants, so I did not explore it further.

❖ Inelegant design

Identifying a research design provides researchers with a roadmap or guide to follow with their project. Alternatively, if a researcher wants to deviate from the normal guide associated with a design, at least in knowing what is typical they would understand why and how they are creating a new path or improvising with it (Berbary and Boles, 2014).

This study has highlighted for me exactly how much I have to learn about research design, especially using qualitative data. I am not sure that I had a clear idea of a 'typical' design so had no clear idea of whatever deviations I was taking. I think that the obvious concern with my study was the number of different methods employed to gather data. It was a naive researcher's mistake that more data would mean deeper understanding of the research focus. I should have done a lot more research on the variety of methods for collection of data and a lot more research on data analysis before I even attempted to write my research proposal. If I had built a more comprehensive understanding of methodology before beginning the study, I may have been able to create a more connected, cohesive study. My reflexive journal reveals these personal doubts early in my research in weeks 1 and 2.

Excerpt from Reflexive Journal Week 1 - Learning as I Go.
Questions

I am not 100% sure what to do first with the data - perhaps my first run through will be to analyse the frequency of key vocabulary? I need to do some reading about analysing qualitative data. The Silverman book will be particularly helpful, I think.

Excerpt from Reflexive Journal Week 2 - More Learning
Methods

Q - So far, how would you assess the methods you are using?
I have too many but I am not sure where the useful 'stuff' is coming from yet. I actually like the simplicity of the PANAS questionnaire but I know that tool is a negative issue for college. I have a suspicion that when I have a chance to skim the data already collected that photographs may be the most useful. I know that photographs are used a lot as data collected from children. This is perhaps because they are not yet able to express themselves as clearly as they would like and photography is a way for them to 'say' what they want to say. Being that I am working with children, and photography is one of the ways I have asked them to record their interest and engagement, it would make sense that it may turn out to be the most useful.

For Example, …

➢ Due to the age of the participants, I could have focused on only photographs as data collection.

➢ I could have done more research on reflexive photography before writing the proposal (Schulze, 2007).

> ➢ I could have explored the idea of photo elicitation (Loeffler, 2004) with post photograph interviews to explore for deeper meanings.

> ➢ To take the student perspective further, and in order to ensure that the participants were genuinely empowered and guiding the research, I could have had the students participate in the labelling and categorization of the photographic data. In a study of well-being (Gabhainn and Sixsmith, 2006), this complete process was, in my opinion, used to good effect.

A coordinated study using photography as the core could have been less disordered. However, a focus on photography and a more elegant structure is maybe something to aspire to in a further study. The purpose of this study was to find out what influence nature had on the young adolescent learners in our context. This could then lead into the development of a Nature Based Learning Support Programme around things that students are interested in and engage with. I am not sure that the study was elegantly 'coiffured' but I do know I got the information that I, and the school community, needed to move forward with the support programme.

Conclusion

Despite feeling that my study was somewhat inelegant, and that future studies I undertake will be more cohesively 'styled', this study has proven to be incredibly effective. It has highlighted that there is a gap in our support system at school and that Nature Based Learning can fill that gap for a diverse range of students. The influence of nature, on our students, in our context, at this time, were highlighted in this summary video that I created for the school management.

 Click on the link: NBL for Admin (8:11)

Here I summarised the themes that I identified and why they are important for us in our context. Due to the positive feedback from students, parents, classroom teachers and management about the study, it has brought Nature Based Learning to the forefront of the school's thinking. Further evidence for the study's impact is that there have been six significant outcomes, developing from the major themes emerging from the study, figure 28, which highlight the reach and impact of this investigation in this school setting. These are (1) further groups taking up the NBL programme, (2) students advocating for the NBL programme, (3) appointing an NBL co-ordinator, (4) NBL becomes part of the school's vision statement, (5) Positive feedback from external bodies about NBL, and (6) the school management team prioritise NBL in the curriculum. Details and evidence below:

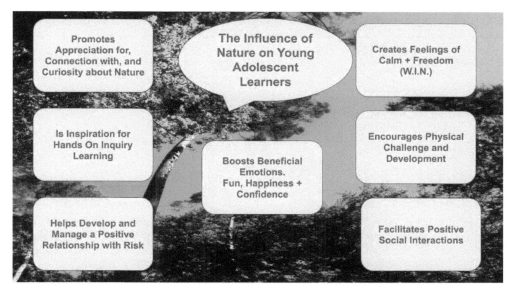

Figure 28: Summary of themes identified in the study about the Nature Based Learning programme at this school.

Significant outcomes of the Nature Based Learning programme and material developments in school educational planning for the future

1. Further groups for Nature Based Learning as support

We have now completed the second and are in the middle of the third group of students for Nature Based Learning as support. The 'programme' is being overwhelmingly positively received by all stakeholders. For example this email from parent volunteer chaperone after a trip with group 2:

Sent: 23 March 2023 13:45
Subject: Thank you for a great Nature Based Learning class!

Hello Gail,
I wanted to let you know what a wonderful time I had with you and the five wonderful fifth graders! The nature-based learning day was awesome! I enjoyed the bus and tram rides, climbing, falling :) and lunching in the beautiful outdoors! The planning and organizing that you put into this is amazing and the kids really do appreciate what you do for them. To hear the stories of the students' growth and to be a small part of it was very rewarding!

As a parent… I hope ~~Name~~ in the fourth grade (next year) will have the opportunity to do something like this. I also wonder if this can be duplicated in middle school. ~~Name~~ would truly benefit from a program like this.

I copied some folks to this email that I believe share the value of this experience and to show off my cool (and school appropriate) photo!

I hope nature-based learning grows and look forward to helping again next trimester! Have a great weekend!

And a copy of an email between myself and the Assistant Principal i/c curriculum:

Sent: 22 May 2023 09:05
Subject: Written Comments?

Hi ~~Name~~
If you can find time, would you please write a couple of brief comments about any positive affects you have seen or have heard about, related to NBL as support.
I think that written evidence from you in my conclusion may be effective.
Thank you in advance,
Gail

Sent: 24 May 2023 10:43
Subject: RE: Written Comments?

Hi Gail,

- Other teachers have found it extremely beneficial for the students they work with. From single-subject teachers such as music to the homeroom, the benefits of NBL has been lauded for its ability to help students' overall wellbeing. Some of the benefits noted have been increased focus, self-confidence and mindfulness. One teacher highlighted that they believe NBL has been so beneficial for students that every student should go out once a week. I have noticed these children being more confident and engaged at school.
- Parents of children that have taken part in NBL also speak highly of it. Especially with the change they have seen in their children's confidence to try new things and their overall self-esteem. Some of the parents were originally unsure about their child not being in their normal classes for a day a week for six weeks. However, once it began, the response has been overwhelmingly positive.

A copy of email from school counsellor (who attended every trip):

Sent: 25 May 2023 23:27
Subject: Re: Comments

Hi Gail,
I wanted to get some of my observations down for you tonight.

Overall, I think every student has benefitted positively from the nature-based learning. This has become evident through talking with the students and observing them in their interactions and explorations. The more the students gained experience of going into nature, the less anxious they became. A few of the students have spoken to me about feeling constricted in the school. In nature-based learning, they see it as a path to freedom and being able to 'breathe.' Many of the students have expressed the desire to continue the NBL or wanting to return to it again.

One of the most interesting things I have observed is the autonomy for the students to explore their interests. For some that meant building dams and trying to contain water using natural materials, others it was focusing on the most minute details they could observe in plants or insects, and still others it was finding places to balance on or places for quiet and just being. Some students set personal challenges for themselves such as how far can I throw a stick, or how high can I climb. Often when setting these challenges, they would reflect on what they did in order to evaluate what they could do better and then set a new challenge for themselves.

The students have also shown growth in independence of moving from asking 'Can I' to

'I'm going to explore here.' As each cohort has gone, the students have also become much more reliant on themselves for problem solving than expecting the teacher to solve problems.

Another skill the students have built is their organizational skills. Whether it is making sure they have their things packed at the start of the day or at each transportation stop, the students have been put in real-life situations where organization matters and has a real-life effect on themselves or the group. As the students gained more experience, they became more self-reliant and less dependent on adults for support with organization.

I have also observed the students benefiting from being put in situations where they have to be resilient. For some this came from getting muddy and not enjoying that feeling, and others, it was from trying to make it to the public transportation on time. Some kids had to face resilience by walking down or up a hill and feeling unsure of themselves or climbing a ladder in a cave. Other kids also had to build resilience from exploring new environments, walking in water, or just simply from working with one another.

Empathy and team building have also been a big part of NBL. Students have been in situations where they had to support each other. This has happened through holding flashlights for each other, giving each other a warning about changes in the terrain that they were walking on, helping each other down stairs or hills, working together to achieve the same goal (such as removing a bag of garbage from a pond or building structures from natural materials, creating dams, etc.), or supporting their peers by giving boosts when trying to climb trees or rocks. Students also within the small group have had the opportunity to get to know each other better while engaging with each other outdoors and on the transportation rides.

See you in the morning.

2. Students advocating for themselves to be part of Nature Based Learning

Excerpts from letters sent by two students to their homeroom teachers.

I strongly believe that I should go for the next six weeks with mrs. Keech in nature.

My first reason is that since I'm in that nature club I feel that I'm paying more attention and that I ask more questions in class, I take more notes, I am more enthusiastic about what I am saying, and I raise my hand more.
One example of this is a few days ago we were in math and you told us to talk with our partner and right after I raised my hand super duper quickly because I was really enthusiastic about my thinking. Another example is when we were in reading workshop yesterday. I asked you a clarifying question because i didn't understand. And before I was in the nature club I was scared to ask a clarifying question and I am still a tiny bit.

> My second reason is that it will make me feel more confident at school. I believe that Nature-Based Learning will push me to more concentration and focus on my learning. For example, you may have noticed that each time I need inspiration I look out at the window. It's a habit to look at nature. I think that links back to my main point, nature is the number one help I need. Remember when you told me I was surely attached to nature because it was most of my topics for writing? The only thing I think about when I'm bored is nature. My inspiration comes from nature, everything comes from it.
>
> Finally, my third reason why I should be able to participate in Nature-Based Learning, is that it would decrease my stress. As you know, I am easily stressed by everything. My stress is one of the biggest problems I have had in my life yet. For instance, I even have stress crises, where I cry for no reason. This connects to why I should go to nature-based learning because it would help me get a break and forget my overwhelming challenges. The three things that help me a lot during my stress crises are my family, music, and above all nature. I believe it will do me some good to be able to be outside.

Teachers were impressed with the students' willingness to advocate for themselves and both students were able to join a cohort of Nature Based Learners.

3. Nature Based Learning Coordinator

The data that has been collected and shared with the school community was powerful and persuasive enough to prompt the creation of a full-time role. Next year the school will celebrate its Diamond Anniversary with its first ever full time Nature Based Learning Coordinator - me! Copy of emails from Lower School Principal:

Sent: 27 April 2023 18:07
Subject: NBL

Hi Gail,
Hope you are well! I have some great news to share in that we will be able to extend our NBL offering next year creating a full time NBL coordinator position.
I'd like to meet with you next week (I'll ask Name to set it up) to get your input into the position and job description. I'll share what we have drafted so far shortly.
In the meantime, have a great Friday and lovely long weekend!

Warmly, Name Removed
Lower School Principal

Sent: 27 April 2023 18:09
Subject: Re: NBL

What I also should have said was - this is largely due to your fine work this year and your advocacy for NBL to enhance student learning - so THANK YOU! This never would have even been possible without your ideas in the first place :)

Name Removed
Lower School Principal

---

4. Nature Based Learning is part of the vision statement projects

An excerpt from the Vision Statement Projects document that the Director is currently developing with the leadership team and the School Board:

Desired Result #3: The establishment of a sustainable transdisciplinary framework for transformative real-world nature-based learning.

Desired Result Description: The school will embrace a schoolwide approach to Sustainability that has Nature Based Learning rooted at its core. Our PK to G12 students will experience a unique programme of learning *in, through* and *for* nature that provides them with hands-on learning experiences both outdoors on campus and off-campus in nature. Nature Based Learning will be used to consolidate, extend or totally transform aspects of transdisciplinary learning in the PYP & MYP and in subject specific elements of the IBDP. Furthermore, these experiences will create a context wherein students gain a deeper understanding of the interconnectedness of all living things and the impact of human actions on the environment. This integrated and innovative approach to Schoolwide Sustainability and Nature Based Learning will be a stand-out feature of our school and help us to foster a culture of environmental stewardship that prepares our students to be the sustainability leaders of tomorrow.

---

5. Positive Learning Community Council (LCC) feedback

This is a representative group made up of stakeholders from the whole community. The LCC acts in an advisory capacity to the Director in terms of developing a schoolwide vision for growth, development and success. There are 9 concepts at the heart of the school's new vision:

1. Academic Excellence;
2. Creativity;
3. Diverse Learning Experiences;
4. Extraordinary Teaching;
5. Global-mindedness;
6. Inclusion;
7. Innovation;
8. Personal Development;
9. Sustainability.

Nature Based Learning is one of 6 projects through which the vision will be achieved. The LCC found strong connections between Nature Based Learning and all 9 concepts. They did not find complete alignment in any other project. The strongest connections were with Diverse Learning Experiences; Creativity; Personal Development.

6. Management team prioritisation

The School Management Team is the operational wing of the leadership structure. The other wing is the Educational Leadership Team. In a recent exercise in prioritising the projects, Nature Based Learning came out on top for the Management Team. We are a high achieving, well-resourced supportive school located in a wealthy city. I think that because of this we sometimes forget that we are in fact still an inner-city school. Our clientele does not have economic problems and the country has an incredibly strong healthcare and welfare system so we do not see a lot of the abject urban poverty so obvious and visible in other cities. Nevertheless, the traffic, pollution and rising crime rates are present. In addition, the complete lack of any natural spaces around the campus is an inner-city issue and one that we had not addressed before this study. As a result of this study, moving forward, the students who need time in nature to support their learning, will get it. So will all other students in the school.

References

Atkinson, P. and Hammersley, M. (1998) Ethnography and participant observation (pp.248-261). *Strategies of Qualitative Inquiry*. Sage, Thousand Oaks, CA.

Ballantyne, R. and Packer, J. (2009) Introducing a fifth pedagogy: Experience-based strategies for facilitating learning in natural environments. *Environmental Education Research*, 15, 2, 243-262

Beamon, G.W. (2001) *Teaching with Adolescent Learning in Mind*. SkyLight Professional Development, Arlington Heights, Illinois.

Berbary, L.A. and Boles, J.C. (2014) Eight points for reflection: Revisiting scaffolding for improvisational humanist qualitative inquiry. *Leisure Sciences*, 36, 5, 401-419.

Blunsdon, B., Reed, K., McNeil, N. and McEachern, S. (2003) Experiential learning in social science theory: An investigation of the relationship between student enjoyment and learning. *Higher Education Research & Development*, 22, 1, 43-56.

Braun, V. and Clarke, V. (2006) Using thematic analysis in psychology. *Qualitative Research in Psychology*, 3, 2, 77-101.

Braun, V. and Clarke, V. (2012) *Thematic Analysis*. American Psychological Association.

Caelli, K., Ray, L. and Mill, J. (2003) 'Clear as mud': toward greater clarity in generic qualitative research. *International Journal of Qualitative Methods*, 2, 2, 1-13.

Calogiuri, G. (2016) Natural environments and childhood experiences promoting physical activity, examining the mediational effects of feelings about nature and social networks. *International Journal of Environmental Research and Public Health*, 13, 4, 439.

Campbell, S., Greenwood, M., Prior, S., Shearer, T., Walkem, K., Young, S., Bywaters, D. and Walker, K., 2020. Purposive sampling: complex or simple? Research case examples. *Journal of Research in Nursing*, 25, 8, 652-661.

Capaldi, C.A., Passmore, H.A., Nisbet, E.K., Zelenski, J.M. and Dopko, R.L., 2015. Flourishing in nature: A review of the benefits of connecting with nature and its application as a wellbeing intervention. *International Journal of Wellbeing*, 5, 4, 55-67.

Chawla, L. and Cushing, D.F. (2007) Education for strategic environmental behavior. *Environmental Education Research*, 13, 4, 437-452.

Crabtree, B.F. and Miller, W.L. (2022) *Doing Qualitative Research*. Sage, Thousand Oaks, CA.

Coleman, T.C. (2014) Positive emotion in nature as a precursor to learning. *Online Submission*, 2, 3, 175-190.

Daniel, B.K. (2019) Using the TACT framework to learn the principles of rigour in qualitative research. *Electronic Journal of Business Research Methods*, 17, 3, 118-129.

Duell, N. and Steinberg, L. (2020) Differential correlates of positive and negative risk taking in adolescence. *Journal of Youth and Adolescence*, 49, 1162-1178.

Dweck, C.S. (2006) *Mindset: The New Psychology of Success*. Random house.

Farmer, T.W., Hamm, J.V., Lane, K.L., Lee, D., Sutherland, K.S., Hall, C.M. and Murray, R.A., (2013). Conceptual foundations and components of a contextual intervention to promote student engagement during early adolescence: Supporting Early Adolescent Learning and Social Success (SEALS). *Journal of Educational and Psychological Consultation*, 23, 2, 115-139.

Feilzer, M.Y. (2010) Doing mixed methods research pragmatically: Implications for the rediscovery of pragmatism as a research paradigm. *Journal of Mixed Methods Research*, 4, 1, 6-16.

Gabhainn, N.S. and Sixsmith, J. (2006) Children photographing well-being: facilitating participation in research. *Children & Society*, 20, 4, 249-259.

Galton, M., Gray, J. and Rudduck, J. (2003) Transfer and transitions in the middle years of schooling (pp:7-14): *Continuities and Discontinuities in Learning*. DfES. London.

Gardner, H. (1983) *Frames of Mind*. Basic Books, New York.

Gardner, H., (1991) *The Unschooled Mind*. Basic Books, New York.

Graebner, M.E., Martin, J.A. and Roundy, P.T. (2012) Qualitative data: Cooking without a recipe. *Strategic Organization*, 10, 3, 276-284.

Gray, T. (2018) Outdoor learning: Not new, just newly important. *Curriculum Perspectives*, 38, 1, 145-149.

Hagenauer, G. and Hascher, T. (2014) Early adolescents' enjoyment experienced in learning situations at school and its relation to student achievement. *Journal of Education and Training Studies, 2*, 2, 20-30.

Heerwagen, J.H. and Orians, G.H. (2002) The ecological world of children. *Children and Nature: Psychological, Sociocultural, and Evolutionary Investigations*, pp.29-64.

Hein, G.E. (2001) The challenge and significance of constructivism. *Hands On*, pp.35-42.

Hoeber, L. (2023) 'The best teacher is also a student': improving qualitative research literacy by learning from my mistakes. *Journal of Sport Management*, 1, 1-8.

Holder, M.D. and Coleman, B. (2009) The contribution of social relationships to children's happiness. *Journal of Happiness Studies*, 10, 329-349.

Hough, L. (2022) *A Space for Joy*. Harvard Ed. Magazine, 22(05) online. Available at: https://www.gse.harvard.edu/ideas/ed-magazine/22/05/space-joy (Accessed 1.09.2023).

Jordan, C. and Chawla, L. (2019) A coordinated research agenda for nature-based learning. *Frontiers in Psychology*, 10 March, p.766.

Johnson, R.B., Onwuegbuzie, A.J. and Turner, L.A. (2007) Toward a definition of mixed methods research. *Journal of Mixed Methods Research*, 1, 2, 112-133.

Kaplan, A., Gheen, M. and Midgley, C. (2002) Classroom goal structure and student disruptive behaviour. *British Journal of Educational Psychology*, 72(2), pp.191-211.

Kellert, S.R. and Wilson, E.O. (Eds.) (1995) *The Biophilia Hypothesis*. Island Press, Washington DC.

Kellert, S.R. (2005) *Building for life: Designing and understanding the human-nature connection.* Island Press, Washington DC.

Kellert, S.R. (2008) Dimensions, elements, and attributes of biophilic design. *Biophilic Design: The Theory, Science and Practice of Bringing Buildings To Life*, pp.3-19.

Kohn, A. (2006) *Beyond Discipline: From Compliance to Community*. ASCD.

Kuo, F.E. (2003) The role of arboriculture in a healthy social ecology. *Journal of Arboriculture*, 29, 3, 148-155.

Little, H. and Wyver, S. (2008) Outdoor play: Does avoiding the risks reduce the benefits? *Australasian Journal of Early Childhood*, 33, 2, 33-40.

Loeffler, T.A. (2004) A photo elicitation study of the meanings of outdoor adventure experiences. *Journal of Leisure Research*, 36, 4, 536-556.

Louv, R. (2008) *Last child in the woods: Saving our children from nature-deficit disorder.* Algonquin Books, New York.

Louv, R. (2016) *Vitamin N: The essential guide to a nature-rich life.* Algonquin Books, New York.

Loh, J. (2013) Inquiry into issues of trustworthiness and quality in narrative studies: A perspective. *Qualitative Report,* 18, 33, 1-18.

Lutz, S. and Huitt, W. (2004) Connecting cognitive development and constructivism: Implications from theory for instruction and assessment. *Constructivism in the Human Sciences*, 9, 1, 67-90.

Maguire, M. and Delahunt, B. (2017) Doing a thematic analysis: A practical, step-by-step guide for learning and teaching scholars. *All Ireland Journal of Higher Education*, 9, 3, 21-34.

McKellar, S. (2020) *Peers, Perceptions of Teaching Practices, and Implications for Student Engagement.* Doctoral dissertation, University of Michigan, USA.

Meyer, K. and Willis, R. (2019) Looking back to move forward: The value of reflexive journaling for novice researchers. *Journal of Gerontological Social Work*, 62, 5, 578-585.

Miller, M., Kiverstein, J. and Rietveld, E. (2022) The predictive dynamics of happiness and well-being. *Emotion Review*, 14, 1, 15-30.

Mygind, L., Kjeldsted, E., Hartmeyer, R., Mygind, E., Bølling, M. and Bentsen, P. (2019) Mental, physical and social health benefits of immersive nature-experience for children and adolescents: A systematic review and quality assessment of the evidence. *Health & Place*, 58, 102136.

Nicholson, S. (1971) How not to cheat children, the theory of loose parts. *Landscape architecture*, 62, 1, 30-34.

North, C. (2015) Rain and romanticism: The environment in outdoor education. *Asia-Pacific Journal of Health, Sport and Physical Education*, 6, 3, 287-298.

Pakarinen, E., Imai-Matsumura, K., Yada, A., Yada, T., Leppänen, A. and Lerkkanen, M.K. (2023) Child-centered and teacher-directed practices in two countries: a descriptive case study in Finnish and Japanese grade 1 classrooms. *Journal of Research in Childhood Education*, 1-20.

Parsons, J. and Taylor, L. (2011) Improving student engagement. *Current Issues in Education*, 14, 1.

Patton, M.Q. (2002) Two decades of developments in qualitative inquiry: A personal, experiential perspective. *Qualitative Social Work*, 1, 3, 261-283.

Pratt, M.G. (2009) From the editors: For the lack of a boilerplate: Tips on writing up (and reviewing) qualitative research. *Academy of Management Journal*, 52, 5, 856-862.

Rai, N. and Thapa, B. (2015) A study on purposive sampling method in research. *Kathmandu: Kathmandu School of Law*, 5, 1, 1-8.

Ritchhart, R., Church, M. and Morrison, K. (2011) *Making thinking visible: How to promote engagement, understanding, and independence for all learners.* Wiley & Sons, New Jersey.

Romm, N.R. (2013) Employing questionnaires in terms of a constructivist epistemological stance: reconsidering researchers' involvement in the unfolding of social life. *International Journal of Qualitative Methods*, 12, 1, 652-669.

Schleicher, A. (2018) Educating learners for their future, not our past. *ECNU Review of Education*, 1, 1, 58-75.

Schulze, S. (2007) The usefulness of reflexive photography for qualitative research: A case study in higher education. *South African Journal of Higher Education*, 21, 5, 536-553.

Schunk, D.H. and Miller, S.D. (2002) Self-efficacy and adolescents' motivation. *Academic Motivation of Adolescents*, 2, 1, 29-52.

Seligman, M.E. (2002) *Authentic happiness: Using the new positive psychology to realize your potential for lasting fulfilment.* Simon and Schuster, London.

Sendze, M. (2019) *Case Study of Public Library Directors' Entrepreneurial Leadership Behaviors on Organizational Innovation.* Doctoral dissertation, Grand Canyon University, USA.

Silverman, D. (2021) *Doing Qualitative Research.* Sage, Thousand Oaks, CA.

Struyven, K., Dochy, F., Janssens, S. and Gielen, S. (2008) Students' experiences with contrasting learning environments: The added value of students' perceptions. *Learning Environments Research, 11,* 1, 83-109.

Terry, G., Hayfield, N., Clarke, V. and Braun, V. (2017) Thematic analysis. *The SAGE handbook of qualitative research in psychology*, (pp.17-37). Sage, Thousand Oaks, CA.

Thomas, D.R. (2006) A general inductive approach for analyzing qualitative evaluation data. *American Journal of Evaluation*, 27, 2, 237-246.

Ulrich, R.S. (1984) View through a window may influence recovery from surgery. *Science*, 224, No:4647, pp:420-421.

Van Den Berg, A.E. and Custers, M.H. (2011) Gardening promotes neuroendocrine and affective restoration from stress. *Journal of Health Psychology*, 16, 1, 3-11.

Wells, N.M. and Evans, G.W. (2003) Nearby nature: A buffer of life stress among rural children. *Environment and Behavior*, 35, 3, 311-330.

White, R. (2004) Young children's relationship with nature: Its importance to children's development and the earth's future. *White Hutchinson Leisure & Learning Group*, 1, 9, 215-219.

Zaltman, G. (1996) Metaphorically speaking. *Marketing Research*, 8, 2, 13-20.

Ziller, R.C. (1990) *Photographing the self: Methods for observing personal orientations*. Sage, Thousand Oaks, CA.

Ethics statement: This research was conducted under supervision with ethical approval from the University of Central Lancashire.

Consent and Permissions: All photographs are included with consent/permission c/o International School Luxembourg.

JQRSS Author Profiles

Gail Keech[1] graduated with a B.Ed. (Hons) in PE and English from I.M. Marsh, formerly Liverpool Polytechnic (now Liverpool John Moores University). Since then she has been teaching in international schools around the world including Penang, Malaysia; Kampala, Uganda and Jeddah, Kingdom of Saudi Arabia. Gail graduated from her MA in Outdoor Practice in 2023 at UCLan. Stemming directly from this MA research she is now the Nature Based Learning Lead and Coordinator at the International School of Luxembourg.

Paul Gray[2] is a doctoral research supervisor and Programme Leader for the MA Outdoor Practice in the School of Health, Social Work and Sport at the University of Central Lancashire. Email: pgray1@uclan.ac.uk

Reviewer Comments

A fascinating insight into the thought processes, reflections and learning experiences of a novice researcher undertaking an ambitious research project. Whilst a 62-page journal article may appear daunting, like all good stories, it is an encapsulating read and well supported by a range of engaging and helpful visuals. The narrative is open and honest from the outset, which is to be commended, providing a depth and richness to the research story which can often be left untold, despite its crucial role in situating and contextualising the researcher and the research. It also opens the door to future research opportunities that explore a range of pupil voices on related themes, such as the value of nature-based approaches for all students, different perspectives on what is perceived and/or believed to be nature and creative, nature-based pedagogical strategies that can be implemented in any school grounds. This article provides useful insights to applied and experimental practice alongside practical and accessible methodological theory for a variety of audiences, including teachers, research students and supervisors, parents and outdoor practitioners.

Lawlor, C. and Palmer, C. (2023) 'Being' in the world of football scouting - an exercise in storied and performed data. *Journal of Qualitative Research in Sports Studies*, 17, 1, 107-126

'Being' in the world of football scouting - an exercise in storied and performed data

Craig Lawlor and Clive Palmer

(University of Central Lancashire)

Keywords: *football, scouting, recruitment, phenomenology, lived experience, song writing*

Abstract

For the scout, the heady responsibility for recognising footballing talent in young players is melded with the promise of their potential success, or even greatness in the game. However, implicit of the scout's role and duty, once talent is spotted, is to pass that talent on to others to nurture, for example, by coaching staff at clubs or academies. This common obligation in scouts for 'letting go' characterises their existence, often in want of recognition for their claims-to-fame, for success stemming from their wisdom and insight to the game. Therefore, ironically, a scout's actions seem to be underwritten by a sense of loss, apart from the brief claim that 'I discovered genius'. This paper reveals aspects of this vicarious lived experience by means of data presented in story and song, collected through a phenomenological lens. The stage is set first by an exposition of the scout's magical [under]world and working conditions, followed by a methodological synthesis of the phenomenon itself, scouting, with relevant theory. Then the story: *Taking in a game: a glimpse through the lens of a Nowhere Man* is followed immediately by the song: *40p a Mile and a Sausage Roll*. These refined presentations of data invite the reader onto the terraces alongside the researcher, and then to participate in the reflection of 'being there', as a researcher engaged in *'scout-ology'*. In conclusion, the paper highlights how from the moment of the highly prized discovery the scout seems committed to live in the shadows, understood only by their own community, to continue their vigil, constantly scoping for talent on the football horizon, for glimmers of hope.

Introduction

Such men are central to the mythology of modern football. Scouts may be marginalised, professionally, but they possess the power of dreams. There is no textbook for them to follow, no diploma they can receive for their appreciation of the alchemy involved in the creation of a successful player. Their scrutiny is intimate, intense, and highly individual. They must balance nuances of character with aspects of pre-programmed ability and fit them to the profile and culture of the clubs they represent (Calvin, 2013).

This quote from Michael Calvin's (2013) seminal book captures the essence of the aptly named *Nowhere Men*, football's hidden tribe of talent scouts; faceless and nameless. Calvin contends everyone knows what scouts do, but no one truly knows

JQRSS Article No: 5/9-17-1-2023-PG[109]-166
ISSN: 1754-2375 [print] ISSN: 2755-5240 [online] Copyright ©: CC-BY-NC-ND
Web: https://uclan.academia.edu/ClivePalmer/Journal-of-Qualitative-Research-in-Sports-Studies

why they do it, and no one knows who they are. Aside from this book by Calvin, another by Cotterill (2021) and other popular journalistic sources, academic literature pertaining to the role of the football scout is relatively sparse (Lawlor, Rookwood and Wright, 2021). Consequently, there is little theory to draw upon when it comes to the practical implementation of scouting and recruitment practices. Perhaps more pertinent is the lack of knowledge of what constitutes a scout, governs their practices and their life-worlds. What is it like to be a football scout? What does it mean to be in the scouting world? This article explores the lived experience of scouts and in doing so, methodologically represents a fundamental shift in research approaches away from a scientised investigation or systematic analysis of what constitutes effective or efficient practices in scouting and recruitment, towards understanding the lived experiences of those embroiled in the scouting world. Through the exploration of phenomenological practices, this article has begun to tell their story.

When undertaking research from a phenomenological perspective, a review of relevant literature should portray the taken for granted meanings and assumptions that make up the knowing of practice (Smythe, 2011). Whilst in this article, creative qualitative methods and performed data are used, it is important first and foremost that the perspectives of professional football scouts' life-worlds are explored. Like Calvin's (2013) appraisal above, and almost a decade later, Cotterill (2021:137) offers a similar assessment of the football scout:

> The image of the scout persists, as the mysterious loner in a flat cap skulking around crumbling stadia, scribbling on bits of paper.

In the highly commodified and dynamic industry that professional football has become, it could be imagined that the 'football scout' would be a highly attractive and appealing role for many football enthusiasts. Calvin (2013:3) again examines this assumption stating that being paid to watch 10 games per week would be the sort of fantasy that sustains the average football fan, but he offers a word of warning about the disconnected lifestyle, 'the long, family unfriendly hours where scouts eat on the run, live on their nerves and receive a relative pittance'. In the academic domain, Griffiths and Bloyce (2022) recently explored the motivations of 12 unpaid football scouts working at professional clubs. They came to similar conclusions, that scouts engage in 'hope labour' due to their desire to work in the industry because of their 'love of the game' and 'quest for excitement'. However, the majority were ultimately disappointed, and their fantasy-laden thinking which led them to engage in unpaid labour failed to result in a paid role, often due to a culture of nepotism where a small, tight-knit network of 'insiders' guard against outsiders.

Referring to Calvin's (2013) description of the scouting experience, there is a lack of understanding of the scout's role and thus, a lack of guidelines and training programmes for scouts. Christensen (2009) states that individuals who engage in player identification possess an eye for talent where scouting is a visual experience, a gut feeling, something seen with the mind's eye (Christensen, 2009). The scout is neither rational, nor objective in their selections which are governed by 'what feels right in the heart and stomach' (Lund and Söderström, 2017:248) where existing beliefs, assumptions, values, knowledge, and past experiences all affect the way in which talent spotters observe performance (Golik, Blanco and Czikk, 2017). In popular culture, the 2001 film *Mike Bassett England Manager* (Barron, 2001) did little to promote player identification and selection as a systematic, error-free process, where the clichéd 'names on the back of a cigarette packet' leads to the inadvertent selection of unknown, out of shape, and past-their-best 'Ron Benson' and 'Tony Hedges' for the England National Team. All this represents some of the taken for granted stereotypes of football scouting, i.e. that scouting is mysterious and non-systematic in nature.

James (2023) points out that the football scouting industry is constantly evolving as data analysis and 'the stats' are driving the way players are identified. For fans and practitioners alike, it seems the hope is that player data and analytics will transform football scouting in the same way that sabermetrics did for baseball, championed in the film *Moneyball* (Briley, 2013). Currently, there is limited evidence of this in the academic literature although several authors contend that the use of player data in the identification process does yield benefits (Schumaker, Solieman and Chen, 2012; Gerrard 2017). Thus, for the processes and products of scouting talent in football, the overall picture may have become a little murkier if we accept that numerical data, complex algorithms and persuasive predictions adds to the sorcery of scouting, which if coupled with the alchemy of the faceless scout, we may reasonably have little faith that football clubs are going to identify players more effectively or more consistently than ever before.

This brief review of literature in a narrow field of research leads us to conclude that scouts are, generally male (see *Nowhere Men*), watch multiple games of football per week, spend long, lonely hours on the road hopping from ground to ground and possess some form of magical insight through a trained eye and a gut feeling. This still leaves us pondering, who, actually, are these scouts? Do they really perform magic? If they do, then why aren't they well-paid and world renowned? Why do they do their jobs at all? How did they develop their alchemy? Is there a hierarchy of chief scout wizards? This article, which is part of a wider doctoral research project, explores through a phenomenological lens what it means to be a football scout, to uncover the experiences of those who live in this world, to explore and potentially erode some of these taken for granted assumptions, whilst inviting the reader into the scouting world, to create their own interpretations from scouts' experiences.

Methods

Phenomenology is the study of 'what gives itself' of the experience as it is lived. van Manen (2017) encourages us to seek and ask, what is this experience like? If we consider that a scout's eye for talent is governed by the culture in which they are immersed, their previous identifications and personal interpretations (Lund and Söderström, 2017; Larkin *et al.*, 2020), then a phenomenological investigation which explores this culture and individuals' lived experiences is appropriate. The challenge, according to van Manen (2017) is to uncover and recover lived meaning from experiences without objectifying or turning lived experiences into positivistic themes, sanitised concepts, objectified descriptions, or abstract theories. Therefore, this research seeks to uncover what it is like to be a football scout and how scouts experience their world. Our intention is to impart something of this lived experience through the medium of story and song, that follow below.

The idea of 'being' as a motivation for this study comes from Martin Heidegger's epoch-making work around *Dasein* or being-there (Heidegger, 1927 / 1962) which signifies that as humans we are always experiencing our world in a context which influences our experience (Smythe, 2011). Therefore, *Dasein*, always 'is'. In 'being', we are always open to the things, thoughts, feelings, people that 'call' or have, and are forgetful or ignorant of all else that is 'there' but does not claim our attention. Other methodologies may seek to remove the issue from its context but phenomenology, in contrast, accepts that not only can we never escape context but that the 'there' of being makes the experience what it 'is' (Smythe, 2011). Thus, this article stems from wider research that is a study of being-in-the-scouting-world. Hermeneutic phenomenology, more specifically, is an ongoing, creative, intuitive, and dialectic approach which challenges pre-determined rules and research procedures, signifying a freeing from the dichotomous right and wrong way of doing things (Crowther, Ironside, Spence and Smythe, 2016). It endeavours to investigate the covered over, taken for granted or the silenced amongst theoretical discourse.

The initial focus of the wider research project was to identify 'effective' and 'ineffective' scouting practices, but it was soon apparent that this was a fruitless endeavour with a plethora of factors contributing to 'good' and 'bad' practice. For instance, one may assume that 'good' scouting results in 'good' recruitment and thus 'good performance', not so. From reviewing literature, completing field observations and drawing on the author's own experiences in the field, reflected upon and captured in first-person narratives, there are a range of variables and factors which can affect this complex, dynamic process, especially if it is to be regarded as being 'successful' (Stephenson, 2012). For instance, there are countless potential players a club could identify, but with so many games for scouts to watch, on top of deciding which players to watch at those matches, is challenging. Following the initial identification stage of what matches and what players, there is a targeting process where multiple scouts must corroborate to decide which players they should attempt to acquire for given teams. Then, there are recruitment factors relating to transfer fees, contracts, wages, agents' fees; all this proceeding the actual process of player integration and the potential relocation of the player at a new club, and potentially their family, to a new location. It is also assumed that the player will just 'fit in' to the new club culture, be selected by the Manager or Head Coach to play, receive appropriate training for their development and avoid injury. Thus, the general idea that 'good' or 'bad' scouting in some way exists and can be identified, monitored and adjusted in the current era, is at best, ambitious. For example:

'Discovering genius' – hope labour

Affirming the stereotype and fuelling folklore about scouting, famously, is Bob Bishop, the Manchester United scout who in 1961 'discovered' the 15 year old George Best in Belfast. Bishop's telegram to United manager Matt Busby read: *I think I've found you a genius.* His local club in Northern Ireland, Glentoran, had previously rejected him for being too small and light (Barret, 2019).

Claims for 'discovering genius', on the basis that 'it takes one to know one', may be part of the problem, not the solution for football scouts generally. Some of the variables mentioned here became apparent during field research, indicating that the richness, and real value of this study lay in exploring the ambiguous, often challenging nature of football scouting with regard to how scouts exchange their social capital, make decisions and exert influence and power over others, all constituting part of their life-world experience as a football scout.

Research design and participants

Lived situations are unique and dynamic and therefore an analysis and presentation which mirrors this dynamism is required (Smythe, 2011). A significant advantage of this philosophical and methodological framework is that researchers' horizons of understanding are acknowledged as entwined with the project, as Smythe (2011) points out, we are bound to our own pre-understandings which will always shape our thinking. Reflexivity therefore plays a central role in the researcher's attempts to keep a check on their preconceptions (Horrigan-Kelly, Millar and Downing, 2016). This reflexivity not only allows for the interrogation of the researcher's understanding of things, but it also helps to bring to the fore the researcher's values, beliefs and motivations (Finlay, 2008; Clancy, 2013). Hence, the lead author's 13 years working in professional football and 7 years enmeshed in the scouting industry is acknowledged and valued rather than bracketed away and disconnected from the research process, something which is more common in Interpretive Phenomenological Analysis (Smith, Flowers and Larkin, 2021).

Contrastingly, in Hermeneutic Phenomenology, the researcher does not attempt to bracket or adopt a Husserlian phenomenological reduction where preconceptions and pre-understandings are put aside to pursue the interpretive work in an unmediated way (Crowther and Thomson, 2020; Dowling, 2007). For Heidegger, it is the individual's situated 'being-the-world' with their own fore-structures of understanding that allows them to understand and question the world from a certain vantage point (Heidegger, 1927/1962). For example, in reflexive notes it was recorded,

> My attempts to bracket out my understandings and pre-suppositions after 7 years in the scouting world are proving impossible, they are part of me.

Smythe (2011) therefore challenges us to become aware of our prejudices and alert the reader as to how the study may have been influenced. In Hermeneutic Phenomenology, the main quest is to provide the audience with an account in which they can engage so they can experience the phenomena as lived by others. Our aim in this article is to communicate those experiences through personal narrative (story), and music (song), which are integrated with and from experiences in the field.

A period of ethnographic observation took place between January 2020 and February 2022, followed by a series of semi-structured interviews (n=8). Through immersion in the experiences and examples of others, phenomena began to develop from the interplay between the data and the interpreter. Rather than seeking to identify effective scouting processes and practices, such as looking for pragmatic efficiencies in scouting, it was decided to reflect upon the phenomena of scouting itself, the lived experience, and what emerged were aspects of meaning which scouts attributed to their experiences. It was discovered there was evidence of scouts being undervalued, unappreciated but still finding meaning in their roles, some still active after many decades in the field. Of course, some accounts have been omitted in line with phenomenological enquiry where van Manen (2017) advises that examples are illustrations, they have the capacity to add new knowledge but can be left out without harming the text, whilst also preserving and protecting the situation being researched.

Interpretation and presentation: story and song

Stories are an increasingly common methodological device in socio-cultural research (e.g. Sparkes, 2002; Gunaratnam and Oliviere, 2009; Rooney, Lawlor and Rohan, 2016), and crafting stories is congruent with the philosophical underpinnings of Hermeneutic Phenomenology (Crowther, Ironside, Spence and Smythe, 2016). Shared stories give testimony to past events and experiences, shedding light on what is known but also what is covered over or forgotten (McAdams, 1993). Therefore, in the first instance, our findings are presented in a creative nonfiction piece (Gerard, 1996), a story where readers are invited to delve into a football scouting experience and make their own meaning from the account, after meeting the scouts that haunt the terraces. By using such creative methods here, the claim is not to state what is true or wholly representative for scouts everywhere but rather, to open a conversation with readers as to possible understandings (Smythe, 2011). As phenomenology deals with narratives, stories, poetry, and anecdotes, not with codes or objectivist data (van Manen, 2017), it is appropriate to interpret experiences and participant responses as 'meaning units' (Giorgi, 1970; 2009) or 'phenomenological examples' (van Manen, 2017). The word 'buytendijk' refers to phenomenology as the science of examples (van Manen, 1997) where 'the example lets the singular be seen' (Agamben, 1993:22). These examples or meaning units therefore shine a light within the research, guiding the reader to the experience, to see what the researcher sees, with an open invitation to think together, to acquire a deeper insight and awareness about a shared phenomenon.

The story below, is followed by a song, written and performed by Craig Lawlor in 2023, to a large and appreciative audience at a research conference, figure 1.

Figure 1: Craig Lawlor (2023) performing the song *'40p a Mile and a Sausage Roll'* as part of his doctoral research and data analysis: *An investigation of scouting and recruitment in men's professional football: issues and future directions.* Graduate Research School Annual Postgraduate Research Conference, University of Central Lancashire, 3rd-4th May.

[Photograph credit: Mervyn Clarke and Helen O'Donnell]

40p a Mile and a Sausage Roll, takes some of the meaningful themes from the story and from the field data in this research, to invite the reader once again into the football scouting world. The 'chorus' or repeated refrains in the song invite the reader (or audience when performed) to vocally contribute, physically including them to become part of the performance and be drawn closer to the messages which the song hopes to impart. This is a form of Participatory Research Method e.g. see Cargo and Mercer (2008), Bergold and Thomas (2012) and Burns, Howard and Ospina (2021). There is a gathering conversation around music and song as unique forms of qualitative inquiry which historically, have received limited attention (Carless, 2018). As Douglas (2020:59) states,

> Song writing is so alluring and challenging; you don't know what you will find and in terms of my own reflections, not only do I interpret song as an engaging form of dissemination, but the crafting of lyrics and an appropriate melody are extremely useful methods of analysis and interpretation, a process where the phenomenon can begin to show itself.

Dahlberg, Dahlberg and Nystrom (2008) discourage the researcher from reaching an understanding too quickly, carelessly, or slovenly, something they refer to as 'bridling'. Similarly, van Manen (1997) also discourages researchers from reaching premature understandings of the phenomenon in question, in short, to avoid jumping to conclusions. Song and story writing can be seen as a form of reflexive practice which avoids early conclusion and deeper refining of data, which aligns with the hermeneutic circle; the ongoing, attentive, circular movement between part and whole (Gadamer, 1988). For example, in song, the composition of both music and lyrics prompt ideas around theme and repetition, rehearsal and shared or participatory methods to impart ideas and interpretations of data. However, as progress is made through a topic, experience or phenomenon, it may be realised that initial assumptions were too narrow, and this triggers a greater understanding of the whole. Crowther and Thomson (2020) state that the hermeneutic circle describes three fore-structures through which individuals come to understand and interpret their life-world:

1) *fore-having* is the background context of pre-understandings,

2) *fore-sight* relates to how an individual always enters an experience with a specific viewpoint and

3) *fore-conception* is an anticipated sense of the interpretations that will be made (Heidegger, 1927/1962).

The aim, therefore, is to prevent interpretations being generated only in what is already known, rather it is about uncovering what is hidden and lies beneath. To provide an example of how the researcher's preconceptions of scouting connected with the experiences of participants from interviews, Craig reflected on his years in scouting that *'at times I felt paralysed by ambiguity' [as reference to Simone De Beauvoir's writing around existential phenomenology - see Bakewell, 2016]*. Due to his experiences in the field, there were undoubtedly times when the research was deductive in nature but due to the scarcity of literature in the field, a process of induction, too, had to occur. The process therefore could be classed as abductive, sitting somewhere between induction and deduction, a common and central facet of hermeneutic phenomenology (Wiltshire and Ronkainen, 2021). Therefore, when examples such as the one identified in the brief quote below came forth, it was possible to combine the first-person narrative and 'data' collected in the field, to form the results:

> [from field notes:] We still don't know our roles. On the day the new guy came in, he should have sat us down and said 'Your role's this, you do that' but that never happened. We still need that to happen because no one knows what they're meant to be doing.

Further examples such as this ambiguity of role and purpose will be apparent in the following section. We therefore invite you, the reader, to experience the football scouting world, and explore what it means to be a football scout through story and song.

Story

Taking in a game: a glimpse through the lens of a Nowhere Man

I walk up the damp concrete steps from the concourse and the cold winter wind hits me, as does the sound of 90s Britpop over the old tannoy and I squint in the light of the floodlights high above the damp and muddy playing surface. I make my way down to my seat; notebook, pen and team sheet, the scout's toolkit, in one hand, polythene cup in the other – not sure yet if it's tea or coffee, I just said 'yes' to the lady in the lounge when she asked if I wanted a drink. I make my way past the seated fanatics, head-to-toe in replica hats, scarves and coats and the familiar smell of meat pies and Bovril. Down to my right I see them, the scouts, my peers, the Nowhere Men. I decided to wear my nice coat and smart shoes tonight, I don't know why, it's bloody freezing. I suppose it's so I look a bit more 'professional' because I want to feel professional, like I've made it, like I'm a somebody. I do look a bit out of place though, everyone else is in big, warm coats and hats.

I make my way to row J, seat 37 where I sit down, two seats down from a scout I don't know. He's youngish, young for the industry anyway, probably mid 30s. He doesn't say a word and doesn't look up. His eyes flick between his phone and his notepad where he's already busy taking notes. We're all here to make notes about players in the game but the game hasn't even started yet, I've got no idea what he's writing.

I'm sat in front of three old-timers, residuals, the backbone of the industry – Hitchcock, McIntosh, and Morris. Morris is the first to pipe up, 'Here, did you hear about Nigel? He's got the sack, he found out he'd lost his job from Sky Sports News!' McIntosh replies, 'Aye but they've agreed to keep him on part-time, haven't they, not bad, gets £20K to go to a few games a week and just chuck a report in'. Hitchcock wipes his nose and intervenes, 'Still, better than what happened to Bob, he got sacked by text! It's a bloody disgrace'. The three of them ramble on incessantly as the teams complete their final preparations ahead of kick off.

I avert my attention from the old timers and notice Summers sat on his own, smartly dressed, newly whitened teeth and he's on the phone. He was a hero in his playing days, I remember watching him on tele when I was a kid and in a funny way it gives him this aura of greatness. I've got no idea if he's any good at scouting, but he sure looks the part. He's talking numbers and work permits, probably speaking to an agent, he seems to know his stuff. He doesn't look up from his pristine leather boots as the teams enter the field of play. I hear Hitchcock's voice again, 'I've only come to watch him', pointing at a name on his team sheet. He's not in the starting eleven. 'What a waste of time' he says indifferently shrugging his shoulders, 'He'll probably only get 10 minutes at the end!' McIntosh replies sharply, 'Aye but you'll leave on 70 minutes anyway, so it doesn't matter if he comes on or not!' The three of them laugh. 'Alright then, who are you watching Macca?' asks Hitchcock mockingly, 'No one really, I wanna get a look at Thompson, he'll never play for our lot, he can't play in a two, but I'll put my report in anyway just to cover myself'. 'We've watched him a few times Macca, half of our lot like him, the other half don't', responds Morris quickly, 'they keep telling me everything he can't do, why not tell me what he can do! Scouts don't do that enough these days'. They all nod in unison.

The game kicks off. I hear a rush next to me as Townsend, one of the good guys, middle aged, former analyst squeezes into the seat next to me. 'Evening. Didn't think I was going to make it, just got here from an Under 23s game', he says, panting. 'Managed to get something to eat on the way here though, so that's a win, I'll put that on the expenses!' He immediately opens a professional looking folder full of scraps of paper, team sheets, jottings of formations and other ambiguous scribbles. 'I see we're sat behind the geriatrics' he says with a laugh and immediately starts writing on his pad with an expensive looking biro. He's writing a report on every player tonight. 'Two or three lines on every player, that's what you need to do' is one of his signature phrases.

The game isn't great, there's no real ebb or flow, the ball changes hands frequently on a bobbly, muddy pitch. Both sides are jam packed with older players who've made their money and careers in the higher leagues and don't look too enthusiastic about a lower league game on a wet December night in the northwest of England. There's a smattering of interesting players, an 18-year-old on loan from a top division side, a few Academy graduates in their early 20s but they can't impose themselves on such a disjointed game. I look down at Summers, he's on his phone again. He can't have watched more than 5 minutes so far in the first half. Townsend nudges me, 'Look at that twat, some scout he is, he's been on his phone the whole time'. He shakes his head with his eyes still fixated on the game, 'Apparently, he's on £100K. He only got the job because he used to play with the gaffer there. Classic football nepotism, what a joke. I hear he's on the take as well'. I ask him what he means, he replies, 'He's using the same agent all the time, Jake reckons he's taking a cut of every deal!'

There's a break in play due to a heavy tackle and the players jog over to the dugout for a mouthful of water and some angry exchanges with their respective managers. I take a moment to listen to the old boys sat in front, it's typical scouting chat. 'That centre half's got a foot like a sheriff's badge! He nearly took someone's head off with that pass earlier' laughs Hitchcock. Then Morris responds, 'Yeah, but he's better than the lad they've got at centre back, look at him (pointing), bloody lazy' which was more racial slur than any serious assessment of physical effort, and totally oblivious to the fact that the player in question is born in England and of African descent. 'Speaking of which, have you seen Godson at our place? He's a lazy git, he's alright on the ball but he doesn't want to defend', quips McIntosh angrily. 'Yeah, heard he's got a bad attitude Macca?' asks Hitchcock with a sharp turn of his head. 'Oh aye he has, so the Gaffer tells me. He couldn't tackle a fish supper, he's weak as piss!' The three laugh in unison as the play gets underway again.

'How bad's this?' Townsend asks about the game as we near half-time. I've lost count of the number of times I've checked my watch and rubbed my knees to try and warm myself up. 'Look at him! He's having an absolute nightmare!' shouts Morris as a midfield player tries to turn and run back on the heavy playing surface, 'My missus would beat him in a race and let me tell you, she ain't quick!' The rear-guard laugh and nudge each other as the ball goes out of play for yet another throw-in.

After a spirited three minutes of stoppage time the half-time whistle blows, 0-0. The fans clap with the same enthusiasm that Townsend and I feel as we trudge up the steps and into the lounge, where there's a crinkled A4 sheet of paper stuck down with blue tack displaying: Scouts and Media, clinging to the door. Hitchcock, Morris, and McIntosh are already in there with their cups of tea and curled up cheese sandwiches. Townsend and I sit on a separate table. You can still hear the three old timers chatting away, 'How's the new bloke at your place? The new Head of Recruitment or whatever' asks Morris. 'Seems alright' replies Hitchcock, 'I've not met him yet but he was alright with me on the phone'. 'You want to see if you can get more out of him than 40p a mile and a sausage roll on the way home' responds McIntosh, with a laugh and a mouthful of sandwich.

Johnny comes and sits next to us, 'Alright guys?' I don't know his surname, just the club he works for. He's in his early 20s, wet behind the ears, carrying an iPad. 'What do you think of Dickinson?' he asks about the 18-year-old loanee. 'He's okay' replies Townsend, 'But he can't get into the game'. Johnny responds sharply, 'His stats are amazing, one of the best in the league for his attacking output'. You can almost feel people's eyes roll as they're sat around the table. 'How are things at your place Johnny?' asks Simon who's a Recruitment Analyst in his mid-30s. 'Not great. I'm working with a really boisterous Manager' Johnny replies, lowering his head. 'I'm sat in with the coaches and everyone's got an opinion. It wasn't like this at my last club, it's incredibly stressful'. 'How did you get that job, Johnny?' asks Townsend. 'I just rang the Chairman up, went in for a chat and he gave me the job. It's great, I love it' says Johnny, with an unconvincing smile, 'It doesn't feel like a job to me, it's an unhealthy obsession. I'm at this game tonight, one tomorrow and two at the weekend'. The conversation ends with some unenthusiastic nods of the head and an equally uninspired 'great' from Townsend.

I look round the room, there must be 40 scouts here. The majority sit hunched over their cups of tea and sandwiches. Two former players-turned-scouts stand by the door exchanging war stories. 'It's bloody crap this game' one of them says. I recognise his face but don't know the name, 'I'm getting off at 65 minutes'. The other, Gaz, replies 'I won't be far behind you, I'm at the training ground tomorrow then off up to Scotland on Thursday'. I feel a hand on my shoulder, it's Smogga. Mid-60s, former council worker, good, honest bloke. 'Hello young man' he says with a smile, we shake hands and exchange some scouting small talk, 'Going well your lot? What's the new gaffer like? How's Will getting on? Heard about Nigel?' He starts telling me all about his current role, like many on the job, it doesn't sound great. He continues, 'We still don't know our roles. On the day the new guy came in, he should have sat us down and said, "your our role's this, you do that" but that never happened. We still need that to happen because no one knows what they're meant to be doing'. I nod away and try and provide some reassurances, but I know it's the same story for a lot of us, 'I'm getting 25p a mile at the moment and going to the same bloody grounds every week. It's ridiculous' he says with a frown. Over the old tannoy comes a crackled message, 'Please welcome the players back onto the pitch' and the Nowhere Men make their way onto the concourse and up the crumbling steps to their seats.

The temperature has dropped, the players look a bedraggled bunch as the referee gets the second half underway. The two former players, Gaz and his mate have come and sat just behind Townsend and me, cups in hand. They're chatting away, 'Listen, nothing ever really gets done with the players you flag up. It all gets lost in data doesn't it?' says Gaz flippantly. 'You're right there. It's like when I signed

Jimmy C., we had a load of reports saying he was no good with the ball and couldn't defend but I goes into the Gaffer and says, "Listen, he can run, don't worry about that" and look at him now Gaz, it was a great signing'. Townsend nudges me and winks. 'That's your only currency isn't it? saying 'I signed him', but we all know it's never just one person, it's the whole scouting team, the coaching staff, the Sporting Director or whoever' he says wryly, 'classic ex-player chat'. The next minute a heavy tackle flies in and both sets of players surround the referee. I look around, the scouts are on the edge of their seats, almost like fans, except Summers of course who's still on his phone. 'Ehh Gaz, I love it when a game gets tasty' he says excitedly. All of a sudden, the game springs into life and there's goalmouth action, chances for both sides, bookings being handed out left right and centre. The emotion of the game is infectious and the Nowhere Men have started to take a real interest.

The game reaches the 77th minute and it's still 0-0. A fresh-faced lad steps off the bench and takes his tracksuit off, it's Gerry Jordan, the player Hitchcock has come to watch. I look over to the three old boys, they're already heading up the concrete steps to the exit. Hitchcock looks round at the pitch and sees Jordan ready to come on, 'Bloody typical' he says, throwing his arms in the air as he trudges up the steps. 'Don't worry Hitchy' says Morris calmly, 'You'll get a chance to watch him another time. It's late and you've got a long drive ahead of you'. The nameless scout on the other side of me looks me in the eye and smiles, 'Can you believe it? He's come all this way to watch one player and he's not even going to get to see him'. I smile and laugh in agreement. 'Chris Dennis by the way' and he says which team he works for, we exchange a few pleasantries, establish our mutual connections which is serious currency in this game. 'I'm from an analysis background, me' he says with almost an embarrassed air, 'But scouting's a different ballgame altogether'. We both turn back to the action as the home side miss a guilt-edged chance at goal. 'I get no direction from the club really, I'm just here taking the game in and making as many notes as I can. I put my report up on the system but I've got no idea if anyone reads it'. I nod sympathetically, I know that feeling. 'Here, can I get your number? I'll give you a bell sometime'. We exchange numbers, unaware of just how valuable that connection could be in the future.

'Here lad, are we getting off?' says Gaz behind. 'Too right, you said you'd be away by the 65th minute'. The ball rolls out of play for a throw-in. It's minute 81 now and there's a mass exodus. 'Nice to meet you, I'll give you a call' says Chris as he shakes my hand and jogs up the steps. Summers has gone too. There's only me, Townsend and young Johnny left. Johnny's tapping away on his iPad, oblivious to those pushing past him in a rush to get to their cars. 'He's naïve but credit to him he sticks around and does the job' says Townsend.

Minutes pass slowly as the players tire and the pitch worsens. I decide it's my time to go. There's nothing for me to see here but I never go before 87 minutes, it feels wrong to go any sooner. I make my way out as quickly as I can, past the stewards and those still busily working in the concourse and into the rain. As I hear a rambunctious response from the crowd following what I can only assume to be a heavy tackle or a poor refereeing decision, I bump into Harold, a scout for a Premier League club, smoking a cigarette on his way to his car. 'What did you think of Dickinson tonight?' I tell him my thoughts. 'I love him, me, I absolutely love him' Harold responds after expelling a plume of smoke into the cold night air. 'He's got everything, he's big, quick, strong, direct, mobile, sharp…' He carries on in this fashion for another minute or so, listing a plethora of synonyms for the word 'fast' before we part ways and he heads down a side street. 'I prefer parking here, you can get on the motorway quicker. Ta-ra mate'. I feel my phone vibrating, it's an unknown number, I answer, it's Chris Dennis. 'How bad was that? I couldn't take anymore of that game' he says. 'How did it finish up?' I tell him I don't know, I've left early too. 'I've not got a clue why I was there mate, we've always looked at much better leagues and players than that, but this new fella's come in and he wants us to look at the lower leagues, it's bizarre'. Chris clearly wants to talk as I reach my car, open the door and jump in as quick as I can with my coat still on and put the heater on full blast. 'I've watched these teams for years, I watch them on video too, I know who the best players are but when I put them forward, I get a blank look or get told they're shit. The club's an embarrassment'. I'm getting another call, it's my boss, Warren. I need to take it, I apologise to Chris and tell him I'll call him back soon. Warren's on his way back from another game. 'Well the game wasn't great but it was competitive enough, Jennings did well, the Gaffer likes him, I think we might try and take him in January'. I don't really like Jennings personally, but I responded something like, 'Okay, yeah, great'. I don't want to disagree with him really, he's the boss and what he says goes. 'Who did well at your game?' I tell him about Dickinson, the 18-year-old loanee, he replies coldly, 'Nah, don't like him unfortunately'. I try to change the subject onto players we both like or players I think he likes but he's fairly non-committal. 'Where are you on Saturday?' he asks. I tell him, my heart sinks as I utter the name of that club. Early in my career I would have felt excited about going to a game at that place, but it's a long drive and I'm pretty confident there's no players of interest for us there. 'Should be a good game that, make sure you report on Potter' Warren replies sharply. Again, a player I've watched before who I don't think is good enough to be signed, 'No worries, will do' I mutter. 'Okay pal, I'll see you next week for that scout's meeting. Cheers mate, bye…bye' and hangs up.

The End

Song

'40p a Mile and a Sausage Roll'

Music and lyrics composed by Craig Lawlor, 2023

(Chant/folk beat in the style of Bob Dylan or Billy Bragg)

We're just a bunch of *Nowhere Men* finding players here and there
When I see a talent I stop and stare
When they do something unique it really makes me smile
As long as I get my 40p a mile

Chorus/refrain (all):
40p per mile and a sausage roll, my data reveals my professional role,
Questions and motives and identity, the real outcomes of my… 'Scout-ology!'

It's not a science, we're not flying to the moon
But the Manager, Chief Scout and I aren't singing the same tune
When I stop and think about it, I don't really know my role
But at least I get expenses and a sausage roll

There's a player here today he's big, he's quick, he's strong
But my line manager and I don't get along
One day it might culminate in an ugly club wide fight
Cos I'm sick of watching Accrington every Tuesday night

Chorus/refrain (all):
40p per mile and a sausage roll, my data reveals my professional role,
Questions and motives and identity, the real outcomes of my… 'Scout-ology!'

I'm not sure what I'm doing here we have no philosophy
It's feels like I'm paralysed by ambiguity
Did you hear about Bob? He got sacked by text
And now I'm wondering if I'll be next

I do it for the buzz – Wow we've got someone!
I watch players all day but the job's never done
When football's good - It's great, it's unbelievable!
But our targets are unrealistic and unachievable

Chorus/refrain (all):
40p per mile and a sausage roll, my data reveals my professional role,
Questions and motives and identity, the real outcomes of my… 'Scout-ology!'

I want it to go on for as long as it can - I love it!
But most days I feel like a hypocrite
Scouting is a privilege - The best job in the world!
This is what it's like being-in-the-scouting-world

I'm growing tired and weary of going to these games all alone
I've never met my boss but he seems nice on the phone
I don't know who I'm watching and what's worse I don't know why
But at least the club will pay for my butter pie

Chorus/refrain (all):
40p per mile and a sausage roll, my data reveals my professional role,
Questions and motives and identity, the real outcomes of my… 'Scout-ology!'

If you're not sure about being a scout, you should get out now
All those ex-players are holier than thou
I spent years in the industry, I don't want to stand here and gloat
But for my hard work I got a Blackburn Rovers coat

Conclusion

From the story and the song we see the confusion, the angst, the enthusiasm (and lack of), the anxiety and ambiguity, the heart sinking feeling of being-in-the-scouting world. We experience the paradoxical nature of being a football scout, clinging on to meaning which is not in the successful recruitment of players, it's not the glamourous role some may perceive it to be. The reality is that scouting comes with little recognition or reward for the majority. However, we see the shared, lived scouting experience where groups of scouts gravitate towards similar, likeminded people, where despite some conflict and loneliness, they find meaning in being a football scout. As Heidegger states, being is always being-with, all our lived experiences are shared with, and in relation to others (Heidegger, 1927/1962). We also see scouts striving to survive in an unstable industry, fearful of losing their job, or their life as they know it. Again, paradoxically, they seem to do it for the love of the game, the thrill of the fight, but they still leave the matches early.

Aside from challenging the researcher's preconceived ideas of the role of the football scout and presenting novel results relating to being in the football scouting world, this article calls for further inquiry into, and use of, creative methods in dynamic socio-cultural settings, as it gets to the heart of the experience, and seemingly tells us more about the realities of the lived experience. Creativity in research is so often dismissed (Braben and Dowler, 2017) but it is hoped this article has evidenced the value of this ongoing, reflective approach to uncover lived experience and meaning, particularly in the philosophy and methodology of Hermeneutic Phenomenology. All the findings; principally the story and the song, are crafted from legitimate qualitative data but expressed in a more accessible, less distant, more inclusive manner. It is hoped the reader might have felt accompanied to walk through the scouting world, and maybe relate to other scouts' experiences through creative descriptions. As Smythe (2011) encourages, we should open ourselves up to a journey of thinking as our knowing emerges. This allows a reconnection with what it means to be human, discover afresh what is already known but perhaps forgotten, hidden or put aside. It exposes vulnerability and resilience, dread and hope, sadness and joy. It identifies things celebrated and things despaired of, and crucially in this context, it reveals the experience of what it means 'to be' in the scouting world.

References

Agamben, G. (1993) *The coming community.* University of Minnesota Press, Minneapolis, MN.

Bakewell, S. (2016) At the existentialist café. Vintage, London.

Barrett, J. (2019) *The story of George Best, part one: 'I think I have found you a genius' – the telegram that led to the legend.* Sunday Post online, posted: 6th September. Available at: https://www.sundaypost.com/fp/i-think-i-have-found-you-a-genius-the-telegram-that-led-to-birth-of a-legend/ (Accessed 21st October 2023)

Barron, S. (2001) *Mike Bassett England Manager* [film: 89 mins] dir: Steve Barron. Artists Independent Productions, Film Council, Hallmark Entertainment. UK.

Bergold, J. and Thomas, S. (2012) Participatory research methods: a methodological approach in motion. *Historical Social Research*, 37, 4, 191-222.

Braben, D. and Dowler, R. (2017) *Peer review processes risk stifling creativity and limiting opportunities for game-changing scientific discoveries.* London School of Economics, posted 17th Sept. https://blogs.lse.ac.uk/impactofsocialsciences/2017/09/17/peer-review-processes-risk-stifling-creativity-and-limiting-opportunities-for-scientific-discoveries/ (Accessed 14.11.2023)

Briley, R. (2013) Review of *Moneyball* dir: Bennett Miller, and *Trouble with the Curve* dir: Robert Lorenz. *NINE: A Journal of Baseball History and Culture*, 21, 2, 182-188.

Burns, D., Howard, J. and Ospina, S.M. (Eds.) (2021) *The SAGE handbook of participatory research and inquiry.* Sage, Thousand Oaks, CA.

Calvin M. (2013) *The Nowhere Men: the unknown story of football's true talent spotters.* Random House, London.

Cargo, M. and Mercer, S.L. (2008) The value and challenges of participatory research: strengthening its practice. *Annual Review of Public Health*, 29, 325-350.

Carless, D. (2018) 'Throughness': A story about song writing as auto/ethnography. *Qualitative Inquiry*, 24, 3, 227-232.

Christensen, M.K. (2009) An eye for talent: Talent Identification and the 'practical sense' of top-level soccer coaches. *Sociology of Sport Journal,* 26, 3, 365-382.

Clancy, M. (2013) Is reflexivity the key to minimising problems of interpretation in phenomenological research? *Nurse Researcher*, 20, 12-16.

Cotterill, J. (2021) *Anatomy of a football scout.* Camara Brasileira Do Livro, Brasil.

Crowther, S., Ironside, P., Spence, D. and Smythe, L. (2016) Crafting stories in hermeneutic phenomenology research. *Qualitative Health Research,* 27, 6, 826-835.

Crowther, S. and Thomson, G. (2020) From description to interpretive leap: using philosophical notions to unpack and surface meaning in hermeneutic phenomenology research. *International Journal of Qualitative Methods,* 19, 1-11.

Dahlberg, K., Dahlberg, H. and Nystrom, M. (2008) *Reflective lifeworld research* (2nd ed.). Studentlitteratur, Lund, Sweden.

Douglas, K. (2020) Singing in troubled times. 'This country' reflections on song writing and singing qualitative research (Chapter 4). In, Denzin, N.K. and Salvo, J. (Eds.) *New Directions in Theorizing Qualitative Research: The Arts.* Myers Educational Press, USA.

Dowling, M. (2007) From Husserl to van Manen: A review of different phenomenological approaches. *International Journal of Nursing Studies,* 44, 1, 131–142.

Finlay L. (2008) A dance between the reduction and reflexivity: explicating the 'phenomenological psychological attitude'. *Journal of Phenomenological Psychology,* 39, 1, 1-32.

Gadamer, H.G. (1988) On the circle of understanding (pp:55-66). In, Connolly, J. and Keutner, T. (Eds.) *Hermeneutics versus science? Three German views.* University of Notre Dame Press.

Gerard, P. (1996) *Creative non-fiction, researching and crafting stories of real life.* Story Press, Cincinnati, Ohio, USA.

Gerrard, B. (2017) The role of analytics in assessing playing talent (pp. 423-431). In, Cobley, S., Schorer, J., Wattie N. and Baker, J. (Eds.) *Routledge Handbook of Talent Identification and Development in Sport.* Routledge, Abingdon.

Giorgi, A. (1970) *Psychology as a human science: A phenomenologically based approach.* Harper & Row, New York.

Giorgi, A. (2009) *The descriptive phenomenological method in psychology: A modified Husserlian approach.* Duquesne University Press, Pittsburgh.

Golik, M.N., Blanco, M.R. and Czikk, R. (2017) On the trail of line managers as talent spotters. *Human Resource Development International,* 21, 3, 232-253.

Griffiths, J. and Bloyce D. (2022) 'If you haven't got the contacts… you have no choice': A figurational examination of unpaid work in football scouting in men's professional football in England. *International Review for the Sociology of Sport,* 58, 1, 87-107.

Gunaratnam, Y. and Oliviere, D. (2009) *Narrative and stories in health care: illness, dying and bereavement.* Oxford University Press, Oxford, UK.

Heidegger, M. (1962) *Being and Time.* (Trans: J. Macquarrie and E. Robinson). Harper & Row, New York. (Original work published 1927).

Horrigan-Kelly, M., Millar, M. and Dowling, M. (2016) Understanding the key tenets of Heidegger's philosophy for phenomenological research. *Journal of Qualitative Methods,* 15, 1, 1-8.

James, S. (2023) *The reality of being a scout in 2023: 'You do it for love - not money.'* The Athletic. online. Available at: https://theathletic.com/4131355/2023/01/30/transfer-window-football-scouting/ (Accessed: 19th October 2023)

Larkin, P., Marchant, D., Syder, A. and Farrow, D. (2020) An eye for talent: The recruiters' role in the Australian Football talent pathway. *PLoS ONE,* 15, pp:11.

Lawlor, C., Rookwood, J. and Wright, C. (2021) Player scouting and recruitment in English men's professional football: opportunities for research. *Journal of Qualitative Research in Sports Studies,* 15, 1, 57-76.

Lawlor, C. (2023) *An investigation of scouting and recruitment in men's professional football: issues and future directions.* Graduate Research School Annual Postgraduate Research Conference, University of Central Lancashire, 3-4 May.

Lund, S. and Söderström, T. (2017) To see or not to see: Talent Identification in the Swedish Football Association. *Sociology of Sport Journal,* 34, 248 -258.

McAdams, D.P. (1993) *The stories we live by.* Guilford Press, New York.

Rooney, T., Lawlor, K., Rohan, E. (2016) Telling tales; storytelling as a methodological approach in research. *Electronic Journal of Business Research Methods,* 14, 2, 147-156.

Sparkes, A.C. (2002) *Telling tales in sport and physical Activity.* Human Kinetics, Leeds, UK.

Schumaker, R.P., Solieman, O.K. and Chen, H. (2010) Sports knowledge management and data mining. *Annual Review of Information Science and Technology,* 44, 115-157.

Smith, J.A., Flowers, P. and Larkin, M. (2021) *Interpretative phenomenological analysis: theory, method and research.* Sage Publications Ltd. London.

Stephenson, J. (2012) *The scouting and recruitment of professional footballers and the recruitment service.* Fetherbys, London.

Smythe, E. (2011) From beginning to end: How to do hermeneutic interpretive phenomenology (Chapter 12). In, Thomson, G., Dykes, F. and Downe, S. (Eds.) *Qualitative research in midwifery and childbirth: Phenomenological approaches.* Routledge, London.

van Manen, M. (2017) Phenomenology's original sense. *Qualitative Health Research,* 27, 6, 810-825.

Wiltshire, G. and Ronkainen, N. (2021) A realist approach to thematic analysis: making sense of qualitative data through experiential, inferential and dispositional themes. *Journal of Critical Realism,* 20, 2, 159-180.

Ethics statement: This research was conducted with ethical approval from UCLan.

Copyright asserted for music and lyrics: *40p a Mile and a Sausage Roll*, composed by Craig Lawlor.

JQRSS Author Profiles

Craig Lawlor[1] is a Senior Lecturer and PhD researcher in Sports Coaching and Performance Analysis at the University of Central Lancashire. Email: CLawlor2@uclan.ac.uk

Clive Palmer[2] is a research supervisor in the School of Sport and Health and a doctoral education lead in the Graduate Research School for the University of Central Lancashire. ORCID-ID https://orcid.org/0000-0001-9925-2811 Email: capalmer@uclan.ac.uk

Reviewer Comments

This paper brings you up close and personal with the realities and actualities of the football scouting world, affectionately named here as *'scout-ology'*. By employing thick description and inviting the reader into the scouting (under)world, the authors effortlessly evoke a sense of *being-there*. Through the immersive experience of storytelling and song, the authors capture the essence and complexities of football scouting; from witnessing casual forms of racism and sexism to the micropolitics and nepotism associated with a tight-knit network of 'insiders'. Notably, the authors make a meaningful contribution to a somewhat neglected area of research. By applying novel methodological approaches, they push open the door into a research area still in its infancy, whilst, at the same time, applying these novel methodological approaches helps them to gain increasing traction in contemporary qualitative research. While this paper is based on data that is both context- and geographically-bound, it certainly *gets to the heart of the experience* of football scouting. Now that the authors have 'submitted their report', it is for the wider football and research community to 'take notes' and offer some clarity to a scouting world shrouded in ambiguity.

Cunningham, D., Grecic, D and Richards, P. (2023) Decision-making in rugby and implications for coach education: the elicited case of naturalistic, differentiated and disruptive decision-making. *Journal of Qualitative Research in Sports Studies*, 17, 1, 127-152

Decision-making in rugby and implications for coach education: the elicited case of naturalistic, differentiated and disruptive decision-making

Darren Cunningham, David Grecic and Pam Richards
(University of Central Lancashire)

Keywords: *Shared mental models, coach developer, sensemaking, team sports*

Abstract

Decision-making in team sports has attracted significant interest over recent decades by those in pursuit of excellence. None more so than by the three authors who have worked, researched, and supported coach and athlete development in this area cumulatively for over 60 years. This paper therefore presents an amalgamation of learning in the form of a retrospective narrative discussion around the key tenants of Decision Making (DM) with the sport of rugby union being utilised as the exemplar. Specifically, here the first author is asked to reflect upon his life in sport as a rugby player, coach and coach education tutor against various DM frameworks and debates which have shaped his own development. The second and third authors act as critical friends and provide additional research context within each section's discussion. Interestingly a landscape is presented where Decision Making emphasis has generally been placed upon the offensive phase of the game which has in-turn driven coaching pedagogy and attention of those engaged in these sports. The authors therefore propose that this focus is too limiting, and that coach education provision needs to explore decision-making in more depth to differentiate the types of decisions being made and the DM processes that underpin them. They describe the merit of Naturalistic Decision Making and the use of Shared Mental Models as valuable lenses by which to view DM in team sports and on which to base future coach learning. Finally, the authors introduce an additional element to the team DM arena, that of Disruptive Decision Making and offer rugby exemplars of how NDM and SMMs can provide the foundations upon which coaches should base their practice. The authors make a call to action for coaching to address a wider taxonomy of decision-making within team sports' training and match contexts. Recommendations are then provided for how coach education might better develop the DM practices of both coaches and their athletes.

Introduction

Rugby like all team sports shares the complexity and challenges of understanding in-action competitive DM. The complexity of the DM process within

JQRSS Article No: 6/9-17-1-2023-PG[110]-167
ISSN: 1754-2375 [print] ISSN: 2755-5240 [online] Copyright ©: CC-BY-NC-ND
Web: https://uclan.academia.edu/ClivePalmer/Journal-of-Qualitative-Research-in-Sports-Studies

a coaching context presents coaches and applied specialists with a range of multifaceted challenges. Each DM challenge requires a bespoke approach to understanding the individual, team, situation, and context in which they are all executed (Richards, Mascarenhas and Collins, 2009). A major challenge therefore facing coaches and specialists working within the professional game, is to understand the complexities of not only DM, but the specific types of DM skills required in the sport and how we integrate this understanding into the coaching process. Recent research into rugby union is starting to highlight the importance of DM development (Morgan, Mouchet and Thomas, 2020; O'Connor and Larkin, 2015) and offers coaches valuable insights and frameworks on which to reflect and guide their future practice (Light, Harvey and Mouchet, 2014; Mouchet, 2005; Mouchet and Duffy, 2018). Despite this progress the authors are still aware of issues around the content, philosophical basis and focus of many rugby coach education programmes and therefore aim to shed further light on what could be included to inform and develop future practice in both player and coach DM. Therefore this paper presents a phenomenological account of current rugby DM coaching and coach education practice, and recommendations for change are made based on the experiences, work, and research of the three authors. In turn the paper presents; an overview of current rugby coach education practice, a debate on the complexity of DM within this context, alternative DM paradigms that could add value to practice, a new area of DM exploration, and then finally discusses the implications of this paper's findings.

Methods

Phenomenology as a methodology adopts a subjective epistemological position, aligned with Husserl's (1999) descriptive phenomenology, that promotes and then interprets the participants' lived experience (Allen-Collinson, 2009). Our research takes this approach to study the experiences of the first author whilst enacting, coaching, or educating about, rugby decision making. We have developed this phenomenological outlook to respond to existing calls to 'look inside' coaches lived experiences when trying to explain and understand the decision making (DM) process (Lyle and Vergeer, 2014), as well as researchers' requests for an approach that can more effectively account for the subjective dimensions of coaching in real contexts (Light et al., 2014). A challenge to researchers working in phenomenology, however, is to identify the most appropriate data collection methods to gain access to the subjective human experience in sport situations (Varela and Shear, 1999). Within rugby this has often been through the use of personal narratives (Grecic, 2017; Mouchet et al., 2014; Mouchet and Duffy, 2018; Wilkinson and Grecic, 2019). The value of personal narrative is well established in sports coaching research with Smith and Sparkes (2016) arguing that it provides a valuable alternative to positivist methods. Jones (2009) goes further and suggests that personal narrative offers a deeper enquiry into what the coach may see, think and feel, going beyond the surface level of coaching and its social interactions. Such narratives can be elicited in various forms. For the purpose of this study, we explored a number of different forms of interview research used in sport to gain deeper insights and facilitate learning (Cronin and Armour, 2017; Jenkins, 2018; Thomas and Grecic, 2020). We selected the explicitation interview method (Vermersch, 2009) for describing the practice of introspection as it had been used in rugby decision making research previously (Mouchet *et al.,* 2019), and it allowed reflections on specific singular events (DM episodes, coaching acts, and individual education courses). Of course, this is not a new idea within the sports coaching and decision-making domains. Often deep retrospective interviews have been utilised to dig deeper into coaching behaviours (Gilbert *et al.,* 2009; Partington and Cushion, 2013; Stone *et al.,* 2021) as well as how high-level coaches / experts make their decisions (Collins *et al.,* 2015. What is novel about our approach however is the use of critical friends during the interview process to shape the first author's reflections against key singular events that would best inform practice and extrapolate forward into the future of rugby coach education. The co-authors, both of whom have over 30 years' experience of working and researching in sports coaching, play the role of 'devil's advocates' as they probe into the 'what' and 'how' of the first author perceptions to facilitate deeper interpretation of the 'why' and ultimately his re-conceptualisation of DM practice.

Trustworthiness: In line with the method selected we note the view of Vermersch (2012) who offered specific internal measures to judge the value of the research. These 'checks' serve to validate the fact that the subject, when he speaks about his experience, feels subjectively in touch with it. Specifically the measures to judge such work are; 'singularity' – that each event is a single act that was accessed and reflected upon; 'presentification' – that there are sufficient details to offer the depth of perception of the lived experience; and 'memory' – there is evidence of the subject's ownership of their reflections (I... we... did / felt / thought X or Y) (Vermersch, 2012). Additionally, if readers are seeking further specific criteria that are appropriate to judging this study given its particular qualitative focus and purpose, we direct them to Smith and McGannon (2018) and their evaluation around the depth of description we present, how the data makes the reader feel, and the study's findings' potential for naturalised generalisation (Smith, 2017).

Results and Discussion

The results below are based on elicitation questioning surrounding 4 specific DM contexts and events in the first author's playing, coaching and coach educating career. Key memories and interpretations from each experience were further explored following discussion with the co-authors. Segments of responses and selected deeper reflections are presented to shine a light into the first author's world.

The topics raised are then supported by key academic literature and current learning about the topic so that the wider playing and coaching fraternity can see how our research endeavour links into decision making in rugby.

Event 1:	**'The catalyst for exploration'**
Role:	**Player**
Context:	**Top of table clash to decide the title – 22nd November 2003**

Q: Can you describe when you became interested and most aware of decision making in rugby?

Yeah. Well, you see, to illustrate what I'm talking about, it was the top of the table clash. We actually played on the same day in 2003 when England won the World Cup. That's how I remember it so vividly because the World Cup final kicked off early and then we played it straight after. Both teams had won eight games, so I thought it was a big top of the table clash but unfortunately, we came out second best, but just by a couple of points, because of me and my decision.

Q: So how were you coached decision making as a player?

No, not a lot to be honest. Our coaches at the time were ex-players who were good motivators. They were good trainers as such, as I like to call them *the trainers* rather than coaches. We never really got coached any sort of decision making. We were told that we had to play a certain way and there was a certain game plan that we had to stick to and we had to be in a certain part of the field for certain phases and stuff. So, we didn't really get that much autonomy when it came to making decisions. It was more we had to play it to a script.

Q: And how did that make you feel as a player at that time?

At that time to be honest with you, I probably liked it. When I played a bit at a lower level, we were just sort of chucked out onto the pitch. So, it was more, like it felt a lot more organized. And at the time, I think a lot of the higher-level teams were playing to scripts but it was sort of the first time I had. So, in a way it felt good. It felt like we were playing to what we thought our strengths were [pause]. Umm, but it was also in a lot of the games we played, (it) was also the strengths of the opposition as well, and we didn't really have any sort of coaching or training in how to make decisions on what to look for to make the decisions. If you know what I mean?

Q: I think so... can I take you back to one particular decision you recall...

Yes, I can remember one, it actually haunts me to this day to be honest, because if I had done what I thought was right to do at the time, we probably would have won the game. We only got beat by a few points... It was a kick forward and we chased the kick down. I think the scrum half flicked the ball up to another player who passed the ball out to me, and there was me and another player outside of me in support and he was, ... he was like a rocket. The game plan was to get the ball wide and to get the ball to this player. And I remember getting the ball and thinking I've got to get the ball to him. Even though we only had one (defender to beat) and there was two of us against one. Their fullback was coming across from the right-hand side and I remember thinking to myself, 'you know the game plan', got to get the ball to Alan. And then, as I went to pass, I saw the defender slip off me. As soon as I saw him slipping off me (and moving so he could make a tackle on Alan) I knew it was too late. I had already made the decision and the ball was leaving my hands. Whereas normally if I saw that, i.e. I saw them running and over pursuing, I would have just looked (faking a pass) and then come back with the ball myself, and go in under the post (to score). I would definitely have beaten them. But because of what was I was thinking about - playing to the script, making sure I got it to the right people, I gave it (the ball) to Alan but the player who ran straight past me made the tackle because he had a good angle on him. But, you know, even to this day, I still have nightmares about it because I know I could have just pulled it back and gone under the posts and scored.

Reflection: *My interest in decision-making is constantly growing and this incident stimulated that interest even further. Looking back, I was hugely unprepared as a player, given the complexity of the game and the decisions that players are expected to make. It is criminal how unprepared we as players and the coaches were at the time. There were other key incidents too and light bulb moments when I finally realised that I could make decisions on the pitch and influence the game whilst it was happening. I remember vividly a 10 (play maker on opposing team) giving me the run-around by making-decisions based on where I was positioned and what I was doing (as an opposing defender). He was scanning for me all the time, but I realised what he was doing and tricked him by giving him false cues. Looking back these are the things that drove my interest in decision-making and the search to learn how to do it better.*

Arguably, one of the toughest and most physically demanding of team sports rugby union is a dynamic, territorial, high-impact collision sport that requires its players to possess a variety of sport specific motor skills such as passing, catching, kicking and tackling (Dunn, 2006). Physical qualities such as speed, strength, power and aerobic endurance are also essential to rugby performance (Tierney and Simms, 2018). Furthermore, in line with the dynamic nature of the sport, players need the ability to make rapid, effective decisions to give themselves and their team the best chance of success (Tierney and Simms, 2018). Therefore, DM in rugby union is as important as it is complex, with outcomes significant to the team's overall chances of success. This complexity is the direct consequence of two teams of 15 players competing in a match, within the pre-determined laws of the game, both teams working towards the same performance goals of scoring more points than the other. Outwitting the opposition and winning the match requires the integration of physical, technical, tactical and psychological components. The complexities of competitive sport are built from a combination of patterns of action and behaviours within a continuously changing environment (Passos *et al.,* 2008). Players are faced with complex in-game DM in dynamic environments (Zsambok, 1997) where time pressures and limited information affect players to make quick decisions to good consequences (Amalberti, 2007; Klein *et al,* 2007; Klein, 1993).

Traditional concepts have often defined DM as a 'bit of a gamble', a kind of utility analysis where a number of options are assessed against certain information and an action choice is selected by its perceived likelihood of success (Schraagen, Klein, and Hoffman, 2008). A large amount of DM research, however, seems to focus on motor control and argues that individuals possessing superior motor skills often display a greater ability to anticipate the intentions of their opponents and therefore choose a more effective action in response (Roca, Ford, McRobert, and Williams, 2011). While these theories of DM offer value and certainly must be considered, they are all too often explored controlled laboratory experiments, and therefore do not explore DM in a real-world context. Conversely, in uncertain and ambiguous operational settings, decisions must be made in highly complex situations and under extreme time constraints that make them very difficult to replicate in a controlled laboratory setting (Orasanu and Connelly, 1993). More specifically, we argue that the various types of DM processes within rugby (and other team sports) require differentiating and classifying so that they can be better explored and developed. Such classification of DM would include:

1) Differentiating individual and team DM
2) Individual and team intersecting DM
3) DM in closed context (e.g., line outs, set plays)
4) DM in open context (e.g., open play)

Recognising this complexity of DM in rugby union we would further sub-divide attention to the following categories:

a) In possession DM
b) Out of possession DM
c) DM in transition

We recognise that the emphasis of research in team sports has predominantly been on the 'in-possession' aspects of DM with little, if any work, focusing on the opposition DM within the 'out of possession' phase of the game (Richards, Penrose and Turner, 2015).

Event 2:	'Looking for help'
Role:	Coach Education Learner
Context:	Advanced and Performance Coach Award Assessment Days

Q: After your playing career you took up coaching. What did DM practice look like in at the start of your coaching journey?

There was one particular time we were playing, it was Jed Forest against Galashiels. A big local derby and we actually did end up winning the game, but only just. And there was a decision made but funnily enough, it wasn't by me, but I was well, I was trying to make the decision. Because I kind of guessed what the guys were gonna do, we had quite an easy (penalty) kick that would take us like a try ahead if you know what I mean. And I tried to make that decision and get them to kick for goal and they didn't. They decided to go to the corner and he just completely screwed his kick and kicked the ball dead. So… So I wasn't very happy about that but, basically it was that I tried my best as a coach to allow the players to make decisions on the field themselves as I knew it was the right thing to do. The only thing was, in all the training I had had as a coach, I'd never really been coached on how to coach decision making.

Reflection: *I always wanted my players to make good decisions and to play what's in front of them, but I knew I didn't really understand how to work on this in training. As a coach I was making a lot of the decisions for them, just as my coaches did for me, in the warm-up, pre-game, during the game, and penalty options. I developed a huge interest in decision-making and started to research it and try different methods of coaching it. At my next club, I started to have team discussions before and after training about decision-making and the players really bought into it. It seemed to provoke a lot of thought and the players seemed to start making better decisions during game play, in training as well as in games. We won 100% of our league games that year, so it obviously worked in some way, but I still didn't know if what I was doing was correct?*

Q: You later developed your coaching by taking the higher advanced and performance awards. Can you look back on those specific courses and events and how they delivered DM content?

On the Level 3 (Advanced Coach course) I honestly can't remember anything being done about decision making and, like I said earlier, decision making was a real interest of mine. It has been for years. I think I probably understood the game emphasis across the levels. A lot of a Level 1, Level 2 and a fair bit of Level 3 to be honest is about the game, about actually playing the game and coaching the game as such. When you get to the Level 4 (Performance Coach course) it is a little bit more about analysis and real details of the game rather than just playing. I can't actually remember anything being said about actual decision making. I do remember the reasons that got me interested (in decision making on the courses) was because they used to say 'this is a decision-making activity' or 'decision making drill' right? So, you needed as a coach to have some decision making for your Level 2 assessment for instance. And then they would give you, they would literally give you a book with different drills on how to coach decision making. I would just sit looking at them and think to myself. How on earth is that teaching decision making? Yeah. And I'm not even making a decision. I'm doing what they're telling us to do - out of a book.

It didn't ring true like. It just wasn't decision making. It was putting you into a situation where (the player) had to make a decision, but it wasn't actually coaching you how to help the player make that decision correctly, how to facilitate that with your players.

Reflection: *Over my career I have taken and passed all the levels of the rugby union's coaching awards on offer in the UK (Level 1,2,3,4). I have also delivered and co-delivered these awards as an RFU and SRU coach educator. Although the lack of decision-making content entirely at the lower levels can be justified as the* *basics of safety, organisation and planning take precedence, it is such a key area of the sport that its omission worries me and almost reinforces some very outdated views that rugby is simply about being able to perform well established moves, skills and structures. In recent years these lower level courses have concentrated more on the coaching process, developing relationships, creating learning environments, ensuring psychological safety etc., but how to facilitate and support decision making is still glaringly missing from the curriculum. In my experiences there is a focus on testing players decisions but not delving into what, how or why we make those decisions. Only one view is offered to the coach, ecological dynamics, constraints led, environmentally initiated. It is also deemed the decision making is good if the outcome was what coach had pre-determined for that activity, and there is nothing mentioned on what contributed to the decision-making. I always reflected on these sessions and thought about the complexity of the game and realised there was no discussion about the importance of experience, cognition, or memory.*

Q: Were there any specific theories of DM promoted and explained during the course?

Yeah, yeah, yeah. It was all about constraints. It was all that was covered. Basically, the the course information said that it's all based on constraints. But (the RFU) is (the only organisation) where you can get that qualification (to coach rugby at higher levels) if you coach decision making the way they are. If you don't it's then they'll say, well, that's not how you've been told how to coach decision making. So, it's almost indoctrinated into you how to coach decisions.

Q: What about when you went on the highest-level coaching course (Level 4 Performance Coach Award)?

The only decision making that really was touched on was X. He was one of the tutors on the course as it happened. Again, I never realized at the time, but now looking back and knowing what I know now, it was almost shoved down my throat. It was more like affordance driven, like how the environment drives the decision making, i.e. it was more constraint led. So putting certain constraints on the games to force certain scenarios and force players into the making certain decisions - all based on dynamical systems.

To be fair, I wasn't that aware of any anything else at the time. I remember I used to think to myself about it all the time, about how or what I could do to make my decision making as a player better. Of course, at that time I thought the Level 4 is going to teach me how I could coach decision making to my players and make them better decision makers. That's why I got so interested in it. And then I basically went along with it again, this is what everybody has to do because it's your badge at the end of the day, if you don't do it (their way).

Q: And do you still think and coach that way, using the ideas you learnt on those courses?

Not at all. I still had my experiences that had given me an idea of what was actually needed. I also started to think about doing a Prof Doc to develop my thoughts on decision making and explore decision making through experience or through memory or through, cognitive stuff. I remember saying to me it's a little bit of everything, whereas some theories say it's just hard and fast. I think you need a little bit of everything, you know, mental models, situation recognition, I think situation recognition is absolutely huge in in team sports, just recognizing situations, understanding situations.

Reflection: *While completing the Level 4 coaching course, the game was broken down into specialist technical or tactical areas and presented in the classroom via lectures, specialist coaches and guest speakers. I remember thinking to myself, if at the highest levels of competition decision-making is key to success, then why is there only one approach skimmed over during the course?*

Within the Rugby Football Union (RFU) competency-based certification awards, there appears to be a mismatch between the performance demands facing coaches and the professional development available to prepare practitioners to coach within the modern game (Thomas and Grecic, 2020; Wilkinson and Grecic, 2021). Research suggests that competency-based courses seem to fall short in meeting the development needs of elite coaches, particularly their ability to address 1) the complexity of DM within rugby from a playing perspective, and 2) the theoretical mechanism, enabling rugby union coaches to understand how they themselves, can most effectively develop DM skill in their performers (Collins, Burke, Martindale, and Cruikshank, 2015). Such shortcomings and limitations are presented by Collins *et al,* (2015) as a failure to consider the wider complexities of DM in rugby. Cushion (2009) however argues that these coach development programmes are designed to develop coaches' understanding of pedagogy and education, that subsequently allow them to deliver high quality practice sessions in a positive learning environment. We argue that such context although informing pedagogy and technical skill development, does so in isolation of the subject matter of DM.

Those working in rugby union, as in all team sports, share the complexity and challenge of understanding in-action competitive DM. The complexity of the DM process within a coaching context presents coaches and applied specialists with a range of multifaceted challenges. Each DM challenge requires a bespoke approach to understanding the individual, team, situation and context in which they are all executed (Richards, Mascarenhas and Collins, 2009). The major challenge therefore facing coaches and specialists working within the professional game, is to understand the complexities of not only DM, but the specific types of DM skills required in the sport and how this knowledge can be integrated into the coaching process. At present we argue that the competency-based focus of many sports' coaching qualifications and frameworks such as the RFU's Advanced Coaching and Performance Coaching Awards, and other sports who also adopt the United Kingdom Coaching Certificate (UKCC) framework, do not facilitate the opportunity to embed 'in-game' DM. Indeed, many of sport's governing body courses have traditionally considered the coaching act, and specific areas such as DM, as generic processes. In this way the applied content of the coach education curriculum can be perceived as one dimensional, with the delivery methods chosen deemed suitable for all coaches, in all circumstances, regardless of their respective sport. Of course common sense would tell us otherwise (Lyle, 2002), and we present the argument that such a 'one size fits all approach' is limiting the ability of coaches to effectively coach DM. Thankfully coaches' bespoke needs are finally being recognised by studies such as the recent UK Sport Pathway Coaching Position Statement (UK Sport, 2020). Here we believe that the ability to develop DM skills of coaches and performers, in the precise context they are needed, should be one of the key areas addressed by future coach learning.

Grehaigne, Godbout, and Bouthier, (2001) note that despite the importance of effective DM for successful team performance outcomes DM appears to be given very little emphasis in many sports' coaching accreditations other than being linked to pedagogical practices embedded within an ecological systems and non-linear framework (Kinnerk *et al.*, 2018; Light and Evans, 2020; Stone *et al.*, 2020). Nowhere is this more evident than within the English RFU's higher-level coaching awards (Advanced Coaching, and Performance Coaching Awards, previously L3 and L4 respectively on the UK Coaching Framework). Within these awards there is no explicit reference to DM development within the RFU's coach developer's tutor packs, although in line with Gredhaigne *et al.'s* (2001) observation, analysis of tutor resources does highlight a singular ecological dynamical system explanation of skill acquisition for player in-game DM (Davids *et al.*, 2013; Passos *et al.*, 2008; Renshaw *et al.*, 2009). Although this ecological theory can make a valuable contribution to performers' development, we argue that it is limited and does not address the full complexity of the DM process, but rather offers a singular lens by which to view the concept of decisions. These two concepts, decisions and decision making (DM) are fundamentally different. Decisions are the course of action taken, whilst DM is the process through which the decision is made. Within coach education, understanding the process of DM is essential, as focusing on the decision outcome can be flawed, as no one singular decision is definitively correct. There may in fact be several options to achieving the desired outcome. Unfortunately a streamlined approach using a single theoretical framework is frequently witnessed within coach education, and specifically with the approach taken to develop DM skills in performers. Although the ecological approach is undoubtedly valuable in rugby given the importance of players being able to react to the uncertain and ever-changing decision at-action environment (Mouchet and Duffy, 2018; Passos *et al.*, 2008), the theory needs to be integrated with other approaches that present a clear outline to how DM skills can be developed. Richards *et al.*, (2016) warn against exploring one theory only in isolation as this will inflate its contribution to the concept of DM. It is therefore proposed that sport and rugby union specifically should consider a broader range of concepts and theories. We propose that Naturalistic Decision Making (NDM) should be more fully utilised to underpin work in this domain. NDM provides an integrated range of models and theories (Richards and Collins, 2020) which address cues and situational factors and explains how these are both executed at an individual and team level (Richards *et al.,* 2009) through the process of sensemaking (Richards *et al.,* 2012). This would seem to be of great value for all those wishing to gain a greater insight into how best develop DM in rugby.

What is Naturalistic Decision Making (NDM)?

NDM has been described as making decisions by the application of experience in unclear, dynamic field settings that are recognisable and important to the decision makers (Lipshitz, Klein, Orasanu and Salas, 2001; Zsambok and Klein, 1997). In other words, NDM is the study of how people function in their normal, real-world surroundings or at least a simulated scenario, preserving important aspects of their normal setting, actually make decisions (Zsambok and Klein, 1997). It is argued that experienced decision makers do not actually compare available options from a list of possibilities, but through previous knowledge and experience, recognise patterns and evaluate subsequent options by envisaging the possible outcomes of the situation (Klein and Hoffman, 2008). The decision maker assesses possibilities and advances by anticipation to minimise the complexity of the situation and instead of using reflective processes to save resources, a more independent level of behaviour is applied (Macquet and Fleurance, 2007).

Decision complexities in sport: integrating theory and practice

The relevance of NDM is essential to both understanding aspects of DM in sport (in possession, out of possession and transition; Richards *et al.,* 2009) with a range of theoretical approaches of NDM being of significant to informing the discussion. The following section will therefore provide a brief overview of these approaches. However, it is relevant to outline that the key theoretical approaches which will be explored later in this paper: *Recognition Primed Decision Model,* Klein (1993); *Situation Awareness,* Endsley (1988); *Sensemaking,* Dervin (1983) and *Mental Models* Johnson-Laird's (1983); *Shared Mental Models* (SMM), Cannon-Bowers, Salas and Converse's (1993) should not be viewed in isolation of each other. Richards and Collins (2022) proposed that the theoretical approaches from NDM all make a valuable contribution to enhancing our understanding of DM processes and should be explored collectively, in doing so the complexity of DM in sport can be more effectively understood. DM is undoubtedly of significance in the world of elite sport. As mentioned earlier, Kaya, (2014) argues that the quality of the DM by the participants, individually and collectively, determines the level of success. The following discussion will present an overview of NDM approaches in context of rugby before the theoretical foundations provided below are presented in context of 'out of possession' dimension of the game. Data from Morgan *et al.,* (2020) study highlighted various methods that coaches working with the French national rugby teams utilised to facilitate more effective DM utilising pre, during and post competition / training coaching interventions. An interesting finding of their study was a focus 'on the ball' rather than on wider aspects of the game. Indeed, from the first author's experience when he has been exposed to sporadic DM training sessions in rugby, there also has seemed to be a major emphasis on coaching DM from the perspective of when 'in-possession' of the ball and in an attacking context, i.e., beating a defender in a 2 v 1 situation, attacking from the set-piece or playing with fast multi-phase ball. We recognise this is undoubtedly an essential part of the game and must be coached, however, there seems to be a shortfall in coaching effective DM when not in possession of the ball, and during the transition phase of possession. Work by Richards, Penrose and Turner (2015) and more recently Richards *et al.,* (2019) outlined that although attacking ('in possession') and defensive aspects ('out of possession') of the game share commonalities, these two phases of the game (including the third phase of transition) require different thought processes as information is engaged with differently within the DM process.

Competitive sports in general regularly exhibit dynamic settings that display a number of parallels to those that are studied using the NDM approach. The parallel, dynamic setting of a rugby match mimics the characteristics of uncertainty, high stakes, shifting and conflicting goals, multiple participants, and intense time constraints (Macquet, 2009; Zsambok and Klein, 1997) and justify the value of NDM as a paradigmatic approach to DM in rugby union. For example, while operating in open 'phase' play, the attacking team can generate momentum by producing quick ruck ball (recycling the ball back into play from a contest for the ball on the ground), where the time between a tackle being made and the ball being moved away from the ruck may consistently be as quick as 1.5 seconds. This means that the defence must be able to reset, recognise cues and tactical patterns, understand the situation and problems faced and react accordingly within seconds, and all this staying within the laws of the game. We propose that understanding the theoretical concepts that underpins these processes, enables coaches to design and construct an effective pedagogical approach that effectively develop DM in their players and teams.

Event 3:	'Passing on knowledge'
Role:	Coach Education Tutor
Context:	Advanced Coach Award Delivery Session (2016)

Reflection: *Even on the Level 4 course (Performance Coaching Award) how we were introduced to decision-making concepts and theories was very disappointing. It seemed very one dimensional and biased to promoting one 'ideal'* *way of developing players' decision-making through the use of the ecological / constraints approach. We were given supporting research papers to read, presentations to watch and were lectured on the benefits and value of this approach. Much of the coaching behaviours promoted seemed more appropriate to when working with young children or lower level players. Examples of where this had been used with elite players and teams such as the All Blacks didn't take into account our own circumstances and needs but presented this approach as the panacea to all our coaching desires. I've tried this approach in the past with my players, but it has given me more headaches and conflicts than help and support. Some players don't want to be left to work it out for themselves or be guided to reach a certain outcome. They want to know, to feel, to understand and the courses didn't prepare me to best facilitate that learning.*

Q: Following the examples you've given at events as a player, coach, coach delegate etc. is there anything else that you would like coaches to be more aware of to do with decision making?

Yes, well, first and foremost, I think it would be I'd like the coaching culture to be more aware of different ideas of decision making and also, you know… the disruption of decision making. The driver behind my thoughts about decision making is that when two teams play, if every coach in England has gone through the RFU Coaching awards and manual, every coach in England will coach decision making the same way. But, generally speaking, again, from all the research I've done on decision making and probably through my own experiences, the better make better teams decisions and they are generally more successful than the teams that don't make them.

So I still want to coach my players to be better decision makers. But how can I get an advantage? How can I find an edge and get an advantage over the opposition? And one of the things I was thinking of was, well, if successful decision makers make good decisions, if I can do something as a team within the laws of the game to disrupt the decision making of the opposition and make them make bad decisions, its gonna lessen their chances of success. And obviously it's our strength and also increases our chances of success. And that's really what it is.

Reflection: *As a coach tutor tasked with delivering the concept it was very frustrating, what about introducing other concepts and theories surrounding decision-making? The lack of focus on decision-making and how the game has moved on leaves a huge gap in the coaching curriculum. The Level 4 breaks down the game into specific areas with numerous modules providing detailed technical and tactical knowledge and ideas to coaches, most of which were very thought provoking and promoted innovative coaching. I really enjoy watching other coaches' coach, I watch lots of games and pre- or post-match interviews with players and coaches. My interest in decision-making led me to think, in general, if good decision-making equals success, then coaches and players can influence and disrupt the oppositions decision-making, then surely that will decrease the opposition's chances of success against us? This led to my interest growing in how coaches can* *influence and disrupt their opponents, what strategies do they use pre-, during and post match? This is a new area and should be covered in coach education, I call it Disruptive Decision Making.*

Disruption of Decision-Making (DDM)

In the context of elite sport and striving to gain a competitive advantage, athletes and coaches will regularly attempt to exploit their opposition by intentionally causing a disruption to their DM flow (out of possession coaching). This requires the coach to minimise process losses and maximise process gains. It appears that teams will intentionally plan to gain advantages by implementing strategies to cause disruption to the DM of their opposition when they do not have possession. This can force the opposition into states of self-doubt and nervousness, creating anxiety and ultimately poor DM, causing performance errors and resulting with a reduction in their chances of success. Interestingly, however when we hear the word 'disruption', we instinctively think of its negative connotation, which is not always the case. The term disruption can be defined in the Oxford Dictionary of English (2010) as '... a disturbance or a problem that interrupts an event, an activity or a process'. Therefore, it is important to stress that these disruptive tactics and strategies are not violations of the laws of the game and are not to be perceived in any way relating to the promotion of cheating, but instead are recognised as part of high-performance sport. The challenge facing elite teams is not only to design tactical play and to outperform the opposition, but to also be able to deal with the disruptive tactical play implemented by the opposing team.

In recognising that a large percentage of time in rugby involves teams engaging in the 'out of possession' phase of the game, the average being in Super Rugby competition when teams will spend just over 18 minutes or 46% of ball in play time, in the 'in possession' phase of play (Super Rugby, 2020), suggesting that over half the game is spent in 'out-of-possession' and transition phases (56%). Therefore, it is essential that we understand what is occurring in these phases. As highlighted above during a period of being out of possession, a team will be trying to disrupt the opposition to regain possession. For the purpose of this paper, disruptive decision-making (DDM) can be defined as a deliberate process, which can be executed in any context including competition, with the objective of gaining a competitive advantage by disrupting the tactical decision-making of the opposition. Disruption can be of a psychomotor, psychosocial or psychological nature and can be applied both overtly and covertly.

It may however be necessary here to clarify exactly why DDM has been defined in this way. DDM is pertinent to elite rugby union and many coaches will meticulously plan adversative interventions or disruptive strategies for use at different stages of competition. These can occur either before the match, during the match, immediately after or a combination of all three. As articulated in the above definition of DDM, such strategies can be planned and implemented before competition (in the days / hours leading up to the match), during the match, or post-competition (immediately after the match). For example, attempts to use psychological interventions such as 'mind games' or 'gamesmanship' (Howe, 2004; Wright, 1992) may be employed to gain a psychological advantage before competition. Coach education can therefore support the coach with differentiating the different types of DM as outlined in this paper. Specifically, with DDM coach education can assist the coach with understanding how to 'manage match day performance' (before and after the game) in relation to DDM and also how to manage DDM within the game, which is a particular focus for this paper.

Managing DDM in the game incorporates the NDM theories outlined above for in possession play. The complexity of the situation is still driven by Shared Mental Models as players actively seek to identify the cues (Recognition Primed Decision theory) which are related to tactical plans (Situational Awareness) that have been agreed as a team (sensemaking). For example, a team out of possession might try to disrupt the opposition's DM by showing a picture of defensive weakness in a certain area of the pitch, therefore inviting the opposition to attack that area or misleading them into a situation where the ball carrier will be isolated, and the defence can regain possession of the ball. In engaging in this type of disruption the defensive team is perceiving information about the team in possession and contextualising this within their own tactical plan (SMM), with the objective of regaining possession. This short overview relating to the scenario, disguises the complexity of this process, but it is hoped that the intricacy of the situation can be appreciated by the reader and will be addressed in more detail in future papers. However, the point which is pertinent here, is that the comprehension of such complex aspects of play requires a high level of engagement and learning through the process of coach education. Therefore, by presenting only a singular lens from one theoretical framework, as part of a coach education course, does not equip coaches with the skills to effectively coach all aspects of DM within a rugby context.

Event 4:	'Applying learning and experience'
Role:	Experienced Coach
Context:	New squad's first training camp

Q: Moving forward to your present coaching practice and DM, can you talk me thought what your work looks like now in this area?
> With the Army (rugby team), because I get them for a full week, we have lots of meetings, forwards meetings, team meetings and we do team building. We talk through things a lot, about why and how we're trying to develop it (decision making).

In the talks I try to give them a mental picture of what we actually want from them in certain situations. I'm not dictating to them what they're doing, but it's like, you know, in this situation, we need to come up with a way for doing x, y or z. As one specific instance, the hooker (forward player who hooks the ball back at a scrum), I would sit down with (the players) and say right, if they lose a hooker to a yellow card for 10 minutes how are we going to play now? What will you do and what will you change? And a lot of the time the players will say to me well, you know, it depends. What they do depends on whether one of the back rows may be able to play there, so he might just slip straight in and hook and I'll say 'Right, so what would we do in the scrum? How are we going to attack them? What can we do differently. I'll talk to players and try to draw it out of them what they know and what they can do. But also because of the time I've got, I'd also sit and talk to players to help them make those decisions. But they would be made before the game if you like, almost like rehearsed decision making.

Q: That's interesting, but do you also prepare them to be able to make decisions in the game?

Yes, yes, definitely. Well, we'll do that in training. I'll put time constraints on different things. We do a lot of scenario work. So, I'll say a likely scenario on the field, may be you know, that we're four points down, it's the final two minutes of the Army v Navy game and we have to score a try. We're in this position. We've got a man down. We've got two men in the bin. How would we plan and go through different scenarios and then sometimes the players will come up with an idea and come up with an option to play a certain way or do a certain thing. And I'll probably not agree with it or I haven't agreed with them all, so I'll say we'll look at it. Let's have a look and see what it is, how that looks, see how it feels. The players then go through it and then if it's executed well, I'll get them straight back into the little huddle and just see how does that feel? You know, do you think that will work with a live defence? Right. We're going to put more pressure on you here, so I'm letting the defence up against them (much closer).

On the attack I just do different scenarios too and put them in to play around with timings and letting people go offside, having certain people who can just go beyond the laws so they can just do whatever they want and then we work on how we're going to counteract that. If it happens in the game.

Reflection: *My interest in decision-making and all the reading I have done to find out more is clearly evident in my coaching practice. The decision-making concepts, theories and new ideas that I have researched while working on my Professional Doctorate are fully applied in the way that I work with my players on and off the pitch. We work together on developing mental models and shared mental models. Also, I spend a lot of time talking to the players and reviewing their individual and team performances with an explicit focus on decision-making, directing awareness, highlighting relevant cues. I am always looking to develop new training practices to prime players and give a greater depth of understanding. All the things I never had as a player. Lastly, I have a huge interest in using decision-making, or maybe more specifically disruptive decision making where we work to develop any practices, such as deception, cue distortion, or psychological intervention, pre-match, during or post-match to gain a strategic advantage. I have* *researched a number of decision-making concepts, and recognise that all have at least some value, however I have really nailed my colours to the naturalistic decision-making ideology.*

We acknowledge and recognise the importance of the ability to react to uncertainty in competitive situations whether caused by tactical disruption or other means and want to address the complexity of this process in more depth, to support the development of coaches and players alike. The complexity of DM requires a multitude of lenses to understand how DM presents in sport. From a strategic level, there is the need to design and operationalise Shared Mental Models (SMM) which shape the performance vision or 'alpha vision' (Richards, Collins, and Mascarenhas 2016), and therefore inform what information is attended to and the decisions that are made. This in itself is an extremely complicated activity and requires dual 'top-down' and 'bottom-up' processes, which integrates the experiences of players, coaching staff and specialists. The reader is referred to Richards and Collins (2020) for a theoretical account of the paradigms involved. In addition, the integrating reflective practice to develop team DM (see the five-stage model by Richards, Collins and Mascarenhas, 2016) provides a clear staged approach to developing DM skills for all phases of the game, including in-possession, out of possession and transition.

Mental Models (MM) and Shared Mental Models (SMM)

A fundamental theory supporting the effective delivery of pedagogical process aimed at developing DM skills relates to the construction of Mental Models (MM) and Shared Mental Models (SMM). SMMs not only provide a blueprint to inform the progression of practices, but also shape the content of what information in the performance setting is attended to. A Shared Mental Model (SMM) can be defined as (Cannon-Bowers *et al.,* 1993:221):

> Knowledge structures held by team members that enable them to form accurate explanations and expectations, and, in turn, coordinate their actions and adapt their behaviours to the demands of the task and other team members.

A large amount of literature surrounding mental models (MM) concentrate on individual cognitive performance, acquiring systems knowledge, and individual systems interaction (Salas, Stout and Cannon-Bowers, 1994), nevertheless, such research also highlights that the concept of SMMs may be applied to facilitate coordinating actions within a team setting, assisting teammates to predict what each other need and do in order to function together as a team (Jonker, Birna Van Riemsdijk, and Vermeulen, 2010). As such, it is argued that team performance is heavily reliant on team members sharing an understanding of the team itself, team objectives, the roles of teammates, individual roles, and the task to be executed

143

(Richards *et al.,* 2016). Team members therefore draw on common or shared understanding of the situation, in the form of a SMM.

Within a coaching context research has indicated that the integration of a SMM into the performance setting not only provides a framework to shape pedagogical delivery, but also accelerates and improves the DM skills of the individuals and team collectively (Richards *et al.,* 2012). The coach's initial vision of performance (SMM) which is constructed at the start of the performance cycle contains the detail of what aspects of performance will be developed during the season. This vision has been referred to as the 'alpha version' (Richards *et al.,* 2009). The 'alpha vision' (SMM, or performance vision) is sub-divided into smaller performance 'chunks'. These performance chunks (normally 3-5 components) are those items that have been identified by the coach as being essential in securing performance success and that can delivered in a progressive and sequential manner. For example, in rugby one might be playing from receiving a deep kick and a second might be attacking from a lineout. These sub-components of the performance vision (alpha vision) contain the detail or roles of team players, skills-sets and what information is needing to be attended to (Richards *et al.,* 2016). Interaction between the coaches and the players, empowers the players to understand and adapt the 'alpha version', and align it to their own ideas and agreed perspectives as a team, resulting in subsequently giving ownership of the 'in action' version of the performance vision, known as the 'beta version' (Richards *et al.,* 2012). The beta vision of performance (formally the alpha vision) acts as a blueprint to structure pedagogical practices and shape what content information is attended to and priorities during a rugby match/training and which integrates the players perspective.

SMMs are integral to efficient group interaction, team training and competent performance (Cannon-Bowers *et al.,* 1993; Klimoski and Mohammed, 1994; Richards *et al.,* 2012). SMMs are argued to have great importance for effective shared situation awareness (Endsley, 1995; Endsley and Jones, 2001) which is deemed essential for teams performing tasks in rapidly shifting, real world environments, such as emergency response groups, military units and high-performance sports teams (Young and McNeese, 1995). Hence, a coach's understanding of how to design and develop SMMs will improve both the effectiveness and outcome of coaching pedagogy. SMMs are relevant as they enable performance decisions to be agreed as a team, and understood in detail and complexity. SMMs also enable the phase of the decision to be examined in detail (Richards *et al.,* 2009; 2012) providing a vehicle for both the integration of theory, and therefore an enhanced understanding of how that knowledge can be used by practitioners to develop decision-making skills in individuals and teams.

Recognition Primed Decision-making (RPD): Klein's (1993) RPD model demonstrates how experience and pattern recognition is used in the DM process, to avoid time-consuming investigative strategies associated with traditional judgement and DM, where there is a necessity to select the most appropriate response from a large range of options (Klein, 1993; Klein and Hoffman, 2008). The RPD model depends heavily on the experience and expertise of the individual, acknowledging a typical human perception process known as pattern recognition (Youguo *et al.,* 2008). This generally refers to the process of comprehending interesting patterns and cues, and matching it with (recognising) information already stored in long term memory as a MM or SMM. In simple terms, the decision-maker deliberately assesses a mental representation (MM), and forms expectations of future states. Recognising a representative course of action and responds appropriately (Klein, 1997). From a shared or team perspective, as individuals become more aligned in their understanding of the team and its objectives, SMMs are further developed (Converse, Cannon-Bowers and Salas, 1991) which adds further support to the inclusion of SMMs as a theoretical concept that is essential for coaches to understand in multiple contexts, but more especially within the coaching and development of DM. Integrating RPD into the coaching curriculum would enable coaches to connect SMM to visual search patterns, as information deemed to be important in the performance environment can be primed and used to accelerate the operationalisation of in game DM (Richards, *et al.,* 2012).

Situational Awareness (SA): Endsley's (1988) model of SA is described as the collecting of information from the environment, and the comprehension of this information in context of the performance setting. Formally, SA has been defined as 'the perception of the elements in the environment within a volume of time and space, the comprehension of their meaning and the projection of their status in the near future' (Endsley, 1988 p. 97). SA theory outlines three levels of situational awareness. Level 1 involves the perceptual elements within the situation. Without possessing the fundamental ability to perceive cues, patterns or any other important information within the performance setting will increase the chances of forming an inaccurate representation of the situation (Endsley, 2000). However, Sarter and Woods (1991) argued that a relatively inexperienced practitioner might be able to achieve Level 1 SA and possess a basic perception of the situation when there is no pressure, fatigue or other distractions applied. Level 2 refers to the understanding and integrating the information and is frequently referred to as comprehension. SA is a construct that incorporates far more than 'just' perception, including the combination and interpretation of information with relevance to the practitioner's objectives (Sarter and Woods, 1991). Someone possessing Level 2 SA will have the ability to, through the process of pattern recognition, understanding and evaluation, develop effective meaning and significance from synthesising the Level 1 data received. Finally, the most advanced level of Endsley's (1988) model of SA, Level 3 requires the projection of future status and actions of situational elements. Quite simply, someone possessing Level 3 SA could be described as 'being ahead of the game' (Sarter and Woods, 1991) and have the ability to predict the most likely future outcomes within the operational environment and virtually eliminate any shocks or surprises (Endsley, 1995). This will be executed by incorporating the ability to understand the meaning of the presented data and compare it with a set of operational objectives in order to effectively predict future states that will be valuable to DM (Endsley, 1995; Sarter and Woods, 1991).

Rugby players must show a constant awareness of their surroundings and visual displays presented by the opposition to achieve SA (James and Patrick, 2004). Valuable information will be displayed to the players in the form of offensive / defensive set-ups, formations, field position, ball location, type of ball (set piece / phase or transition), player location, velocity, ability, and match (weather) conditions. Perception, and comprehension of these presented 'pictures' are essential to anticipation, DM and future actions. For example, a defender within the defensive line must perceive their direct opponent's movements and actions while maintaining focus on their defensive duties and simultaneously perceiving other, both offensive and defensive players' movements, ball location / movement / speed and direction. Success for the defence would require the defensive players to make sense of the presented information, as such that the opponent's movements may be coordinated with other attacking players and ball movement (James and Patrick, 2004). This information is compared to the opposition's previous actions and behaviours in similar situations, and subsequently supports the DM process facilitating the anticipation of the likely outcomes of the opponents attacking strike. The inclusion of the theoretical understanding of SA into the Coach Education curriculum would therefore not only enhance the understanding of coaches to develop more effective on field decision-making but also layer the complexity of information in a progressive and logical manner.

Sensemaking: Weick (1995) referred to sensemaking as 'how we structure the unknown so as to be able to act in it' (Ancona, 2011:3). Simply described, sensemaking is how people 'bridge the gaps' and make sense of situations, it's how they construct information that is missing and make decisions on how best to use that information (Dervin, 1983). Within a sporting context sensemaking is essential within the DM process. Richards et al., (2009; 2012) outlined that sensemaking has two key components of noticing (attending to key information) and framing (framing the information in context of the tactical philosophy of the team). The integration of sensemaking into the coaching process empowers the performer (and members of the team collectively), to be guided to perceiving key information in the performance setting, in context of the game plan and tactical playing philosophy. Sensemaking is therefore informed and driven by the SMMs, which shape what information the players and team need to prioritise and attend to. Additionally, Klein *et al.,* (2007) described sensemaking as the framing and re-framing of information and postulated that sensemaking commences as soon as there is a perception of defective data or an unexpected event within the existing frame.

The theoretical concepts outlined above are relevant for all phases of the game, in possession, out of possession and transition. As noted previously, over recent years, researchers have directed their attention to applying these theories to attacking aspects of the game. This influenced and enhanced our understanding of how to coach 'in possession' DM. Coaches therefore need to differentiate how we coach in possession and out of possession phases of the game, and as a result coach education is required to provide the pedagogical understanding of what this involves and how it is done. To address this challenge, the paper will next consider out of possession phase in relation to DM and specifically the role of disruption of DM before concluding with recommendations for coach educators and coaching programmes.

Recommendations to enhance decision-making in rugby coach education

Looking back on events, reflections, and interpretations provides a valuable lens to look forward into the DM needs of the sport and coach education in particular. Coach education should improve the coach's ability to establish and develop their knowledge and understanding of how to create an integrated vision of performance (an 'alpha' vision, see Richards *et al.,* 2009).

Establish the ability of coaches to: 1) Design SMMs and 2) develop a team SMM to shape and guide the DM of players. Specifically, this will provide coaches with a structure to guide how their 'alpha vision' and subsequent 'beta vision' (with constant collaboration of coaches and senior players) can be used to form their own club's blueprint to coaching, and structure training sessions that can effectively develop DM skills. Also, outlining what information is important, what information is attended to, and how it is prioritised (Richards *et al.,* 2016). Specifically, what is important here is the sense of empowerment and player buy in to the creation and maintenance of SMMs (Richards *et al.,* 2012). Developing the coach's recognition that DM is bespoke to phases of the game, match situations and areas of the field. For example, the process of DM in rugby will differ between a set piece situation, where the setting is less deviating and controlled; and any transition (counterattack) or multiple phase aspect of the game that is more uncontrolled and chaotic.

Develop coaches' understanding of SMM: the way they are designed and how they are constructed, coaches will be able to develop a proposal, which can be used to structure the content of DM practices that they deliver to their team. Such a blueprint could and should be used by their National Governing Body's coach developers in partnership with their coaching candidates to help structure and develop the content of DM modules within their coach education courses.

Conclusion

The Explicitation interview method provided a valuable insight from lived experience, supplemented by facilitated reflection and critical friends' commentary. Findings have identified a number of key learning points that could be considered to support and enhance how the sport is coached. A major challenge of DM in rugby union (as with many team sports) is the numerous situations and phases which present themselves, all requiring a different type of decision to be made, either in a more linear controlled situation such as set piece (scrums, lineouts, kick-off's), or a more dynamic, chaotic situation such as open play. This distinction in itself requires coaches to differentiate the skills within their coaching pedagogy, as to how they design their learning environment. Furthermore, coaches are encouraged to differentiate how coaching in different phases of the game is addressed, for example offensive, defensive and transition play. The complexity of understanding this taxonomy of decision-making requires a closer alignment from practice and theory as pedagogical practice can be designed more effectively if they are informed by theory. As coach education frameworks are perceived as one of the major influencers that provide guidance on how to coach, it is essential that such coach education programmes provide the content for not only the design of practical exercises, but the theory that underpins the rationale of those exercises. Additionally, we argue that a further sub-division is needed, where decision-making is explored at a granular level resulting in the identification of range of decision-making skills required in sports. This would enable coach education to not only support the development of new coaches entering into sport but also enhance the practice of more experienced coaches and support their continued learning in this domain. This paper therefore highlights the valuable role that coach education plays in this process but the requirement that they do so, not from a 'one size' fits all lens but one that recognises the complexity of the concept of DM.

References

Allen-Collinson, J. (2009) Sporting embodiment: sports studies and the (continuing) promise of phenomenology. *Qualitative Research in Sport, Exercise and Health*, 1, 3, 279-296.

Ancona, D. (2011) Sense making: framing and acting in the unknown (Chapter 1, 3-19). In, Snook, S., Nohria, N. and Khurana, R. (Eds.) *The Handbook for Teaching Leadership.* Sage Publications Inc., Thousand Oaks, CA.

Amalberti, R. (2007) La Maitrise des Situations Dynamiques [Control of Dynamic Situations]. *Psychologie Francaise,* 46, 107-118.

Cannon-Bowers, J.A., Salas, E. and Converse, S.A. (1993) Shared mental models in expert team decision making (pp. 221-246). In, Castellan, N.J. (Ed.) *Individual and group decision making: Current issues.* Lawrence Erlbaum, Hillsdale, New Jersey.

Collins, D., Burke, V., Martindale, A. and Cruikshank, A. (2015) The illusion of competency versus the desirability of expertise. *Sports Medicine*, 45, 1-7.

Converse, S., Cannon-Bowers, J.A. and Salas, E. (1991) Team member shared mental models: a theory and some methodological issues. *Proceedings of the Human Factors Society Annual Meeting*, 35, 19, 1417-1421.

Cronin, C. and Armour, K. (2017) 'Being' in the coaching world: new insights on youth performance coaching from an IPA approach. *Sport, Education and Society*, 22, 8, 919-931.

Cushion, C. (2009) Modelling the complexity of the coaching process. *Soccer Journal*, 54, 8-12.

Davids, K., Araujo, D., Correia, V. Vilar, L. (2013) How small sided and conditioned games enhance acquisition of movement and decision-making skills. *Sport Science Review*, 41, 3, 155-161.

Dervin, B. (1983) *An overview of sense making research: concepts, methods, and results to date.* International Communication Association Annual Meeting. Dallas, TX. USA.

Dunn, J. (2006) *Coaching decision making in rugby* [online]. (Accessed 10th November 2023). https://d26phqdbpt0w91.cloudfront.net/NonVideo/b347f85d-88ff-4082-b850-cb327cc2ce7f.pdf

Endsley, M.R. (1988) Design and evaluation for situation awareness enhancement. *Proceedings of the Human Factors Society Annual Meeting*, 32, 2, 97-101.

Endsley, M.R. (1995) Toward a theory of situation awareness in dynamic systems. *The Journal of Human Factors and Ergonomics Society*, 37, 1, 32-64.

Endsley, M.R (2000) Theoretical underpinnings of situation awareness: a critical review (pp:3-32). In, Endsley, M.R and Garland, D.J. (Eds.) *Situation Awareness Analysis and Measurement.* Lawrence Erlbaum Associates, Mahwah, New Jersey.

Endsley, M.R. and Jones, D.G. (2001) Disruptions, interruptions and information attack: impact on situation awareness and decision making. *Proceedings of the Human Factors and Ergonomics Society Annual Meeting*, 45, 2, 63-67.

Gilbert, W., Lichtenwaldt, L., Gilbert, J., Zelezny, L. and Côté, J. (2009) Developmental profiles of successful high school coaches. *Int. Journal of Sports Science and Coaching*, 4, 3, 415-431.

Grehaigne, J.F., Godbout, P. and Bouthier, D. (2001) The teaching and learning of decision making in team sports. *Quest* [00336297], 53, 59-76.

Grecic, D. (2017) Making sense of skill: a personal narrative approach. *Journal of Qualitative Research in Sports Studies*, 11, 1, 33-48

Howe, L.A. (2004) Gamesmanship. *Journal of Philosophy of Sport*, 31, 212-225.

Husserl, E. (1999) *Basic writings in transcendental phenomenology*. Indiana University Press, USA.

James, N. and J. Patrick. (2004) The role of situation awareness in sport (pp: 297-316). In, Banbury, S. and Tremblay, S. (Eds.) *A Cognitive Approach to Situation Awareness*. Routledge, Abingdon.

Jenkins, S. (2018) Working with coaches and their teams in youth and collegiate sport in the USA: An interview with Dr Andy Gillham. *Journal of Sports Science and Coaching*, 13, 3, 305-314.

Johnson-Laird, P.N. (1983) *Mental models: towards a cognitive science of language, inference, and consciousness*. Cambridge University Press, Cambridge, UK.

Jones, R.L. (2009) Coaching as caring (the smiling gallery): accessing hidden knowledge. *Physical Education and Sport Pedagogy*, 14, 4, 377-390.

Jonker, C.M., van Riemsdijk, M.B., and Vermeulen, B. (2011) Shared mental models. In, De Vos, M., Fornara, N., Pitt, J.V., Vouros, G. (eds) Coordination, Organizations, Institutions, and Norms in Agent Systems VI. COIN 2010. Lecture Notes in Computer Science vol 6541. Springer, Berlin.

Kaya, A. (2014) Decision making by coaches and athletes in sport. *Procedia-Social and Behavioural Sciences*, 152, 7, 333-338.

Klein, G (1993) Naturalistic decision-making implications for design. Klein Associates, Fairborn, OH

Klein, G. (1997) The recognition-primed decision (RPD) model: Looking back, looking forward (pp:285-292). In, Zsambok, C. and Klein, G. (Eds.) *Naturalistic Decision Making.* Erlbaum Associates, Mahwah, New Jersey.

Klein, G. and Hoffman, R.R. (2008) Macrocognition, mental models, and cognitive task analysis methodology (pp. 57-80). In, Schraagen, J.M., Militello, L.G., Ormerod, T. and Lipshitz, R. (Eds.) *Naturalistic Decision Making and Macrocognition*. Ashgate, Hampshire, England.

Klein, G.A., Phillips, J.K., Rall, E.L. and Peluso, D.A. (2007) A data-frame theory of sensemaking (pp.113-155). In, Hoffman R.R. (Ed.) *Expertise out of context: Proceedings of the Sixth International Conference on Naturalistic Decision Making*. Lawrence Erlbaum Associates, NJ.

Klimoski, R. and Mohammed, S. (1994) Team mental model: construct or metaphor? *Journal of Management,* 20, 2, 403-437.

Kinnerk, P., Harvey, S., MacDonncha, C. and Lyons, M. (2018) A review of the game-based approaches to coaching literature in competitive team sport settings. *Quest,* 70, 4, 401-418.

Light, R., Harvey, S. and Mouchet, A. (2014) Improving 'at-action' decision-making in team sports through a holistic coaching approach. *Sport, Education and Society*, 19, 3, 258-275.

Light, R.L. and Evans, J.R. (2020) A Freirean perspective on indigenous players' journeys to the NRL and AFL: From freedom to oppression? (Chapter 7 pp: 20-28). In, Light, R.L. and Curry, C. (Eds.) *Game Sense for Teaching and Coaching*. Routledge, London.

Lipshitz, R., Klein, G., Orasanu, J. and Salas, E. (2001) Taking stock of naturalistic decision making. *Journal of Behavioural Decision Making,* 14, 331-352.

Lyle, J. (2002) *Sports coaching concepts: A framework for coaches' behaviour*. Routledge, London.

Lyle, J. and Vergeer, I. (2014) Recommendations on the methods used to investigate coaches' decision making (pp:121-132). In, Potrac, P., Gilbert, W. and Denison, J. (Eds.) *Routledge Handbook of Sports Coaching*. Routledge, London.

Macquet A.C. and Fleurance P. (2007) Naturalistic decision-making in expert badminton players *Ergonomics*, 50, 9, 1433-1450.

Macquet, A.C., (2009) Recognition within the decision-making process: a case study of expert volleyball players. *Journal of Applied Sports Psychology,* 21, 1, 64-79

Morgan, K., Mouchet, A. and Thomas, G. (2020) Coaches' perceptions of decision making in rugby union. *Physical Education and Sport Pedagogy*, 25, 4, 394-409.

Mouchet, A. (2005) Subjectivity in the articulation between strategy and tactics in team sports: An example in rugby. *Italian Journal of Sport Sciences*, 12, 24-33.

Mouchet, A., Harvey, S. and Light, R.L. (2014) A study on in-match rugby coaches' communications with players: A holistic approach. *Physical Education and Sport Pedagogy*, 19, 3, 320–336.

Mouchet, A., Morgan, K. and Thomas, G. (2019) Psychophenomenology and the explicitation interview for accessing subjective lived experience in sport coaching. *Sport, Education and Society*, 24, 9, 967-980.

Mouchet, A. and Duffy, P. (2018) Rugby coaches' perceptions of their in-competition role. *Sports Coaching Review*, 9, 1, 24-47.

O'Connor, D. and Larkin, P. (2015) Decision Making for Rugby (pp:102–112). In, Till, K. and Jones, B. (Eds.) *The Science of Sport: Rugby*. Crowood Press, Wiltshire, UK.

Orasanu, J. and Connolly, T. (1993) The reinvention of decision making (pp. 3-20). In, Klein, G., Orasanu, J., Calderwood, R. and Zsambok, C. (Eds.) *Decision Making in Action: Models and Methods*. Ablex, Norwood, New Jersey.

Oxford Dictionary of English. (2010) 3rd edition. *Oxford University Press*. Oxford.

Partington, M. and Cushion, C. (2013) An investigation of the practice activities and coaching behaviours of professional top-level youth soccer coaches. *Scandinavian Journal of Medicine and Science in Sports*, 23, 3, 374-382.

Passos, P., Araújo, D., Davids, K. and Shuttleworth, R. (2008) Manipulating constraints to train decision making in rugby union. *Int. Journal of Sports Science and Coaching*, 3, 1, 125-140.

Renshaw, I., Davids, K., Shuttleworth, R. and Chow, J. (2009) Insights from ecological psychology and dynamical systems theory can underpin a philosophy of coaching. *International Journal of Sport Psychology*, 40, 4, 580-602.

Richards, P., Mascarenhas, D. and Collins, D. (2009) Implementing reflective practice approaches with elite team athletes: parameters of success. *Journal of Reflective Practice,* 10, 3, 353-363.

Richards, P., Mascarenhas, D. and Collins, D. (2012) Developing rapid high-pressure team decision-making skills. The integration of slow deliberate reflective learning within the competitive performance environment: A case study of elite netball. *Reflective Practice,* 13, 3, 1-18.

Richards, P., Collins, D. and Mascarenhas, D. (2016) Developing team decision making: A holistic framework for on-field and off-field coaching processes. *Sports Coaching Review,* 6, 1, 57-75.

Richards, P., Penrose, S. and Turner, M. (2015) *Developing Team Decision Making Capabilities in elite football Youth Academy Players.* Cluster for Research into Coaching: International Coaching Conference, 9-10 September 2015, Manchester Metropolitan University, Crewe, UK.

Richards, P., Collins, D. and Robbins, M (2019) *Accelerating team decision-making: Integrating a slow, deliberate, off-field learning environment with rapid on-field, in-action decision-making, in elite netball players.* 14th International Conference on Naturalistic Decision-Making, San Francisco, California. 18th June.

Richards, P. and Collins, D. (2020) Commentary: team cognition in sport: current insights into how teamwork is achieved in naturalistic settings. *Frontiers in Psychology,* 11, 81.

Richards, P. and Collins, D. (2022) Shared Mental Models (Chapter 13, pp. 199-214). In, Collins, D. and Cruickshank, A. (Eds.) *Sport Psychology Essentials.* Human Kinetics, Champaign, IL.

Roca, A., Ford, P., McRobert, A. and Williams, A. (2011) The processes underpinning anticipation and decision making in a dynamic time constrained task. *Cognitive Processing,* 12, 3, 301-310.

Salas, E., Stout, R. and Cannon-Bowers, J. (1994) The role of shared mental models in developing shared situation awareness. In, Gilson, R.D., Garland, D.J., & Koonce, J.M. (Eds.) *Situation Awareness in Complex Systems.* Embry-Riddle Aeronautical University Press. Daytona, Florida.

Sarter, N.B. and Woods, D.D. (1991) Situation awareness: a critical but ill-defined phenomenon. *International Journal of Aviation Psychology,* 1, 1, 45-57.

Schraagen, J.M., Klein, G. and Hoffman, R.R. (2008) The macrocognition framework of naturalistic decision making (pp. 3-25). In, Schraagen, J.M. Militello, L., Ormerod, T. and Lipshitz, R. (Eds.), *Naturalistic Decision Making and Macrocognition.* Ashgate Publishing, Aldershot, UK.

Smith, B. and Sparkes, A. (2016) *Routledge Handbook of Qualitative Research in Sport and Exercise.* Routledge, London.

Smith, B. (2017) Generalizability in qualitative research: misunderstandings, opportunities and recommendations for the sports and exercise sciences. *Qualitative Research in Sport, Exercise and Health,* 1, 10, 137-149.

Smith, B. and McGannon, K. (2018) Developing rigor in qualitative research: problems and opportunities within sport and exercise psychology. *International Review of Sport and Exercise Psychology,* 11, 1, 101–121.

Stone, J., Rothwell, M., Shuttleworth, R. and Davids, K. (2021) Exploring sports coaches' experiences of using a contemporary pedagogical approach to coaching: an international perspective. *Qualitative Research in Sport, Exercise and Health,* 13, 4, 639-657.

Super Rugby (2020) *The Power of the Pacific* [online]. Available at: https://super.rugby/superrugby/fixtures/archives/2020-super-rugby/ (Accessed 14.11.2023)

Thomas, B and Grecic D. (2020) Into the Abyss: a study to inform and develop a bespoke athlete transition model for professional rugby. Part 1: establishing a theoretical framework to guide the investigation. *Journal of Qualitative Research in Sport Studies,* 15, 1, 295-312.

Tienrney, G.J. and Simms, C.K. (2018) Can tackle height influence tackle gainline success outcomes in elite level rugby union? *International Journal of Sports Science and Coaching* 13, 3, 415-420.

UK Sport (2020) *UK Sport Coach Development Team and EIS Performance Pathways.* Pathway Coaching Statement. English Institute of Sport, Sheffield.

Varela, F. and Shear, J. (1999) First-person methodologies: What? Why? How? *Journal of Consciousness Studies,* 6, 2-3, 1-14.

Vermersch, P. (2009) Describing the practice of introspection. *Consciousness Studies,* 16, 10, 20-57.

Vermersch, P. (2012) *Explicitation et phénoménologie.* PUF. Paris

Weick, K.E. (1995) *Sensemaking in Organisations.* Sage Publications, Thousand Oaks, CA.

Wilkinson, S. and Grecic, D. (2019) Talent development for professional rugby league: observations and analysis from a career in rugby's high-performance environment. *Journal of Qualitative Research in Sports Studies,* 13, 1, 153-174.

Wilkinson, S and Grecic, D. (2021) A realist framework analysis of rugby academy managers' duties and roles: the ABC's and D's of Talent Development (Attitudes, Behaviours, Challenges…and Development needs). *Journal of Qualitative Research in Sport Studies,* 16, 1, 200-221.

Wright, J.J. (1992) Gamesmanship or cheating: how far should coaches go to gain an edge? *Strategies (08924562)* 6, 21-22.

Youguo P., Wenzhi, L., Mingyou, L. and Jianping L. (2008) Theory of cognitive pattern recognition (Chapter 17 pp:432-462). In, Peng-Yeng. Y. (Ed.) *Pattern Recognition Techniques, Technology and Applications.* I-Tech, Vienna, Austria.

Young M.F., McNeese M.D. (1995) A situated cognition approach to problem solving (Chapter 12). In, Hancock, P., Flach J., Caird J., Vincente K. (Eds.) *Local Applications of the Ecological Approach to Human-Machine Systems.* Lawrence Erlbaum Associates. Mahwah, New Jersey.

Zsambok, C.E. (1997) Naturalistic decision-making research and improving team decision making (pp.111-120). In, Zsambok, C.E. and Klein, G. (Eds.) *Naturalistic Decision Making.* Lawrence Erlbaum Associates, Mahwah, New Jersey.

Ethics statement: This research was conducted with ethical approval from the University of Central Lancashire.

JQRSS Author Profiles

Darren Cunningham[1] is a UKCC Level 4 Rugby Union coach with experience from grassroots to elite level. From his PGDip and MSc in Coaching Science he is currently working towards his Professional Doctorate in Elite Performance at UCLan.

David Grecic[2] is the Head of Research and Innovation in the School of Health, Social Work and Sport. His research specialisms include coaching consultancy, Physical Education and International partnerships in Higher Education. Email: dgrecic1@uclan.ac.uk

Pam Richards[3] is a Reader in Decision-Making and Interoperability at UCLan. She is also a Chartered Psychologist and supervises doctorial students in high-pressurised team decision-making, in addition to consulting in military and emergency domains.

Reviewer Comments

This paper affords a rare, first-person glimpse into the complexities of decision making in rugby union. The narrative-interview style makes the reasoning clear and accessible, often on contentious issues such as education and autonomy in the game, and beyond. Given that decision making in sporting contexts is often not very clear, this exposition allows the reader to follow a thread of motives that can be traced between the narrative response and detailed reflection. Good methodological choices to conduct this research are key to yielding these valuable insights. The transition in perspectives from player to coach in rugby union is especially impactful, providing strong evidence to support the authors' claims to include decision making in formal coach education programmes from grass-roots to elite levels. This has the potential to improve experiences of playing, coaching and spectating in high-quality sport.

Carruthers, P., Palmer, C. and McKeown, M. (2023) Empathy Machines: using theatre
and film in the training of compassionate and reflective health professionals.
Journal of Qualitative Research in Sports Studies, 17, 1, 153-170

Empathy Machines: using theatre and film in the training of compassionate and reflective health professionals

Pete Carruthers, Clive Palmer and Mick McKeown

(University of Central Lancashire)

Keywords: *performative research, mental health, nurse training, theatre, storytelling*

Abstract

Me: Hi, welcome to my abstract, shall we get straight into it?

You: Erm, Ok?

Me: We only have 300 words, so there's no time for pleasantries.

You: Oh right, I'll be quiet then.

Me: No, it's a dialogue, you have to talk.

You: Why is it a dialogue?

Me: It'll make sense in a minute.

You: Right.

Silence -----------------------

You: Erm… what are you researching?

Me: I'm glad you asked! I'm exploring the use of film and theatre as a pedagogical tool within the training of compassionate and reflective health professionals.

You: Sounds interesting.

Me: I think so.

You: What's involved?

Me: I've written and produced a few films and a play that have been used to train health professionals, mainly around mental health and neurodiversity. I'm asking people who experienced this to share their thoughts, helping me to evaluate how effective it was, and also how it differs from more traditional teaching methods. I'm particularly keen to learn how these stories (the films and the play) affected their own personal stories, and simultaneously, how hearing their stories affects my story as a researcher. Hence why I'm using Dialogical Narrative Analysis as my primary research methodology.

You: Ahhhh… so that's why this is a dialogue!?

Me: Bingo.

You: That makes sense now. How will you share your findings?

JQRSS Article No: 7/9-17-1-2023-PG[111]-168
ISSN: 1754-2375 [print] ISSN: 2755-5240 [online] Copyright ©: CC-BY-NC-ND
Web: https://uclan.academia.edu/ClivePalmer/Journal-of-Qualitative-Research-in-Sports-Studies

Me: Well one key thing I'll share is a best practice model for using film and theatre within the training of health professionals, but the main element of the synopsis will involve me writing and performing a new play that will communicate the key findings, once again, as a story.

You: That's really unusual… hang on, is this a play?

Me: It's more of a short scene, but yeah, if you like.

You: I didn't consent to...

Me: Sorry, that's 300 words.

Introduction

Hello everyone, my name's Pete Carruthers and I'm a writer, actor, director and producer. But to make that a bit neater, let's just say I'm a storyteller.

© 2023 NWPPN (Northwest Psychological Professions Network).

Above: Pete, addressing the audience at the Northwest Psychological Professions Network 10 Year Celebration Event. Keynote speaker. (Carruthers, 2023a).

Photographs: Peter Carruthers: tree fish productions: private collection.

So let's get one thing straight, this isn't just an introduction, this is Act 1 – the Setup. Today, my story begins with a question:

What is the most important characteristic of any healthcare professional?

The clue for me is in this bit (care). Or more specifically, do we want our healthcare professionals to be compassionate? Is that important? Let's look at nursing as an example. This is the Nursing and Midwifery Council's (2018) standards of proficiency for registered nurses, and this is what they say on the very first page about the role of the nurse in the 21st century:

The role of the nurse in the 21st century

Registered nurses play a vital role in providing, leading and coordinating care that is compassionate, evidence-based, and person-centred. They are accountable for their own actions and must be able to work autonomously, or as an equal partner with a range of other professionals, and in interdisciplinary teams. In order to respond to the impact and demands of professional nursing practice, they must be emotionally intelligent and resilient individuals, who are able to manage their own personal health and wellbeing, and know when and how to access support.

Registered nurses play a vital role in providing, leading and coordinating care that is *compassionate, evidence-based, and person-centred.* Brilliant, there it is in black and white, right from the off (compassionate). And I think it goes hand in hand with person-centred too, because I don't think you can really have one without the other. For care to be compassionate and person-centred, we need nurses who can engage *emotionally* and have *empathy*.

But how do we practice compassion? How do we teach people to engage emotionally? Is empathy something you're just born with? Or can it be created?

These kinds of questions are driving my current doctoral research into the training of compassionate and reflective health professionals, using film and theatre or 'empathy machines' as I have called them, a phrase coined from Roger Ebert to signal how important these qualities are in health care, and how in training we might nurture these qualities.

This is Roger Ebert, the best known and, for many, the greatest film critic of all time. This is one of his most famous quotes:

Roger Ebert (1942 – 2013)

'Movies are the most powerful empathy machine in all the arts' (Ebert, 2005).

Wow, an empathy machine, just what we were looking for! He goes on…

'When I go to a great movie I can live somebody else's life for a while. I can walk in somebody else's shoes. I can see what it feels like to be a member of a different gender, a different race, a different economic class, to live in a different time, to have a different belief' (Ebert, 2005).

And more wisdom…

'The great movies enlarge us, they civilize us, they make us more decent people'.
(Ebert, 2005).

Let's see how this plays out in a movie-landscape:

'When I go to a great movie I can live somebody else's life for a while'

© Aronofsky (2011)

'I can walk in somebody else's shoes'

© Berger (2022)

'I can see what it feels like to be a member of a different gender'

© Soderbergh (2000)

'a different race'

© Peele (2017)

'a different economic class'

© Baker (2017)

'to live in a different time'

© Gerwig (2019)

'to have a different belief.'

© Kaye (1998)

'This is a liberalizing influence on me'.

© Darabont (1994)

'It gives me a broader mind'.

© Villeneuve (2017)

'It helps me to join my family of men and women on this planet'.

© Spielberg (1993)

'It helps me to identify with them'

© Forman (1975)

'so I'm not just stuck being myself, day after day'.

© Weir (1998)

'The great movies enlarge us'

© Jenkins (2016)

NB: The film stills in this article are used for scholarly, academic purposes, supporting the key messages of this ongoing doctoral research. They are incorporated under Fair Use / Fair Dealing agreements to 'stimulate discussion' (SCMS, category ii: 2010:182) in the critical review of education and training for Health Care professionals. The authors thank the creators of these fine works to help communicate the findings of this innovative research.
See: https://www.cmstudies.org/page/fair_use

'they civilize us'

© Loach (2016)

'they make us more decent people'.
(Ebert, 2005)

© Capra (1946)

Now, given that I've built that up quite a lot there, it might surprise you that I disagree with Ebert on this. OK, I don't completely disagree, but I think he's missing something important. I do agree with him that movies, or films as they should be called, are incredibly powerful empathy machines, but I think films share this power with another artform, theatre.

© Price (2012)

'Mike' in *Fallout*

So for ten years now, I've been creating film and theatre with the specific aim of maximising empathy and compassion in existing and future health professionals. Here I am as 'Mike' in a short film called *Fallout*. And the more I work in this way, the more excited I get about the results. In fact I'm now so excited about it, that I've taken, what is for me, the terrifying leap into the abyss of academic research. Yes, this is the inciting incident that sends our protagonist on his extremely exciting and perilous journey.

That's the title of my thesis is: ***Empathy Machines: Using theatre and film in the training of compassionate and reflective health professionals,*** and these are my research objectives:

> ➤ I want a deeper understanding of how effective this approach is.

> ➤ I also want to understand how and why students respond differently to this approach compared to more traditional ones.

> ➤ And finally, I'm going to co-produce a best practice model for the use of film and theatre in the training of health professionals.

And this is how I'm going to do it, but let's not call it the **Methods Section,** let's call it Act 2- the Confrontation

Now, for those of you who are not familiar with the PhD by Portfolio pathway, what it essentially means is that three *linked and distinct* projects constitute the main body of the thesis, plus a synoptic report that leads the reader through the whole thesis. Two project areas are retrospective or historical, with a live or prospective project being a direct development from the first two. For my historical projects, project one covers my series of short films around military veterans' mental health, whilst project 2 covers the research and development phases of my latest play called:

The Possibility of Colour

© Carruthers (2022)

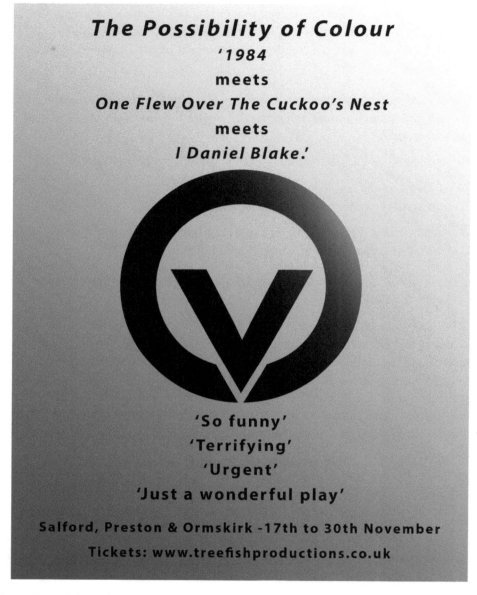

The Possibility of Colour

'1984

meets

One Flew Over The Cuckoo's Nest

meets

I Daniel Blake.'

'So funny'

'Terrifying'

'Urgent'

'Just a wonderful play'

Salford, Preston & Ormskirk -17th to 30th November

Tickets: www.treefishproductions.co.uk

Flyer: *Possibility of Colour,* live performance, and audience participation in research

The live project focuses on the recent professional tour the play. I've actually been writing this play, on and off, since 2008. It's been created with input at every stage of development from student nurses, health professionals, academics and people with lived experience of the themes explored within the play. As a key part of the tour, Health Education England (Carruthers, 2022a) provided funding for 1200 student nurses to attend performances and post-show discussions, and this actually counted as official placement hours towards their nurse training.

Based on the feedback, you can see it was well received, dare I say, impactful. This aspect of 'impact' will be something I hope to convince my funders, my PhD examiners and ultimately the nurses and health professionals who come to see the play, who are striving to support others with mental health issues in daily life.

The Possibility of Colour – North West Tour 2022
(see Carruthers, 2023)

Reviews
- 'A fantastic piece of drama which draws out the joy of everything it is to be human and the value of experiencing the world in your own unique way' * * * * * - North West End

- 'A disturbing and provocative production' - British Theatre Guide

- 'Watching this play is a must' - 10/10 - Writebase

Audience Feedback
- 'Still crying and laughing whilst talking about it the next day!'

- 'Oh my goodness!!! Wow wow wow! That was the best show I have ever seen! It was incredible!'

- 'It was truly terrifying, educational and entertaining. Blew my mind!'

- Average audience score - 4.8/5 * * * * *

Let's move on, what's next in this exciting, white knuckle thrill ride?

(Data collection) ooooo, yes, here we go. Come on! It's like a gritty detective drama now. So much peril!

So from the historical projects I already have lots of audience questionnaires and narrative feedback to include in the analysis. From the live project, each audience member was asked to complete a questionnaire, and a lot of them did. I'm also going to do some 1 to 1 interviews. There will also be the opportunity for participants to offer their creative responses, which could include poetry, paintings, songs, who knows? And once we have all the data collected, we'll then we reach the midpoint of our story. The final bit of Act 2 is the analysis.

I'm using dialogical narrative analysis for my primary research method (Frank, 2005, 2010; Grant et al., 2015). That's because it's all about stories (McAdams, 1993; Gunaratnam and Oliviere, 2009; Rooney et al., 2016). Furthermore it looks specifically at the effect stories have on the audience, which in turn affects me as a researcher and my evolving creative practice. These are forms of Participatory Research (see Cargo and Mercer, 2008; Bergold and Thomas, 2012; Burns et al., 2021). So it's this constantly evolving, back and forth dialogue. And another reason I like this approach is because it perfectly mirrors how I work as a storyteller.

OK, **Results Section.** Or is it Act 3, the resolution?

This is the really exciting bit for me. The main element of my Synopsis (the over-arching report element in my thesis) will involve me writing and performing a new theatre piece that does most of the legwork of communicating the learning from the research. PhD Examiners will be invited to attend a performance of this new piece of theatre ahead of my *viva-voce*. Audience members will also include key stakeholders and contributors throughout the project. Within my thesis there will also be a five-to-ten-thousand-word exegesis explaining the logic of my thought process and my choice of themes and literary techniques.

Finally, as mentioned earlier, I will invite some of the research participants and other stakeholders to co-produce a best practice model for the use of film and theatre as a pedagogical tool for future training. As a sneaky peek of what I expect to find, this is an evaluation report I put together recently using the audience questionnaires from the Northwest tour of the play. This was done independently of my PhD so that I can report to funders on the effectiveness of the project so far (Carruthers, 2022a). I've pulled out a couple of examples that align to the main objectives of the PhD.

In terms of understanding how effective the play is as a pedagogical tool, this question (objective 1) asked audiences if their views have changed after attending the event. Encouragingly, around 40% of respondents said that their views had changed, even including health professionals and lecturers who you might expect to have quite firm views on the themes we explored. Also, for those responding with 'no' or 'uncertain', the vast majority went on to clarify that their views were supported or further strengthened by the event (figure 1: data charts A, B, and C).

Objective 1: Deepening understanding of the effectiveness of film and theatre as a pedagogical tool within the training of health professionals. Have your views changed at all after attending this event?

Figure 1: data distributions of response from the in-theatre questionnaire survey

A: All audience members

B: Student nurses

C: Health professionals and health lecturers

Source: Evaluation Report: *Using theatre drama to educate pre-registration nurses and midwives about mental health.* Health Education England (Carruthers, 2022a).

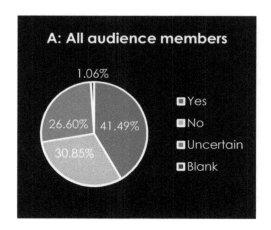

A: All audience members

1.06%

26.60% 41.49%

30.85%

☐ Yes
☐ No
☐ Uncertain
☐ Blank

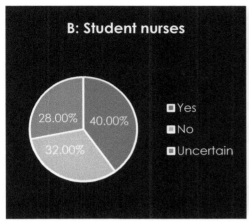

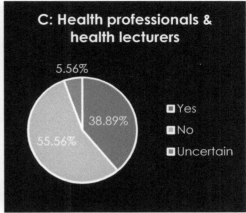

We also had lots of narrative feedback that confirms the effectiveness of this approach. Here are a few examples:

It made me feel the emotions that the patient would feel.

This idea of feeling the emotions of the characters came up quite frequently in the responses, which is exactly what we were hoping to hear. This next one specifically mentions how the event will help them become a more empathetic healthcare professional. Again, this came up quite a lot in the narrative feedback.

As an adult nursing student, this gave me a brilliant exposure to mental health issues, which I feel will help me to become a more empathetic healthcare professional in the future, with the understanding of mental health conditions and their impacts.

Another common theme was this idea of making watching the play mandatory. Whilst this is an encouraging sign of its effectiveness, it also brings up important discussions around whether it is best to offer the experience as an exciting option, rather than forcing people to watch it, especially with respect to some of the themes in the play around coercion and lack of choice.

Thought provoking, emotionally moving, raising plenty of questions and concerns re current and future treatments, using artificial intelligence in healthcare, and lack of alternative methods to recovery. ABSOLUTELY BRILLIANT! This play should be MANDATORY for ALL mental health professionals, student mental health nurses, trainee nursing associates; and an option for other healthcare students.

Several audience members who had lived experience of the themes explored shared that the event had made them feel less alone, more seen and even empowered. This contribution also highlights the need to remember that a large proportion of nurses, particularly mental health nurses, will have lived experience as service users from before or even during their professional careers.

Thank you for bringing this to peoples' attention. It made me feel less alone in the issues I've had and demonstrated it in such a beautiful way.

Other early indicators on effectiveness include that NHS England are very pleased with the impact so far and are keen to support a national tour where thousands more student nurses will attend as part of their training (Carruthers, 2022a). I'm also in early discussions with degree course leaders on how we might use clips from the play to develop new learning resources, such as workshops that focus on specific themes. I made a note of these early impacts in my research notes:

> ↓ NHS England keen to fund a national tour…
>
> ↓ Thousands more student nurses to attend as part of training…
>
> ↓ University degree course leaders keen to develop new learning resources based on clips from the play…

Objective 2: Deepening understanding of how and why student health professionals respond differently to film and theatre compared to the more traditional pedagogical approach.

In terms of understanding how and why students respond differently to this approach, I think more of this learning will come from the more in-depth 1 to 1 interviews, but there are some early narrative comments coming out in my data that give some insight, such as this one.

[The play is a] creative way to see a side of patients which can be difficult to understand in practice.

And this one…

[The play is] an excellent educational tool for students and a window into mental health. Real life experience - delivered in a safe environment.

The key bit here is *'real life experience – delivered in a safe environment'*, which I think is a huge strength of this creative and performative approach versus more traditional teaching and clinical placements. For example, another audience member said,

[The play is] thought provoking and had a lasting learning effect, often the most significant learning is from something that invokes strong emotions.

Objective 3: Producing a best practice model for the use of film and theatre as a pedagogical tool for future training.

And finally, towards this objective there was evidence of the strong emotions invoked by the play that could contribute to longer lasting and more significant learning than can be achieved by more traditional approaches, for example, one trainee nurse said,

Should be compulsory part of training, as it is a creative form of exposure to other fields of practice for Student Trainee Nurses.

Again this idea of the play being compulsory came up frequently, which will need much more thought as the PhD research progresses. However, a Doctor in the audience at one performance said,

> [This play] needs to be integrated with training and Continuing Professional Development of those within the NHS. More specifically the mental health setting.

This theme of using the play within the training and CPD of qualified health professionals came up a lot. And specifically on the use of the post-show discussion, people had suggestions on how to make this element of the research more effective, particularly around having more time to discuss the themes in more depth, and also by possibly structuring the discussions to ensure best use of the time. For example, one trainee nurse said:

> I wish there was more time.

And a Trainee Clinical Psychologist remarked,

> I wonder if there is a way to scaffold the conversation to allow a deeper exploration of some of the really important messages, maybe some pre-prepared remarks, questions or topics which could be used to really get into things more.

Conclusion

Which brings us the final moment of our story today, the climax! **Or a Conclusion.**

To summarise, early signs of the effectiveness of this approach are very positive. There's also enthusiasm from key stakeholders in the health sector and in universities to explore this approach more widely within the training of student health professionals and qualified clinicians.

It's encouraging that this is so far being seen as a positive pedagogical approach by students, health professionals and, vitally, service users with lived experience. If the results continue to be positive, we're potentially pushing at an open door to change how health professionals are trained as there are thousands more placement opportunities needed.

There are already calls for this to be adopted beyond nurse training. Suggestions have included medical students, social work students, paramedics and possibly more.

And that's the end of the story so far. Over to you, this is a dialogue after all.

Thank you.

References

Aronofsky, D. (2011) *Black Swan* [film: 108 mins] dir: Darren Aronofsky. Cross Creek Pictures, Protozoa Pictures, Phoenix Pictures, Dune Entertainment, Fox Searchlight Pictures.

Baker, S. (2017) *The Florida Project* [film: 111 mins] dir: Sean Baker. Cre Film, Freestyle Picture Company, Cinereach, June Pictures, A24.

Berger, E. (2022) *All Quiet on The Western Front* [film: 147 mins] dir: Edward Berger. Amusement Park, Netflix.

Bergold, J. and Thomas, S. (2012) Participatory research methods: a methodological approach in motion. *Historical Social Research*, 37, 4, 191-222.

Blix, B.H., Hamran, T. and Normann, H.K. (2012) Indigenous life stories as narratives of health and resistance: a dialogical narrative analysis. *Canadian Journal of Nursing Research*, 44, 2, 64-85.

Burns, D., Howard, J. and Ospina, S.M. (Eds.) (2021) *The SAGE Handbook of Participatory Research and Inquiry*. Sage, Thousand Oaks, CA.

Capra, F. (1946) *It's A Wonderful Life* [film: 131 mins] dir: Frank Capra. Liberty Films, RKO Radio Pictures.

Cargo, M. and Mercer, S.L. (2008) The value and challenges of participatory research: strengthening its practice. *Annual Review of Public Health*, 29, 325-350.

Carruthers, P. (2022) *The Possibility of Colour*. Directed by Pete Carruthers, tree fish productions, November 2022, New Adelphi Theatre, Salford. Photographer: Carly Altberg.

Carruthers, P. (2022a) Evaluation Report: *The Possibility of Colour* Northwest Tour 2022. *Using theatre drama to educate pre-registration nurses and midwives about mental health,* posted 1st December, Health Education England, [online]. Available at: https://www.hee.nhs.uk/about/how-we-work/your-area/north-west/north-west-news/using-theatre-drama-educate-pre-registration-nurses-midwives-about-mental-health (Acc 2.11.2023)

Carruthers, P. (2023) *The Possibility of Colour, a new play by Pete Carruthers* [online]. Available at: https://www.treefishproductions.com/the-possibility-of-colour (Accessed 31.10.2023)

Carruthers, P. (2023a) *Research puts the spotlight on using theatre and film to train professionals working in health and social care*. National Institute for Health and Care Research, Applied research Collaboration, Northwest Coast [online]. Available at: https://arc-nwc.nihr.ac.uk/news/research-puts-the-spotlight-on-using-theatre-and-film-to-train-professionals-working-in-health-and-social-care/ (Accessed 31.10.2023)

Darabont, F. (1994) *The Shawshank Redemption* [film: 142 mins] dir: Frank Darabont. Castle Rock Entertainment, Columbia Pictures.

Ebert, R. (2005) *Ebert's walk of fame remarks* [online]. Available at: https://www.rogerebert.com/roger-ebert/eberts-walk-of-fame-remarks (Accessed 31.10.2023)

Frank A.W. (2015) What is dialogical research, and why should we do it? *Qualitative Health Research*, 15, 7, 964-974.

Frank, A. (2010) *Letting stories breathe: a socio-narratology*. University of Chicago Press, Chicago.

Forman, M. (1975) *One Flew Over The Cuckoo's Nest* [film: 135 mins] dir: Miloš Forman. Fantasy Films, United Artists.

Gerwig, G. (2019) *Little Women* [film: 135 mins] dir: Greta Gerwig. Columbia Pictures, Regency Enterprises, Pascal Pictures, Sony Pictures Releasing.

Grant, A., Leigh-Phippard, H. and Short, N.P. (2015) Re-storying narrative identity: a dialogical study of mental health recovery and survival. *Journal of Psychiatric and Mental Health Nursing*, 22, 4, 223-286.

Gunaratnam, Y. and Oliviere, D. (2009) *Narrative and stories in health care: illness, dying and bereavement*. Oxford University Press, Oxford, UK.

Jenkins, B. (2016) *Moonlight* [film: 111 mins] dir: Barry Jenkins. A24, Plan B Entertainment, Pastel Productions.

Kaye, T. (1998) *American History X* [film: 119 mins] dir: Tony Kaye. New Line Cinema, The Turman-Morrissey Company.

Loach, K. (2016) *I Daniel Blake* [film: 100 mins] dir: Ken Loach. BBC Films, Wild Bunch, Sixteen Films, Why Not Productions, British Film Institute, Entertainment One, Le Pacte.

NMC (2018) *Future nurse: standards of proficiency for registered nurses.* Nursing and Midwifery Council [online]. Available at: https://www.nmc.org.uk/globalassets/sitedocuments/education-standards/future-nurse-proficiencies.pdf (Accessed 2.11.2023)

McAdams, D.P. (1993) *The stories we live by.* Guilford Press, New York.

Peele, J. (2017) *Get Out* [film: 104 mins] dir: Jordan Peele. Blumhouse Productions, QC Entertainment, Monkeypaw Productions, Universal Pictures.

Price, D. (2012) *Fallout* [film: 10 mins] dir: Dan Price. Black Toffee, SnapperPunchFish.

Rooney, T., Lawlor, K., Rohan, E. (2016) Telling tales; storytelling as a methodological approach in research. *Electronic Journal of Business Research Methods,* 14, 2, 147-156.

Soderbergh, S. (2000) *Erin Brockovich* [film: 130 mins] dir: Steven Soderbergh. Universal Pictures, Columbia Pictures, Jersey Films.

SCMS (2010) Society for Cinema and Media Studies Statement of Fair Use Best Practices for Media Studies Publishing. *Cinema Journal,* 49, 4, 179-185. https://www.cmstudies.org/page/fair_use

Spielberg, S. (1993) *Schindler's List* [film: 195 mins] dir: Steven Spielberg. Amblin Entertainment, Universal Pictures.

Villeneuve, D. (2017) *Blade Runner 2049* [film: 163 mins] dir: Denis Villeneuve. Alcon Media Group, Columbia Pictures, Bud Yorkin Productions, Torridon Films, 16:14 Entertainment, Thunderbird Entertainment, Scott Free Productions, Warner Bros. Pictures, Sony Pictures Releasing International.

Weir, P. (1998) *The Truman Show* [film: 103 mins] dir: Peter Weir. Scott Rudin Productions, Paramount Pictures.

Ethics statement: This research was conducted with ethical approval from the University of Central Lancashire.

JQRSS Author Profiles

Pete Carruthers[1] is a writer, actor, director, producer (and creator of 'tree-fish productions') occasional lecturer, workshop facilitator and PhD by Portfolio research student working across the creative arts and health education at the University of Central Lancashire. Email: PJCarruthers@uclan.ac.uk

Clive Palmer[2] is a research supervisor in the School of Sport and Health and a doctoral education lead in the Graduate Research School for the University of Central Lancashire. ORCID-ID https://orcid.org/0000-0001-9925-2811 Email: capalmer@uclan.ac.uk

Mick McKeown[3] is Professor of Democratic Mental Health in the School of Nursing at UCLan. Mick has consistently supported public engagement initiatives, largely in the field of health and social care, working on projects funded by the NHS, Social Care Institute, Skills for Care, the Higher Education Academy, Wellcome Trust, and the British Council. ORCID-ID https://orcid.org/0000-0003-0235-1923 Email: mmckeown@uclan.ac.uk

Reviewer Comments

Telling a good story is never as linear as it may initially appear and these early acts of research storytelling don't disappoint. I can see a researcher- storyteller confidently playing with narrative devices to explore the interplay between research and story: adjusting levels of dramatisation within act of the research journey. The opportunities for further expanding discussions around the value of participatory change-making in healthcare using theatre or film are clear, as are the challenges. This is a researcher-storyteller who is fully aware of the added complexities of consent and morality which come with the telling, sharing and consuming of these types of narratives. Each read of this dialogue has encouraged new musings: am I reader, audience or character? Are there conflicts for the author in embodying both story and research? Will the empathy machine emerge as character, be scenery or give breath to the dialogue we will encounter? There are clearly plenty more adventures to be had, and so I for one, am looking forward to the next act.

Smith, G., Palmer, C. and Young, K. (2023) Baring one's soul in narrative health research: the enculturation of a health care professional in an island population. *Journal of Qualitative Research in Sports Studies*, 17, 1, 171-186

Baring one's soul in narrative health research – the enculturation of a health care professional in an island population

Glenn Smith, Clive Palmer and Kenneth Young
(University of Central Lancashire)

Keywords: *autoethnography, health care, narrative, storytelling, reflection*

Abstract

Autoethnography demands a high degree of self-reflection and openness about one's own life that is both disconcerting and necessary. Therefore, the presentation of self becomes necessary to inform the reader about the author's positionality in research, but without overextending its scope to the extraneous or sensitive. The utility of the narrative form in autoethnography is discussed in this paper revolving around four short stories including: 1. *Starting Points,* 2. *Arrival,* 3. *Transition to Care Work and Nursing,* and 4. *Professional Initiation.* These auto-narratives are part of a wider study into the enculturation of a health care professional in an island population. These progressive and linked accounts are counterpointed with metanarrative as reflexive explanation of how autoethnography has been deployed as research method. Our paper highlights the potential contribution of autoethnography and narrative research to health practitioners working in socio-cultural and clinical settings. The field in this research is the Isle of Wight, off the south coast of the United Kingdom. Key themes related to this location include its geographical position (i.e. its relative isolation to the mainland), and its role as a social-demographic outlier as foretaste of the future population that the National Health Service will serve (i.e. it's high percentage of retired and elderly people). Consequently there is a wide variance in healthcare needs represented in the Island's population, which are placing new demands on the healthcare workforce to meet those needs in the community. Our paper concludes that the narrative turn through this research is yielding positive insights to how health care is received by those whom it is intended to help, and importantly therefore, how health care professionals might alter their practice in the future, to enhance social approaches in clinical care and therefore to maximize the positive impacts of their actions.

NB: The first author is a PhD by Portfolio candidate at the University of Central Lancashire. PhD by Portfolio requires a collation of personal experiences and professional attainments, upon which a 'retrospective' reflective critique of can be made, in order to guide and inform a new 'prospective' phase of research. This article is part of that process.

JQRSS Article No: 8/9-17-1-2023-PG[112]-169
ISSN: 1754-2375 [print] ISSN: 2755-5240 [online] Copyright ©: CC-BY-NC-ND
Web: https://uclan.academia.edu/ClivePalmer/Journal-of-Qualitative-Research-in-Sports-Studies

Introduction

The presentation of self in narrative is problematic inasmuch as it opens up to accusations of being biased. The subtext of this ethical attack is that there is somehow a morally neutral position from which to assess a research problem. This is clearly a position that can be contested. For example, ask the simple question 'Why ought one take a morally neutral viewpoint?' (Patrick, 2021), and we are left reaching for moral scaffolding to support a morally neutral viewpoint. Despite lacking coherence, this position often leaves the researcher who presents themselves in the narrative, as being under attack.

Autoethnographic process however appreciates that knowledge is partial and situated, and has a viewpoint (Punch, 2012). In contrast to the objectivist, the interpretivist proudly flaunts the colours and hues of their life, that influence and shape their worldview, and epistemological lens. Therefore, embracing these limitations, this account of my culturation into an Island community and health care system is structured as follows:

1. Starting Points

2. Arrival

3. Transition to Care Work and Nursing

4. Professional Initiation

I present each narrative, with questioning about my enculturation into each subculture I visited (Gunaratnam, 2009; Haynes, 2012; Rooney *et al.*, 2016). These questions counterpoint the narrative with my own interpretation of this information. It also demonstrates my commitment to critical thinking about my past, at this moment in time (25 years or more into my career), and not an uncritical and unthinking acceptance of the past, as it was. Critical appreciation of one's own narrative contributes to self-awareness, reflexivity, and empathy for others with shared human experiences (Rosairo, 2023). The colour of the narrative comes, I believe, from presenting the 'situatedness' in such a way as to generate a picture of the journey in the mind of the reader. Times, places and persons are highlighted to situate the derived knowledge in such a way as to make it obvious to a reader the logical and reasonable nature of my own reasoning and conclusions from what I have confronted. I hope that this encourages others to take seriously those touchpoints of their life that informed their own outlook and positionality, and to offer these insights in the knowledge that they help to authenticate their position and view of the world.

Narrative also poses the difficult question of how much one should reveal about oneself (Wolcott, 1983; Gilbourne, 2013). The discomfort of revelation is tempered with the need to present it in such a way to others (eg. Laing, 'The Divided Self'

(1960) and 'The Politics of Experience' 1967) that does not disrespect those being written about, or oneself. Sympathetic disclosure should not however hamper criticality, as this is unhelpful and prevents asking deeper questions that might provide informative insights about oneself and one's worldview.

1. Starting Points

My working life has been on the Isle of Wight, but my life did not start there. My contact with healthcare starts from the age of 5 in the early 1980s, as I recall, having been brought up in Surrey, the width of a field away from the M25. Diagnosed with asthma at the age of 5, I was in and out of hospital for 5 years. This was from my first year in school to middle of middle school. In all, I counted 26 admissions that I can remember. What does this do to one's outlook on life? Well for a start off, it means spending more time in hospital than at school. It becomes part of your life, and to add to that, it normalises it in some respect which I am not sure, had I had less contact with the hospital environment, that it would have done. I have had the opportunity to observe healthcare from the inside for over 40 years. This shapes how you view healthcare in my opinion and how you appreciate it. Not least because the longer you are around healthcare, the farther back you can remember how different it was.

The absence from school is important to highlight too. Unpopular as it was, I spent significant amounts of time on what would now be called colloquially the 'Thickie' table. I was on the same table as people with dyslexia and other learning difficulties as we now understand them. In retrospect largely because of my absences from school, this affected my development or so it appears. I achieved below average in many respects. I didn't know at the time, that I am actually neurodivergent. The label didn't exist to explain my different experience of the world.

You might ask what gives me reason to believe that these prolonged absences caused my suboptimal performance in school to that point? Two things happened close together. The first was my father who was a nuclear test veteran, was diagnosed with inoperable (in those days) lung cancer, and died 6 months later in a hospice. This caused another period of intense contact with healthcare settings. Secondly, my mother and her subsequent partner (who she met whilst my dad was in hospital) went on holiday to Ventnor, on the Isle of Wight and took me out of hospital to go…

As rash as discharging an 8 year old from a hospital ward against medical advice sounds to modern ears, it was probably the best thing that ever happened to me. My symptoms, badly managed in Surrey where the air quality was poor, disappeared in the cool breezy air of Ventnor. Ventnor, the home to the largest respiratory hospital in Europe at one time, proved my symptoms could be more easily controlled. The die was cast and we moved a year later. What subsequently happened was that when my health improved, so it appears, did my academic achievement. Not once from moving to the Island did I then need hospitalisation for my asthma.

Did 5 years of intense contact with hospital settings for both my and my dad's health conditions lead me to become a nurse? The evidence says otherwise. Look up childhood hospitalisation and career change and little evidence emerges to link the two. (Bryce et al, 2023) Irrespective of the general consensus, events conspired otherwise. At school, post GCSEs I went for a music course but never finished it. The reason was my mother had mental health issues and I wasn't able to leave her without support, so there was no question of me moving off the Island. Secondly, one of the issues with that type of employment on the Island is that music and hospitality industries on the Island are seasonal, and you need a more stable source of income to survive. That, and my previous experience probably explains why, when I left school, that I entered health and social care through the route of a Youth Training Scheme. Ironically, this was the career choice suggested to me when I went for careers advice. I had rejected it then perhaps because I was less self-aware of what would suit me. Little did I know then where that choice would take me.

Starting Points was the name I gave to the first descriptive phase of my life. I elected to include reference to my early personal experiences of healthcare, as I genuinely believe this informed my later career choices. It also highlights my positive experience of moving geographically which coincided with improvements in my health. This is an additional derivation from the narrative, the idea that health or ill health can be influenced by where you are geographically, and decisions that are made around where you live can either help or hinder your overall health state (e.g. Department of Health, 2021; Public Health England, 2021).

The geography of the Isle of Wight at the same time constrains and advantages my narrative. Its constraints are geographical and rural, with the isolation compounding the sense of 'other' in relation to the mainland. Historically the Isle of Wight remains less ethnically diverse than other comparative areas of the UK and has traditionally lagged behind in the adoption of innovation in many areas. However in research its isolation and containment can be exploited to produce and test out hypotheses in the microcosm of the Island, the findings of which can be reasonably extrapolated to the macrocosm of the 'north Island' (the rest of mainland Britain).

I also genuinely believe that early contact with healthcare through illness gives you an empathy towards others that someone who does not have that shared experience often lacks (Moudatsou *et al.*, 2020; Guidi and Traversa, 2021). Recent developments of roles in NHS organisations that emphasise the 'lived experience' demonstrate the commitment of NHS organisations to integrating this insight into their service development.

2. Arrival

Coming to the Island in the late 80s was interesting for a number of reasons. Many small businesses still prospered at this point and it was easier to gain work in them. The predominant employers on the Island however have been and still are hospitality and the health and social care sector. Hospitality, as I had already noticed, was seasonal, taking advantage of the beautiful location, Victorian history and interest, and the feeling of getting away from it all when you crossed on the ferry. Seasonality meant you work as hard as you can from April to October, and then have a dry five months with a small hiatus for Christmas visitors to the island, or as we called them, the Turkey and Tinsel brigade. Health and social care however are steadier forms of employment and attract people for that reason.

It could be argued that health and social care is such a predominant employer on the Island as a response to the local demographic. Even in the 80s, the Island attracted the retirement population. People year after year would come over for holidays, only to retire when they didn't have to return for their work. (Department of Health, 2021; Public Health England, 2017). Our move to the Island was precipitated and facilitated by my mum's former work colleagues from Surrey. This is a common experience. One of my school friends from Surrey too moved to the Island and so we knew people here. The transition was eased because we knew others. Our family move was almost an analogous experience to enculturating yourself to an ex-pat community in Spain.

It appears also however that there is a transient population here on the IoW. There are extremes of Poverty punctuated by enclaves of affluence, often not only permanent residents but second homes – the 'DFLs' – Down from Londons, who can be observed during the yearly gathering of the yachting fraternity at the world renowned Cowes week, and the summer months, in their droves coming off the ferries to invade the relative quietude of the Island. Over 90% of the Island remains rural, with isolated villages and hamlets hiding pockets of poor health, poorly kept housing, and erratic employment. Health and social care resources are spread wide and thinly, with surprising variation even in such a small geographical area.

Listening to my own language describing these things, I have become enculturated over these 35 years here on the Island. I too was a mainlander, risking being ignored if I didn't fit in. I too was an outsider, fighting to fit in with the locals. I too experienced the need to be accepted. All of these affect us, affect our ability to function here, and the experience of that process of enculturation geographically and culturally, has its analogies to the ability to enculturate oneself into hospital subcultures. I hadn't really thought of this analogous experience until the exercise of reflecting on my history, but it clearly plays a part.

As I reflect, construct and compose my story, I am becoming aware of the impacts of retelling my story. I note my own language has changed. This is the hand of hindsight at work. Note also I am setting up the themes of enculturation and transitions in this narrative. I purposely wrote this prose to colour in the picture in the mind of the reader, giving them a taste of the environment in which I moved and breathed. This is scene setting for my main research , where I 'reach back in to my autobiographical narrative' to highlight points of learning and scope out potential impacts in the future.

Rural populations differ in many respects from urban ones, the differences being magnified by the geographical isolation of the Island. Urbanised areas attract working populations, but bleed them to the rural idylls on retirement. This attraction of the older retired population against the need for care and hospitality staff creates tension in a population such as the Isle of Wight where need outstrips availability of staff (Public Health England, 2017; Department of Health, 2021).

In contrast to the researcher observing a culture at arms length, the immersion of the researcher in the culture being researched, begs a different reflexive experience. Reflecting upon oneself as the self now reflecting upon the self then, and critiquing one's views then pairs transparency with reflectiveness. Narrative exposition needs to be superimposed with my own criticality to reveal insights that I have derived from these experiences, and how recursive immersion into these recollections reveals more and more of my own views of the subcultures which I immersed myself within (Vryan, 2006).

Offering these insights into my previous experience and work in an Island setting, I hope, underlines how my past work situated on the Island. informs my future work positively. To use understandings derived from the past to inform future hypotheses is in my view intellectually justifiable, provided they are tempered with a willingness to expose them to the crucible of new evidence. This validates these insights, rather than being purely a product of selective memory on my part, unwilling to admit my defects in my approach. To corroborate hypotheses derived from past experience in prospective data collection and research, validates the conclusions that can be drawn. Autobiographical detail is offered in the spirit of transparency to highlight my personal perspective, addressing the criticism that such methodologies are unbalanced by my own narrative, biases and opinions. Presenting oneself in autoethnographic narrative is treated with perceived inferiority by objectivists, a view I firmly reject. Rather, an appreciation of the intersection of the self with the arena under consideration in an open way, as an 'insider' of the subset of systems practitioners offers the 'Heineken' of ethnographic research, views and research insights that 'other methodologies just cannot reach'.

The theme in this element of the narrative also strongly features transitioning as a means of understanding transit between and immersion in cultures. The reader should feel that they are transported to the Island settings in which I worked through the descriptive analysis presented. Against these elements unique to my working journey, I also trust that the universal experience of transition and change resonates enough with the reader that this requires no explanation, but that the landscape of people, places and events needs unpacking to contextualise and situate this transition in a reality that I observed, experienced and interacted with. Narrative in my analysis assumes a certain amount of universal human experience that requires no explanation. This helps to keep the speed of the narrative and the interest of the reader without descriptive detail that detracts from the points I am trying to draw out from the narrative itself.

3. Transition to Care Work and Nursing

Leaving school, my first career move was into the Youth Training Scheme (YTS) for carers (Department of Employment, 1981), which coincided with my first experience in paid care work. I worked in a care home within walking distance of home in Ryde. Care work on the Island in the early 90s was a popular choice for school leavers. The YTS offered such a road into care work. The care home I started in was typical of the 80s and 90s, buildings which were basically converted houses. These had a homely atmosphere but were nothing like the purpose built environments we have now. The ease with which large houses could be extended or converted to small homes would explain why at its height the Isle of Wight had around 150 of these small homes. This number dwindled as the regulations governing the accommodation standards and the need to adapt home environments for increasingly medically dependent residents made the operation of smaller homes untenable. The demands of the regulations outpaced owners' efforts to maintain viable businesses and many businesses closed. Those that were left expanded and extended their footprint, either assisted by being subsumed by larger mainland chains, or by being brought by individuals with expressly commercial interest seeing profit at the core of the enterprise.

As a male school leaver and young carer, it was no use avoiding the stereotypes. Males entering care work were commonly labelled gay, without any recourse to finding out about the individuals themselves. This was not helped by care work then being a predominantly female occupation. I was a minority in this group and had to negotiate enculturating myself into this environment. My gender didn't help. Add to that that the whole point of me being there was actually an apprenticeship in care, I had a lot going on. Firstly, having to negotiate a female dominated environment. Secondly having to go from an academic environment to a vocational environment, and thirdly actually being in a workplace where I earned money full time, rather than the Saturday and evening jobs I had had up to that point. I had worked in a care home kitchen around the age of 16, so I was familiar with the environment but not on the care side.

I moved through three different jobs during those early years post school; care home, then nursing home, then back to care home. My first environment was predominantly older persons with few physical or mental health issues, the nursing home had mainly nursing dependent patients and then the third home had mental health issues. It was around this time I started to become more familiar with the work of the community nursing teams coming in to provide wound care, diabetic injections and other community nursing work. I became aware of the interplay and interdependency between care homes and the visiting professionals that relied on the care home teams to implement the care plans they created. These were my first observed examples of the delegation of nursing tasks to unregistered staff, the thin end of a wedge that would affect my professional life and position as a researcher later. I observed two sorts of nurses, those who wished to delegate everything thus upskilling frontline staff, and those who wished to centralise and control everything unwilling to delegate. This tension has increased over the years in my estimation, something that I constantly questioned and has been central to my work with subcultures throughout my career.

Years later I found this early experience inestimably valuable. You are 'stamped' by this process in some intangible way which is communicated invisibly every time you speak to teams in these arena. This awareness informed my approach to care homes and how I approached enlisting them in the projects we undertook. An experienced insider in this game recognises another experienced insider. Experience cannot easily be counterfeited or faked in the presence of experienced colleagues. People try to do this (and I have met many who try to do this) but end up not sounding authentic. The ring of 'actually having been there and done that' shines through when you relate to these teams having been through the wringer of actually working in them. As I look back, my advice to self (and others) is do not underestimate how valuable this experience is even if it feels that little is gained at the time.

During this time I repeatedly applied to enter the nursing profession, and it took three attempts over four years for me to get in. At the time the first two failures were disappointing but in retrospect it was not the right time for me. I reflected on my early applications, and realised they reflected a lack of maturity on my part. There was no magic moment in which I realised this. The transition and development of my thinking only became apparent when I revisited my previous applications in preparing to apply again. Insights borne of experience and exposure were tellingly not present in my earlier applications, but which I was able to put into words in my successful application.

When I eventually got into nursing, the experience of becoming a student nurse added different colours to my life experience. In my case I continued to work in care environments whilst working as a student nurse, as do many others in the same situation. Nursing doesn't always pay enough, so you continue to work at the same time. For me, this tempered an increasingly academic process with a pragmatic temperament about working with real people.

There is a positive appreciation in this narrative that when one's journey does not go as planned, that it is still beneficial or that helpful insights can still be derived from situations which at the time are perceived negatively. Failing to achieve milestones, such as getting a job interview or getting onto a nursing programme, feel wrong at the time but the insights and improvements one makes as a result of these negative experiences justifies the pain one experiences at the time. Additionally providing examples of where the outcome is unexpected or not in accordance with the intentions of the researcher underlines a commitment to honesty, transparency, and authenticity, with the intention of increasing the reader's trust in the candour of the researcher, who is prepared to bare their soul in the pursuit of truths unearthed from their personal narrative (Gerard, 1996; Mockler, 2011).

I also reflect upon this narrative that I like the term 'ticket collector' that I came upon in my professional career, the idea that one 'collects tickets' (certificates) as one goes through certain experiences to trade them in later, to reach a higher level of professional or personal development. This certainly fits in with the worldview that no insight is wasted provided it is employed in one's own betterment later on.

4. Professional Initiation

There is no other way in my mind to describe entering nursing but the initiation into a professional club, a process of enculturation where one assumes the mantle, and language, and technical paraphernalia of the discipline to which you become devoted. My entry into nursing was on the mental health route, not my first choice, but serendipity was at work. Assumption into this discipline felt like contracting a fungus, a slow rising line of 'mental health

179

nursingness'. Sadly I fought much of it. I didn't realise why at the time I felt so out of place and like the greater fool for questioning basic notions of mental health nursing, such as 'to what archetype does one compare a person's mental health?' or 'if health is relative, who is to define this as healthy and that as unhealthy?' My critique of mental health then reflected my absolutism, and resistance to relativism, in contrast to the process of consensus mental health nursing trusted to inform its views of health and healing, a process I felt was driven by subjectivism Subjectivism, with its lack of commitment to the safe harbour of an anchoring absolute, stalked me and made me feel uncomfortable in the profession I had come in to.

I didn't find a resting place in acute mental health work, and ended up working with people with dementia, at the cross over between mental health and what can be measured objectively with the use of CT scans and mini mental state examinations. It is true to say that my experience of working with people with dementia was fundamental in shaping my view of persons as being persons, not objects, and it shaped my subsequent view of how we should relate to persons. Four years in, and having slogged through a Bachelor of Nursing degree, I pivoted to stroke research, capitalising on my degree with its strong leaning towards research evidence, and started at the hospital, my introduction to the wards.

Stroke research nursing, even before I started Tissue Viability, gave me one key insight that I have held onto ever since. My role followed the entire pathway of a stroke from admission to discharge or sometimes passing away. I observed the interplay between teams, professionals, and patients with their family circles, all in the service of a single pathway. This imprinted upon me the need to enlist all of these subgroups (read subcultures!) in the pursuit of a single goal, and an appreciation of how they need to be coordinated and led for the pathway to work. This insight I drew into my later work in Tissue Viability too.

Moving into Tissue Viability was an obvious transition for me given my previous experience. Older people with dementia and stroke patients often experience leg ulcers from wandering pressure ulcers when they are immobile, and skin tears from their agitation, aggression and from falling, So when the role came up, I was interested in taking my interest in wounds and wound management further. My interview for a post in Tissue Viability was, from my perspective at least, one of those times where you figure you have nothing to lose. I was a complete outsider, as 'mental health nurses don't apply for these positions, don'tchya know??' I also was not attached in some respects to the outcome, I simply was interested in the role and what I could do with it. My three interviewers, a Deputy Director of Nursing, an Education Lead, and a

180

previous Tissue Viability nurse, laughed from beginning to end, not something that reassured me at the time, but the outcome said otherwise.

There was one memorable phrase in my job winning presentation I still carry with me, and only with my delving into autoethnography did I appreciate its significance. I spoke about the wound as a story. The person, and the wound on them, are a story we must discover. This narrative united my presentation, but more accurately, it unified how I saw the world. It was the scaffolding around which all of my subsequent approaches were based, as the story, with its heroes and villains, the events that lead up to the wound, and the touchpoints of victory and defeat in healing the wound, all played out. The heroic endeavour of sometimes healing the wound, sometimes not, inspired my presentation, as it does even now. It also frames my reference to people. Talk to the people first and the story comes out, an important emphasis when it comes to later consideration of my retrospective analysis.

To say that my appointment caused waves is an understatement. 'Mental health nurses don't become Tissue Viability nurses!' Some wards would not even engage with me because of my professional background. This posed a problem for me to get anything done. How would I win them over? How would I engage with them productively? How would I ever achieve anything when it was me against them? Those questions dogged my early years, and I look back at them now with a degree of humour, not something I experienced when I was in the thick of it. How I resolved those issues, and transcended them in some respects sets the scene for my current research and into experiences in a health care system from an islanders perspective.

The narrative is interposed with quotations selectively presented to summarise the story of others, phrases that become memes or posters that one passes in the journey, presented to offer to the reader a taste of what I experienced in these situations. I also propose in the narrative the questions that I posed to myself and which required resolution to move forward. My underlying attitude and feelings, now with a reflective sense of humour, against the underlying angst and anxiety at the time, are compared to offer an insight into my development and relationship to the memory of these events, hopefully again demonstrating a maturity of insight that is afforded by distance from the events themselves and reflection upon them.

Conclusion

The unfolding narrative of my early career is offered to inform the reader and guide them through experiences to which I was exposed which informed my worldview, and to flesh out the landscape in which my subsequent retrospective analysis and prospective research is situated. I deliberately elected to adopt a story telling voice in laying out my positionality, as this, I felt, made it more understandable, dare I say it palatable, to a reader. The reconstruction of these events I appreciate is as much based on my memory as it is on the significance which I ascribe to these personal, temporal and geographical touchpoints. Their exposition is coloured by my view of them. I acknowledge this, but without apologies, as to apologise, to feel abashed as it were, for my view suggests that I think my view of the world is somehow inferior. This is not the point. Quite the opposite in fact as I seek to demonstrate that storytelling is in some sense the most important method for making sense of these events and how they inform my future work.

I intend the theme of storytelling to permeate my description of enculturation, as I propose that this seems to be the method with which one enculturates oneself, by weaving oneself into the storytelling of the culture into which one wishes to enter, sit down and coexist with (Frank, 1995; 2000). An appreciation of this seems to be a novel view of the problem of navigating and coordinating subcultures in the pursuit of cross-cultural goal alignment. Being able to provide an original viewpoint on this issue, and also suggest means with which others facing the same challenges might adopt to achieve cross cultural goals, would seem to me to validate the employment of this pedagogical method.

Avoiding meandering narrative and remaining focussed is a constant challenge. It is rarely, if brilliantly, employed to good effect on occasion (e.g. *The Mezzanine* by Nicholson-Baker, 1988). Stories must have a structure, a beginning, middle, end and moral to the story. The moral, if one would call it that, of the story I present is the adoption of storytelling itself, the exchange of and incorporation into the stories of subcultures, can be utilised effectively to weave them together into a new narrative, unifying individual stories in the achievement of a higher cross-cultural purpose.

Stories, the currency which we exchange in forming and reforming our own and others narratives (McAdams, 1993) may grow in the telling, but this growth is nothing to fear in my opinion. In fact this growth should be celebrated, as I propose this signifies their value increases over time. Expounding them over and over reinforces their significance in defining subcultures, a process that can be influenced positively to the benefit of all involved. The practice of exposition both verbally and in writing adds to the development of this skillset, something that makes autoethnographic analysis both essential and valuable (Gerard, 1996).

Personalisation of care in healthcare relies on the ability to recognise and build upon the stories patients carry with them all the time. Positive appreciation of these stories leads to the ability to incorporate oneself into them in a way that is both therapeutic and affirming. This process is also two way as an informed, alert, reflective practitioner takes as much from these stories as they give to the person to whom they have a duty of care. One need not fear the story telling – one must wield this secret weapon with pride and hone its edge daily.

References

Baker, N. (1988) *The Mezzanine*. Granta Books, Great Britain.

Department of Employment (1981) *A new training initiative: A programme for action [White Paper]*. HMSO, London.

Department of Health (2021) *Health in Coastal Communities: Chief Medical Officer's Annual Report*. HMSO. London.

Frank, A.W. (1995) *The wounded storyteller: body, illness, and ethics*. The University of Chicago Press, Chicago.

Frank A.W. (2000) The standpoint of storyteller. *Qualitative Health Research*, 10, 3, 354-365.

Gerard, P. (1996) *Creative non-fiction, researching and crafting stories of real life*. Story Press, Cincinnati, Ohio, USA.

Gilbourne D. (2013) Heroes, toxic ferrets and a large man from Leeds. *Sports Coaching Review*, 2, 2, 86-97.

Guidi, C., and Traversa, C. (2021) Empathy in patient care: from 'clinical empathy' to 'empathic concern'. *Medical Health Care Philosophy*, 24, 4, 573-585.

Gunaratnam Y. (2009) Narrative interviews and research (Chapter 3, 47-62). In, Gunaratnam, Y. and Oliviere, D. (Eds.) *Narrative and stories in health care: illness, dying and bereavement*. Oxford University Press, Oxford.

Haynes, K. (2012) Reflexivity in qualitative research (chapter 5). In, Cassell, C. and Symon, G. (Eds.) *The Practice of Qualitative Organizational Research: Core Methods and Current Challenges* Sage Knowledge, London.

McAdams, D.P. (1993) *The Stories We Live By*. Guilford Press, New York.

Mockler, N. (2011) Being me: in search of authenticity (pp:159-168). In, Higgs, J., Titchen, A., Horsfall, D. and Bridges, D. (Eds.) *Creative Spaces for Qualitative Researching*. Brill, Leiden.

Moudatsou, M., Stavropoulou, A., Philalithis, A., Koukouli, S. (2020) The role of empathy in health and social care professionals. Healthcare, 30, 8, 1-26.

Rooney, T., Lawlor, K., and Rohan, E. (2016) Telling tales; storytelling as a methodological approach in research. *The Electronic Journal of Business Research Methods*, 14, 2, 147-156.

Rosairo, R. (2023) Narrative approach in qualitative research. *Journal of Agricultural Sciences – Sri Lanka*, 18, 1, doi:10.4038/jas.v18i1.10094

Vryan, K.D. (2006) Expanding analytic autoethnography and enhancing its potential. *Journal of Contemporary Ethnography*, 35, 4, 405-409.

Wolcott, H.F. (1983) Adequate schools and inadequate education: the life history of a sneaky kid. Anthropology and Education Quarterly, 14, 1, 3-32.

Ethics statement: This research was conducted with ethical approval from UCLan.

JQRSS Author Profiles

Glenn Smith[1] is the Clinical Director/Chief Executive Officer, of Lighthouse Medical, providing NHS Dermatology Services on behalf of Isle of Wight NHS Trust. Glenn is also a Post Graduate researcher on the PhD by Portfolio programme at UCLan.

Clive Palmer[2] is a research supervisor in the School of Sport and Health and a doctoral education lead in the Graduate Research School for the University of Central Lancashire. ORCID-ID https://orcid.org/0000-0001-9925-2811 Email: capalmer@uclan.ac.uk

Kenneth Young[3] has a background as a chiropractor with academic and clinical experience in the UK, Australia, and North America. His research interests include knowledge translation, evidence-based practice, professional ethics, identity, and cultural authority. ORCID-ID https://orcid.org/0000-0001-8837-7977 ⓘ Email: kjyoung1@uclan.ac.uk

Reviewer Comments

Reviewer: Glenn bravely embarks on a disconcerting but necessary journey where we, the readers, are invited to share in the richness of his experience. His message is clear, 'It's all about people' and without knowing ourselves and why we do what we do, how are we to relate to others? He powerfully reflects on his early experiences; his asthma and struggles at school, his father's short battle with lung cancer and his mother's mental health issues which led him, unknowingly at the time, into a life of care work. In doing so, he provides ample support for autoethnographic methods, against the naysayers who cling to absolutism and objectivity as he courageously strives to validate relativism and subjectivity in health care research.

Not only does Glenn enculturate us in the Island, curious about the pockets of poor health and poor housing and sceptical of the 'Down from Londons' and the 'Tinsel and Turkey Brigade', he also neatly plots his journey and crucially, shares what it means to be human. At some time or other we all experience being an 'outsider', having to consistently enculturate ourselves. At times like these it is essential we feel vindicated, and we should not be expected to remain neutral and bias-free. We too can begin to understand the value of our experience, however anxious we may feel at the time, reflection is to be valued and we may look back with humour rather than angst, as Glenn does, for it is these experiences that shape us and the way that we interact and interplay with others. Hopefully, for many, this account can be the Starting Point, Arrival, Transition or maybe even Initiation for the recognition of person-centred care and the value of storytelling in healthcare research.

Author Response:

Strange bedfollows - juxtaposing absolutism and subjectivism in autoethnographical research

In Smith *et al.,* (2023), I set out my positionality as a researcher through storytelling and narrative. This was interpreted by my reviewer as setting out a subjectivist and relativist mindset. This worried me as I would never define myself as that, and I admit that this might be a personal discomfort. However on the basis that I must admit to myself that this reaction may not be just something I experience, but that it is something that would resonate with other qualitative researchers, I want to unpack my discomfort a bit, in an effort to mine the autoethnographic gold at the bottom of this particular seam of self-narrative and reflection.

I struggle with the word subjective because it has associations with the idea that a view that is put forward that is described as subjective is somehow of lesser value. One never hears the term "merely objective". The term "merely subjective" can be used pejoratively and colloquially to invalidate the personal viewpoint, as if somehow the fact that a particular experience is only experienced or lived by a few or even one, that this automatically disqualifies that experience as being of value. This seems, to me at least, to be an imbalance.

The subject, as the person who experiences, the indivisible unit of observation and experience that generates the story and narrative, is to me valuable. In fact, I will go further. I suggest that the person is of supreme value in my interpretation, because whilst I admit to subjectivism where it aligns with the goal of recognising the person as a person, I do not subscribe to the automatic assertion that commonly comes alongside this that this infers that I am also a relativist. And that is an awkward juxtaposition. Because to admit that a person is of supreme value commits me to the premise that there is such a thing as an "absolute person". This on the one hand sets out an absolute standard, but on the other links it with personhood, not objectivity, and that is a weird mindset to many academics.

Reductionism, at its roots, reduces phenomena to objects or pieces, the lowest common denominator that can be experienced by everyone. Hence the test of objectivity being the idea that one can experience something independent of time place and person. Relativism asserts no absolute foundation but that all is relative and can be interpreted and that no one interpretation has more validity or value than another. On the one hand this guards against the dismissiveness that can so easily creep in, dismissing the minority view as of no value. But at another level, if all is valuable, none is valuable as there is no absolute comparator upon which to judge. The yardstick that elevates all voices to be listened to simultaneously disavows their value, because to judge value implies a hierarchy with which to judge, and point to one voice over another as being more or less valuable. The Achilles heal of Relativism is that as a viable concept, it has by definition to be relative to itself, which is an absurdity.

The magic trick, if one can call it that, is to simultaneously value the person as an individual, but with supreme value. Whence however, does that value derive from? The answer perhaps can be made in reverse. If one rejects reductionism, as I do, then the opposite in my perspective is to assert a holistic perspective that integrates, and that in my view is the person, who integrates the times, places, and persons, and their significance into the golden thread of narrative. If one rejects relativism, then one must assert an absolute value system. The nexus of these two is the absolute person. And it is this quantum, this idea of the person and their output of stories and narratives that define the value of their existence that seems to me to be the most valuable reason for adopting an autoethnographic approach.

But wait. In the minds of some, this echoes of religion and spirituality. Hadn't we done away with this psychological paraphernalia in the modern world? Well perhaps not. Perhaps that which exited quietly like a true gentleman through the back door when reductionism and relativism took hold, has come back in the front door in the form of autoethnography. And that will disturb some, indeed it may turn the world on its head.

Because to assert this cuts to the root of a particular epistemological issue, which is the value of research against the hierarchy of evidence. The fact that it is even constructed as a hierarchy implies a judgement of value. That which is at the top, the systematic review and meta-analysis of randomised controlled trials, is deemed top notch, and the single case narrated by a sole observer is at the bottom. Yet to assert the value of the individual voice must necessarily involve ascribing value to that which is de-valued in the hierarchy of evidence. Evidence, as the output of observation, derives its value in this hierarchy from the ability of every observer to observe the same thing in the same way. Uniformity and conformity is rewarded. However this is not what a person experiences in real life. The cause effect relationship investigated by a randomised controlled trial is observed in an environment sanitised of complexity and idiosyncrasy, all of which are necessary corollaries of personality and personal stories. Similarities between stories breed resonance, disparities breed counterpoints. The bleaching effect of purging all from a population through exclusion criteria divorces that which is investigated from real life.

That will sound unnecessarily harsh to some, but frameworks wittingly or unwittingly influence people's thinking, and to think of the individual story as being devalued because of the hierarchy of evidence will inevitably, in my view, lead to the devaluing of the person behind that story too. Does someone have the moral courage to call this out? To start a social movement that brands such behaviour as 'merely objective'? Sadly I doubt it. And its effects can be reasonably predicted to be deleterious.

Autoethnography with its appreciation of the quanta of individual stories in my estimation rails against such interpretations, raising as it does the mind of the researcher above objective effects to the one effecting the effects. Agency, as John Lennox puts it, is more important, or just as important, as Mechanism, and Agency can only be investigated and made sense of when one understands the agent, not the mechanism. Autoethnography sneaks inside this barricade to unearth the person behind their output.

Grecic, D., Simões, P., Žlibinaitė, L., Piščalkienė, V., Mattila, M., Tuuva-Hongisto, S., Amoroso, J.P. and Christodoulides, E. (2023) Establishing and delivering sport and physical activity to rural youth communities across Europe: practical learning through 'fire soul' stories. *Journal of Qualitative Research in Sports Studies*, 17, 1, 187-222

Establishing and delivering sport and physical activity to rural youth communities across Europe: practical learning through 'Fire Soul' stories

David Grecic[a], Paula Simões[b], Laura Žlibinaitė[c], Viktorija Piščalkienė[c], Marita Mattila[d], Sari Tuuva-Hongisto[d], José Pedro Amoroso[e], Efstathios Christodoulides[f]

[a] Centre for Applied Science, Physical Activity and Performance, University of Central Lancashire, Preston, UK
[b] Polytechnic of Leiria; and Centre for Business and Economics Research (CeBER), University of Coimbra, Portugal
[c] Kaunas University of Applied Sciences, Kaunas, Lithuania
[d] South-Eastern Finland University of Applied Sciences
[e] Institute Polytechnic of Leiria, CIEQV- Life Quality Research Centre, Portugal
[f] Sport and Exercise Science, School of Science, UCLan, Cyprus

Keywords: *'fire souls', rural areas, community, physical activity, Freytag pyramid*

Abstract

Low levels of youth sport and physical activity is a concern across the world with many strategies implemented to promote its positive benefits and correlation to young people's health and wellbeing. Little data exist on the specific context of establishing and developing sport and physical activity in rural areas, nor on the role undertaken by social actors working to facilitate this within their local communities; the 'fire souls'. The study's purpose therefore was to learn more about FS' work in rural areas, especially relating to activities targeting children and young people, and provide practical insight to guide similar projects in other rural European settings. A qualitative narrative study was conducted that interviewed 42 Fire Souls in 7 European countries using the 'Freytag Pyramid' structure. Following Framework Thematic Analysis the higher order themes; Motivation to make a difference, Challenges to start and maintain, and Overcoming Issues and Maximising Resources were identified. Findings support previous research exploring worker motivation and emphasise the positive role of sport and physical activity in supporting local communities' health, well-being, and cohesion. The study provides original multi-country, multi-site and multi-activity insights, as well as practical learnings to guide future Sport for Development work in rural settings.

Introduction

This study is part of the larger Erasmus+ Sport project; Villages on the Move GO (VOMGO) that aims to promote healthy lifestyle awareness and Health

JQRSS Article No: 9/9-17-1-2023-PG[113]-170
ISSN: 1754-2375 [print] ISSN: 2755-5240 [online] Copyright ©: CC-BY-NC-ND
Web: https://uclan.academia.edu/ClivePalmer/Journal-of-Qualitative-Research-in-Sports-Studies

Enhancing Physical Activity (HEPA), one of the main objectives of European Union sports policy (European Union, 2020). It focuses on supporting voluntary activities in sports and physical activity (PA), social inclusion and equal opportunities for rural citizens so that these are available to all. Initial scoping projects identified numerous challenges to providing sport and PA provision in rural areas, as well as the important role of lone activators, whom the initial project teams termed Fire Souls (FS) (VOMB, 2018; VOMNet, 2018). Robinson and Green (2011) note that in small villages and rural places voluntary sport clubs' activities are at risk and are often dependent on local enthusiasts working alone to make a difference. The previous Erasmus+ Sport Villages on the Move projects (VOM Baltic and VOM Network) substantiated this view and described some of the reasons behind the situation they found, where access to physical activity in rural areas was much lower than that available in more urban surroundings. These studies noted the lack of suitable facilities and instructors, and the limiting factor of the different social environment which made traditional models of service provision unsuitable. A preliminary survey was conducted in rural sport groups in Finland and Estonia by Xamk and Lääne-Viru College, in 2014. Despite the well documented health and wellbeing benefits, children and young people's PA is in decline across Europe, especially in rural and remote communities as is the situation in most regions of the world (OECD, 2023). The purpose of this study therefore was to learn more about FS' work in rural areas, especially relating to activities targeting children and young people, and provide practical insight to guide the creation, resilience and sustainability of similar projects in other rural European settings.

In the context of young people living in rural communities, literature supports the findings of this project's initial scoping study with several barriers perceived to exist that may moderate the success of new activities. In particular, the International Council of Sport Science and Physical Education (ICSSPE) highlight that 'A lot of the time, people in rural communities do not have easy access to transport and must travel to gain access to opportunities. Electricity, internet connection, and running water are also common challenges in rural communities. There is not a lot to do in rural areas … and this can lead to challenges for the community' (ICSSPE, 2021:18). Research substantiates this view with studies identifying issues such as the distance from and access to sport facilities (Steinmayr et al., 2011; Wicker et al., 2009), the lack of time and financial resources available to participate (Umstattd Meyer et al., 2017;), social isolation (Moore et al., 2010; Treadwell and Stiehl, 2015) as well as the absence of local role models and facilitators (Conroy and Coatsworth, 2006; Howie et al., 2020; Rottensteiner et al., 2013) as real and present barriers.

The low level of PA worldwide is a well-documented concern (Council of European Union, 2013; United Nations, 2022; WHO, 2018a, 2018b) with research supporting the World Health Organization's position that worldwide, 3 in 4 adolescents (aged 11–17 years) do not currently meet the global recommendations for physical activity (Guthold *et al.*, 2020). This situation is especially concerning given widespread consensus over the value of sport and PA in facilitating a vast array of health and wellbeing benefits (Pedersen and Saltin, 2015; Schuch *et al.*, 2018; WHO, 2018b) and reducing the impact of non-communicable diseases worldwide (Lee *et al.*, 2012). The low level of PA amongst children and young people is especially worrying due to its correlation with later adult levels of PA. This is even more concerning due to the dramatic 41% reduction in children's PA post the COVID-19 pandemic with vulnerable communities the worst hit (Wilke, 2021) at a time when the pandemic has inflicted a 200% increase in negative mental health issues, particularly anxiety and depression amongst youth (OECD, 2021).

Importantly, research highlights that sport and physical activity can help address this situation with Kellstedt *et al.* (2021:2) noting that young people's PA is 'a high frequency health behaviour'. Unfortunately, however, the positive benefits of such behaviour are differentiated according to a variety of factors, including where young people live, learn and play (Joens-Matre *et al.*, 2008; McCormack and Meendering, 2016). We must, therefore, accept the potential for problems to be compounded amongst young people living in rural areas due to a range of challenges and barriers that they face, many related to lack of access and ease of participation (Eime *et al.*, 2015; Moore *et al.*, 2010; Yousefian *et al.*, 2009). Many organisations are, however, working to address this issue with young people by offering help, guidance and support to promote sport and PA initiatives (e.g., ICCSPE 2021; Mountjoy *et al.*, 2011; UNESCO, 2022; UNICEF 2021; WHO, 2018a). This study, therefore, is informed by sport and PA's use for social development and relates to organisations and projects that use sport as a tool to achieve humanitarian and social change goals (Kidd, 2008). Collectively therefore we consider the project's FS as key members of the Sport For Development (SFD) workforce that drive rural community action.

Welty Peachey *et al.* (2020) noted that SFD has experienced significant advancements in recent years, in both research and practice (Keane *et al.*, 2021; Luguetti *et al.*, 2023; McSweeney, 2020; 2021; Meir, 2022; Smith *et al.*, 2021). In contrast to sport development practices, that focus on the improvement of athletic skills and pathways toward professional sport, SFD is defined as 'the use of sport to exert a positive influence on public health, the socialization of children, youth and adults, the social inclusion of the disadvantaged, the economic development of regions and states, and on fostering intercultural exchange and conflict resolution' (Lyras and Welty Peachey, 2011:311). The United Nations International Children's Emergency Fund (UNICEF) (2021) estimates that around the world, more than 3,000 SFD initiatives exist, run by 2000 organisations in 148 countries defining SFD as 'the use of sport, or any form of physical activity, to provide both children and adults with the opportunity to achieve their full potential through different types of initiatives that promote personal and social development' (UNICEF, 2021:6).

The right of access to sport is mandated in the United Nations Educational, Scientific and Cultural Organization's (UNESCO) International Charter of Physical Education, Physical Activity and Sport and its value is both implicit and explicit within The United Nations 17 Sustainable Development Goals (SDGs). Anecdotally, many pockets of good work are already happening around the world (ICSSPE, 2022; Peralta and Cinelli, 2016; Sport-for-development.com, n.d.; Sumption and Burnett, 2021). Scholars have, however, taken a critical approach to much of the research in this field so far, identifying the neo-colonial tendencies of many SFD organizations (Darnell and Hayhurst, 2012) which has led to the voices of those 'developed' going unheard (Nicholls et al., 2011). They have also challenged an evangelical approach to SFD research in which sport is championed as solving societal issues without having the empirical evidence to substantiate such claims (Coalter, 2007; Sugden, 2010).

As noted above the SFD sector has established nearly 3000 projects worldwide but has been criticised in relation to the types of research findings that are presented. This Fire Souls' study addresses a number of these points. Firstly, it will reflect Nichols et al.'s (2017) call for co-creation of knowledge and give precedence to the voices of those driving the SFD initiatives. Secondly it will uniquely provide multi-venue, multi-project, cross-cultural data collection to offer insights from more than one geographical setting (Giulianotti, 2011). Finally, it will reflect the calls from a range of systematic reviews in the field of SFD which request that more robust evidence can be collected to support further work in this domain (Barkley et al., 2018; Cronin, 2011; Langer, 2015; Whitley et al., 2019).

Overall, then, the purpose of this study is to investigate the Fire Souls' stories in order to positively impact future sport and PA activities for children and young people living in Europe's rural communities.

Method
This research was undertaken as part of the Erasmus+ 'Villages on the Move Go (VOMGO) Project', coordinated by the South-Eastern Finland University of Applied Sciences (Erasmus+ Sports project code Nr. 613004-EPP1-2019-1-FI-SPOSCP). The full project consists of 9 partners from 7 European countries exploring numerous local initiatives and utilizing a culture of experimentation to enhance voluntary activities in sport, facilitating social inclusion and equal opportunities of rural citizens, immigrants and refugees. We accept that there is no single best way to define 'rural' (Coburn et al., 2007) but in order to provide insight

and permit generalisation, we utilise aspects of Galbraith (1992) and Ritchey (2006). The focus of this study therefore was the activities specifically targeted at children and young people in rural areas, delivered by community activists, the FS, who work through sports organisations to promote positive change that solve and address social injustices and challenges in their communities.

The study adopted a relativist ontology and an interpretive position driven by a subjectivist epistemology, thus promoting qualitative means of inquiry. The advantage of qualitative research to the examination of FS work is the presentation of multifaceted, humanly constructed realities, which is achieved through the process of interpreting and interpretation (Sparkes and Smith, 2014). Qualitative research explores the meanings associated with social phenomena, but specifically from the perspective of those who experience it (Malterud, 2001) offering an insider's perspective (Conrad, 1987) against the backdrop of its natural setting (Järvinen and Mik-Meyer, 2020). A central tenet of qualitative research is to explore the meanings that people give to parts of their lives (Taylor *et al.*, 2016) and to seek understanding of individuals' experiences through their own frame of reference (Corbin and Strauss, 2015). Smith (2018) notes that when applied properly qualitative methods can be seen as a reliable way of producing results from a representative sample, that can be generalised to wider populations or contexts. Accordingly, qualitative methods have been chosen to help explore and understand the complex world of the FS in their naturalistic settings so that others may learn from their experiences. The SFD model (Lyras and Welty Peachey, 2011) guided this qualitative project by directing the literature search, as well as informing the findings' analysis and discussion.

Sampling and recruitment

Participants were purposefully sampled by the 9 partners who make up the full VOMGO project. All were identified as expert individuals by each host country partner with initial selections and rationale discussed with all partners until the final selections were made. All FS were working at various sports clubs, rural sport associations, schools, and sport institutions and leading community activities for children from different age groups, including those from socially vulnerable groups such as immigrants and people with disabilities. A total of 42 Fire souls from seven European countries participated in the study. Their data were anonymised and denoted to them in the study by the letters FS and their number 1-42. 17 females (39.5%), 25 males (60.4%), were contacted by the VOMGO partner institution and all agreed to participate in the study. The sample reflected a range of activities, including individual and team sports, as well as indoor and outdoor activities. The demographic characteristics of participants are summarised in figure 1. Prior to data collection, informed consent was obtained from all participants.

Figure 1: Fire Souls' Demographic Characteristics

Country of Firesouls' work	Gender F:female M:male	Years of experience in sport activities	Sport and PA supported and developed	Role	Target group
Finland	F	16	Gymnastics	Coach	Families and children
Finland	F	25	All activities - Physical education focus after school clubs	Activity Leader	School children 7-15 years old
Finland	M	55	Gymnastics	Coach	All ages
Finland	M	55	Biathlon	Leader	Children and high level athletes of all ages
Finland	F	12	Finnish baseball, Pesäpallo	Coach	Children and female adults
Finland	M	35	Football, floorball	Coach	All ages
Finland	F	10	Multi sports	Activity Leader	Immigrant and refugee children and women
Finland	F	30	Cross country skiing, athletics, orienteering, activities for kids	Outdoor Leader	All ages
Finland	M	40	Outdoor activities	Club founder and Outdoor Leader	All ages
Finland	M	25	Lava dancing, floorball, volleyball, cross country skiing	Instructor and Coach	All ages
Lithuania	F	22	Physical activity and movement classes	Fitness instructor	Preschool children
Lithuania	F	27	Aerobics, gymnastics, volleyball	Fitness instructor and Coach	Children, youth, female adults

Lithuania	F	7	Nordic walking, hiking	Outdoor leader	All the community
Lithuania	F	6	Hiking, cycling, volleyball	Outdoor leader and Coach	All the community
Lithuania	F	28	Ballroom dances	Teacher	All the community
Lithuania	M	20	Basketball	Coach	Children and youth
Cyprus	M	20+	Fundamental and Developmental Movement Skills	Movement Instructor	Primarily Children, All ages.
Cyprus	M	20+	Kite Surfing, SUP, Surf	Club founder and Outdoor Instructor	All ages
Cyprus	M	20+	Rhythmic and Artistic Gymnastics	Gymnastics Teacher	Primarily Children and all ages
Cyprus	M	7	Rock climbing, bouldering	Climbing Instructor	All ages
Cyprus	M	15+	Downhill biking	Biking Instructor	All ages
Slovenia	F	26	Martial arts, Functional training	Martial arts teacher	All ages
Slovenia	M	45	Futsal, cycling, hiking, nordic walk	Outdoor Instructor and Coach	All ages
Slovenia	M	16	Basketball	Coach	Children and youth
Slovenia	M	35	Football, volleyball, basketball. Functional exercises for women	Activity Leader and Coach	All the community Female adults
Hungary	M	45	Trail running	Outdoor Instructor	Children and youth
Hungary	M	12	Orienteering	Outdoor Instructor	Children – all ages
Hungary	M	70	Hiking, excursions, orienteering, outdoor sports	Outdoor Instructor	All the community

Hungary	M	50	Swimming, gymnastics, handball, football, PE	PE teacher and Coach	Mainly children and their parents
Hungary	M	45	MTB, trail running, orienteering	Outdoor Instructor	All ages
Belgium	F	15+	Swimming, dance, tennis and gymnastics for people with one or more disabilities	Special Needs Teacher adn Coach	All ages
Belgium	M	33	Archery	Archery Instructor	Mainly children and parents
Belgium	M	23	Gymnastics, acro gym, freerunning / parcours	Gymnastics Teacher	All ages
Portugal	F	33	Dance	Dance Teacher	All ages
Portugal	F	22	Orienteering	Orienteering Leader	All ages
Portugal	M	40	Handball and basketball for people with one or more disability	Inclusion Coach	All ages
Portugal	F	22	Dance	Dance Teacher	All ages
Portugal	F	25	Trail running	Outdoor Instructor	All ages
Portugal	M	49	Race walk, triathlon, athletics	Athletics Coach	Children and Youth athletes interested in competition
Portugal	M	54	Cycling	Cycling	All ages
Portugal	M	40	Caving, outdoor activities, running, trail running	Outdoor Instructor	All ages
Portugal	M	29	Surf, bodyboarding	Surf Instructor	All ages

Data collection

Interviews took place at the FS delivery location at a time deemed convenient by them, often before or directly after an activity or group. Interviews were conducted in person and in the FS' native language by a partner researcher from that country. The interview adopted Gustav Freytag's narrative structure the 'Freytag Pyramid' (Kumaat and Zulkarnain, 2021), to help shape interviews based on how participants made sense of their efforts to facilitate grassroots sport and PA activities in the rural communities they served. This structure was chosen as it provided clearly defined stages by which to explore the FS story and thus scaffold the narrative interview (Francis, 2020). The interviews started with a question to put the participant at ease asking the FS how they first got involved in sport. The sharing of experiences between researcher and participant helping develop rapport and shared understanding. An interview schedule was then followed that took the Fire Souls on a life-cycle journey from activity conception to potential future actions (Campbell, 2014; Freytag, 1900) utilising probes and follow up questioning informed by SFD literature and concepts. Interviews lasted from 20-90 minutes (M=65). All interviews were recorded, transcribed verbatim, and translated into English before analysis.

Data analysis

The study adopted a Framework, Thematic Analysis approach to the data. Framework Analysis (FA) is a series of analytical stages rather than a methodology and offers the flexibility to use both deductive and inductive methods which was required for this study given its aim and purpose (Ritchie and Spencer, 1994).

Spencer *et al.* (2014) describe FA as a matrix-based method comprising five interconnected stages that provide clear guidance on data analysis, from initial collection and management through to the development of explanatory accounts by the researcher. The key tenet of the approach is the development of a 'thematic framework' specific to the research study (Smith and Firth, 2011). This provides the researcher with a defined method to organise data by classifying and labelling data in relation to main themes, concepts, and categories (Ritchie *et al.*, 2010). FA's five stages are the processes of: Familiarisation; Developing a Theoretical Framework; Indexing; Charting; Mapping and Interpretation (Ritchie and Spencer, 1994), with this study following each stage in turn.

1. Familiarisation - The first author read and re-read each transcript and made reflective notes in the margin of each script. These notes related to his own experiences when operating as an activity leader, Physical Education (PE) teacher and coach, but also how the issues and concepts discussed aligned with the SFD literature. 2. Charting / Mapping – a framework was first developed to guide the study's analysis. Following stage one the first and last author reflected on the notes made and how the emerging concepts linked with the Freytag question areas to

195

establish the interview framework (see figure 2). 3. Indexing – raw data units from each interview were deductively 'indexed' and collated together in relation to the Framework categories. Initial comments related to each data unit were noted to support and develop understanding (see Appendix 1 as an example of this process). 4. Triangulation - both authors then analysed the 'indexed' data in each area to triangulate their workings and develop their understanding (Maxwell, 2012). Clusters of raw data that related to common concepts were grouped together to identify the emergent themes. These themes were subsequently 'built up' into larger representative sub-themes which in turn were grouped to establish the higher order major themes. 5. Mapping and Interpretation - our final themes were then described.

Figure 2: Fire Souls: Coding Framework Index from Interview Questions

Interview questions general area of Interest	Emerging topics from initial reading and notes	
1.Genesis of idea	1.1 Initial motivation to start something in their area	1.2 Physical Activity Philosophy
2.Start Up Experience	2.1 Key influences	2.2 Issues
3.Establishment / Nurturing issues	3.1 Challenges faced	3.2 Solutions
4.Outputs of their work	4.1 Impact on Others	4.2 Rewards for Self
5.Future ideas and hopes for their club / community	5.1 How to Sustain club numbers	5.2 Future Development Ideas

Trustworthiness

This study is driven by Maxwell's suggested interpretive, descriptive, and theoretical validity criteria for qualitative research (Maxwell, 2012). We also ask the reader to note Nowell *et al.* (2017) and their work depicting that to be accepted as trustworthy, qualitative researchers must demonstrate that data analysis has been conducted in a precise, consistent, and exhaustive manner through recording, systematizing, and disclosing the methods of analysis with enough detail to enable the reader to determine whether the process is credible. The Framework Analysis (FA) established analytical stages enable others to review how the final interpretation was developed, facilitating transparency of the data analysis process and thus enhancing rigour (Ritchie and Spencer, 1994). FA therefore offers a systematic method that is visual and transparent, enabling the development and maintenance of a clear audit trail from the start of data analysis (Tobin and Begley 2004).

Results and Discussion

Following the framework analysis, 24 emergent themes were established from the raw data codes. These were built up into 9 lower order sub-themes which then created the 3 higher order major themes of: i. Motivation to make a difference, ii. Challenges to start and maintain, and iii. Overcoming issues and maximising resources (see figure 3 with illustrative participant quotations).

Figure 3: Analysis of Fire Souls' work with illustrative participant quotations

Theme	Subtheme	Illustrative Participant Quotations
(i) Motivation to make a difference	**Wanting to make a difference and bring benefits for others** • Give something back to the people and area • Keep things going • Improve lives to build stronger communities • Enable competition success • Share new knowledge	*On many occasions, parents would ask me the following: 'Where about should I take my son for sports?', 'Which is the better sport for my daughter?' etc. This is where my idea was generated from! I wanted to establish an academy that would fill in this gap. I wanted to create a sports academy that would address parents' concerns on sports that would be suitable for their children.* (FS 28) *It is important that local young people are more oriented towards sport and not devote to harmful habits such as alcohol or cigarettes.* (FS7) *It started with the idea and great desire to unite people who educate preschool children, because insufficient attention is paid to the physical activity of children of this age in Lithuania. By uniting such people and setting common goals, it would be possible to achieve even more, expand and coordinate activities, implement the idea of children being active.* (FS3) *I want to do something for the community, I feel like as a kid I got a lot of good things in this association and now I want to give it back. It is a principle, that helps me to be motivated.* (FS4)

	Passionate advocate of Sport and PA values • Help children experience the joy of being active • Enhance social capital • Promote health benefits • Being with Nature	*There is also an emphasis on raising those children to properly behave outside the playground. We try to make these children better people including every person who loves basketball or any other sport.* (FS30) *We also base our actions on well acknowledged sports principles, such as Fair Play. All of our energy is spent to the making of good personalities and characters; we want children and young people to learn how to respect each other, share with each other, claim what belongs to them and not stepping, claim for their rights, negotiate and step back when they are wrong.* (FS34) *They are learning basic motor skills through games, gaining psychophysical abilities, balance and strength which is very important at a young age. Exercise is good for a healthy development and socializing but the main thing is to develop a love for the sport.* (FS24)
	Love of being active and involved in Sport and PA • Previous successes • Identity and self worth • Passion and excitement • Way of life	*I am involved in the sport because I love this and I constantly do my utmost to transmit this love of mine to other people, who may need this extra motive and inspiration to involve in sports, not necessarily with cycling but with any other sport! (FS2)* *I have been doing sport since my childhood. Trainings have taught me to work with perseverance, never to give up any competition but struggle till the end but due to my old age it is not the physical victories, but the health maintaining effects of sport is what I am missioned to pass on. (FS8)*

		I was born with ski equipment on and immediately after learning how to walk I started to ski (FS9).
		As far as I can remember myself as a child, I have always been on a bike! (FS21)
.	**Self-gratification and rewards** • Qualifying for an event • Praise and encouragement from others • Personal and Professional Development • Joy in watching others	*When a relay race starts and the kids are out in the forest, I have 'flow' all the time, I'm running back and forth between the spectator control and the finish line. I cheer for them, and I really love to see that it goes well for them...you can see the joy on their faces, they seem to have performed well, and it seems also that they gave the maximum but also enjoyed it. It gives me a lot of power; their joy radiates back to me. (FS4)*
		The biggest success for the coach is when a medal is hung to its trainees' neck. (FS6)
		You can see various groups enjoying this sport and you are really happy when you see their photos .... I saw a photo that was sent to me and I told myself: 'Wow! Look what I did!' This is the impact, and this is the reward I receive (FS11)
		They deserve to have and enjoy. We see that every day! They come with a smile, they leave with a smile and when on a holiday break, they say they miss us! And this is really great! (FS28)
(ii) Challenges to start and maintain	**Critical supporters to make it happen** • Lockdown and appreciating benefits of PA • Existing Associations and agencies • Significant People /Volunteers/Family/ Board members	*After the quarantine it was even better to meet again. This situation was good for everyone maybe to learn to appreciate this community, which we consider to be permanent. (FS4)* *We have supporters, support from the city or district government, not so much financial as moral support from certain people. But if you do,*

	/Children's parents/ Sponsors	*plan, of course, if there is support from government organizations, mayors, or other agencies, that's important. Then it is easier to involve everyone. (FS9)*
		It is definitely the family because we are all connected to sports and to our sports club. The first one is my wife also the most involved person beside me in this sports club, it is the easiest to solve the problems together and we consult with each other. Of course, there are others, my son and daughters, I have very good friends which help me a lot. This is the only way forward, to do it together. (FS1)
		There is voluntary people, who work with big heart on their leisure time and get amazing results. I want (to)say big thanks for all people working voluntarily in sport clubs (FS39)
	Lessons learnt to build and develop initiatives • Importance of technology / Social Media to promote idea/ Improved processes/Improve communications • Learning from others / Mentors and role models/ Personal development needs • Collaborations / Seeing other examples	*To be interactive all the time and really use a lot of social media because our young people, children love it very much and it is their main source of information. We use YouTube, social networks are used to broadcast matches. There are more plans for the future with the creation of a platform to help organize more and better, but that requires resources and time. We really use and will use it more widely. (FS9)*
		we need to do more cooperation and networking work. It is reasonable to do cooperation with other Sports clubs, people to get new experiences, tips, ideas to develop own work (FS16)
		So, communication has to be good, surplus also the communication within external people. If you're not communicating properly with the local sports service or people and

		schools in the neighbourhood, then you potentially miss out the participants. So, the broad spectrum of communication is important…. good collaboration. Don't minimize, but exchange. Look around closely. What is happening in the neighbourhood? Which needs are there? (FS37)
(iii) Overcoming issues and maximising resources	**Human resources to ensure a legacy** • Managing people • Succession planning • Burn out	*The hardest, the hardest, like every job or volunteer work, it is always managing human resources. (Isabel)* *Building a community is not an easy mission. You have to know how to deal with people: you cannot make them offended, which sometimes is not easy. There are people who think they are the best and know everything. You have to handle these people. You need to create a positive atmosphere and make people feel good. (FS8)* *We are getting older, and our physical abilities are deteriorating and replacement will be required, but there is basically no replacement and it may happen that a very successful sports club falls low overnight. We are working on introducing young people to the system, but there is no one who would take on such a responsibility. Here we have a big problem, and we are not the only club. (FS1)* *Because a lot of people work a lot for the association, but sometimes that much administration wears us out…we need to be careful not to get burned out. Also, if one or two people takes the back of an association (it) is too much work. We need to pay close attention to this so that the division of labour works properly. (FS4)*

	Changing behaviours • Attract participants and helpers • Covid 19's lasting impact • Diversify activities • Enter competitions	*The Coronavirus period placed an emphasis to outdoors activities. It was a step forward to sports as more and more people turned to nature. It has been possibly – besides all the negative aspects – the best period for outdoor activities and physical activities and sports ever! (FS2)* *The biggest challenge is to really be able to make changes on the behaviour of the people you know? Because we, I was saying, everyone knows that the exercise is good, its good for your health, they all know the benefits, there are evidence but then on practice because of lack of time, or lack of, some people point out economic difficulties, there is always a reason for them to not practice (FS32)* *We aspire to offer classes and programmes targeting parents as well, such as outdoors programmes, which are in fashion now, e.g. cross fit. We also aspire to offer programmes for children and parents together, like bike tours and walking tours. We would like to increase the number of sports we offer and expand towards this direction. We would like to invest in second choice sports, the ones that are less promoted, such as squash, baseball, golf, etc. Because sports like football, which are first choice and first promotion sports, are widely promoted. I would also like to include alternative sports as well as general gymnastics sports for both young people and adults (FS34)*
	Lack of Physical resources • Lack of infrastructure • Finances /Bureaucracy	*Indeed, we have plans to establish something of our own. We planned to do it later on and not immediately but based on the current situation and the current developments, it is probably the*

		only solution. Start creating our own place, as soon as possible, will be the *solution to our current situation. (FS28)*
		Of course (our) first challenge is money. Always thinking from where we could get money. Also at the moment municipality finances are weak, so it is really hard to get support from there. (FS15)
		Everything was difficult during the initial stages! For every type of license there was a difficulty laying behind... Whatever official I had to do, for example, for the official papers I needed to have or for a license to use the seaside, there was no easy way, there was always an obstacle there waiting for me (FS11)

Major Theme One: Motivation to make a difference

Within this theme, 4 distinct areas were established. These being (i) Wanting to bring benefits to others, (ii) Passionate advocate of Sport and PA values (iii) Love of being active and involved in sport and PA (iv) Self-gratification and rewards. Data here reflected previous studies that have explored the motivation of those engaged in SFD work such as the activity leaders, volunteers, and scholars (Pink and Cameron, 2013; Smith *et al.*, 2014; Welty Peachey *et al.*, 2014; 2016; 2018). The FS described their intrinsic and extrinsic motivational drivers (Ryan and Deci, 2000) as well as elements of Self Determination Theory (SDT) (Deci and Ryan, 2008), especially relatedness in how attached and passionate they were to their community, the activities they were involved in, and the meaning this also gave to their lives.

(i) Wanting to bring benefits to others. In this specific environment the FS seemed driven to have a positive impact upon their communities as many felt indebted to their club, area or sport and the beneficial influence it had played in their development. For instance, FS4 explained:

> I want to do something for the community, I feel, like, as a kid I got a lot of good things in this association and now I want to give back. It's a principle that motivates me. (FS2)

This impetus presented itself in different ways depending on the particular circumstances in which each FS found themselves and the stage of the community programme, initiative or activity they were involved in (Yu *et al.*, 2023). For some, the immediate need was to keep activities going, for others, it was to gain recognition for their area, or vicariously for their participants via competition success.

> It meant a lot for me, when the team, which I have already prepared for this competition won a championship at the first time. It was a fantastic experience, when I saw it first, that they had stood on the top of the podium. And the guys said that they can also thank me for this. I was a little touched then, it was a really nice experience. (FS4)

Furthermore, being able to bring people together and build stronger community cohesion was seen as a valuable process for the FS. This finding links to sustainable development and the concept of 'naturalness' in the community (Skille, 2015) that derives from a sense of social responsibility and one's goal of social contribution. For example, FS34 explained his personal goal, 'to support society'.

> We make attempts to involve children in participation actions, making them aware of values, not only with regards to sports values but generally. We try to make them aware of societal participation and group participation, so as to prepare them to enter society successfully as citizens. We support active participation. (FS34)

(ii) Passionate advocate of sport and PA values. In line with SFD studies the FS were extremely passionate about the positive impact of sport and PA (Van der Veken *et al.*, 2020; Welty Peachey *et al.*, 2018). Their unique circumstances leading to an obligation to pass on what they had learnt in their lives so their community would benefit. This information ranged from ideas about how to facilitate and manage new activities, events and competitions to simply their own self-discovery of the importance of being actively involved in sport and PA within their rural area's natural environment. FS25 noted that it was her '*desire to share that wellness with other people that you have discovered and not to keep only within yourself*' (FS25). FS26 raised the topic of nature too and how she hopes to promote it in her community, '*we like to share with young people and with the community, as a lot of our sport is done in the nature, it is the respect for it. To leave it how we found it or, if possible, even better*' (FS26). This sentiment is supported by the European Commission's Work Plan with the promotion of Green sustainable projects, one of their key goals is for sport (European Union, 2020). FS19 also had this desire to share his knowledge to help others and described his main goal as to help '*sustain [the natural environment]and stimulate the well-being and physical development of our members*' (FS19). This feeling now has a growing body of research that highlights the benefits of sporting activities and the promotion of blue-green natural spaces for health and development (Gascon *et al.*, 2017; Stangierska *et al.*, 2023).

Linked to this point, the FS recognised sport and PA's potential to achieve a variety of positive outcomes at the community and individual levels (Coakley, 2015). Their stories emphasised the positive impact that sporting activities had brought to their communities reflecting, Wadey *et al.*'s (2020) study that highlighted how such initiatives provide opportunities for collaboration, social equality, health promotion and economic impact. For example, FS3 commented,

> The first benefit is human: they start to know each other... this promotes their physical activity, the joy of movement, and the formation of attitudes towards a physically active life. I think our work is very purposeful, focused and beneficial. (FS3)

Continuing in this vein, the FS noted that they were motivated to support the inclusion of all members of their community. Indeed, research stresses that organised sport can contribute to full and equal participation, strengthening the social ties of people with disabilities, fostering social contacts, and helping establish friendship networks (Albrecht *et al.*, 2019; Darcy *et al.*, 2017). As FS24 reasoned,

> There is a sociocultural factor here. The acceptance of difference, the diversity of both the cultures and the people who participate... So this diversity and the acceptance of difference is an important value. (FS24)

(iii) Love of being active and involved in sport and PA. This sub-theme highlighted the significance of the FS' previous sporting experiences as participant, performer or volunteer on their subsequent career path. For example FS29 explained,

> My opinion is that you don't just decide to work in sport, but that is a way of life. I'm active in sports since a very young age. I started in primary school and led children's groups. Later, I tried some other professions, but I've always returned back to sports because I have never got satisfaction anywhere else. Sport is my life (FS29).

Many FSs often spoke about the great pleasure they found in physical activity as a hobby, while others reported that they were already engaged in volunteering and professional clubs during their childhood or adolescence, *'I started at the age of 15 as an assistant trainer. That way, I also got the chance to train myself'* (FS33). Indeed, being involved in physical activity and sports from an early stage of life seems to be a significant predictor for a lifelong participation in physical activity (Hirvensalo and Lintunen, 2011; Li *et al.*, 2009) and seem to have driven our FSs to help others share in similar experiences. Many felt that being holders of sporting achievements and being recognised at a high level let them succeed at a sort of dual career setting, for example, *'I am professional international football player ... I have been in three women's world championships. One time gold medallist'* (FS7). They felt this also enabled them to act as role models with a potential influence on community members' behaviours (Dix *et al.*, 2010; Storm and Eske, 2021).

(iv) Self-gratification and rewards. The final motivator that emerged from the data was the self-gratification and personal rewards the Fire Souls gained from their work. These ranged from the personal honours and achievements afforded to them whilst others described the recognition they received whilst facilitating activities, as FS28 explained,

> What is really meaningful, and rewarding is the love I get from children as well as the support I get from parents. They acknowledge me, they appreciate the centre and the work that we do. It drives us on. (FS28)

The FS also highlighted the immense joy felt from the results of their actions,

> Also, these kinds of meaningful moments I get when I see people on the sport field, or seeing kids in sport competitions because there, everything is genuine. Kids and youngsters' sports give these special feelings. Powerful and meaningful. (FS16)

Major Theme 2: Challenges to start and maintain

Challenges to start and maintain has three sub themes of: (i) Human resources to ensure a legacy, (ii) Changing behaviours, and (iii) Lack of physical resources.

(i) Human resources to ensure a legacy. With regards to legacy, the FS recognised their responsibility to those that had come before them and the debt they were owed. FS33 described his need '*to maintain the guild and to pass it on to our successors*' (FS33). This desire to sustain what had already been established by themselves and others presented itself in the succession planning of the FS. As FS5 explained, '*The most important plan is to manage the succession of the leadership of (X). My main mission is to find the person who would manage this succession within 5 years*' (FS5). Many of the FS expressed their concern for how difficult this process was for them. As FS20 noted, '*The biggest difficulty is to continue something. It ends being a cycle, people come, and people go but the hard part is to continue*' (FS20). Some of the difficulty in finding their successors was levelled at the lack of young people willing to take on the role, as FS5 explains,

> I would like it not to end. I wish it had young people to replace us and that these activities or even new activities continue. This is what I would like for the future. Let things be maintained, that our children take hold of what we have created. (FS5)

However, the high standards that the FS set themselves and expect of others, as well as their intricate knowledge of what challenges their successors will face, also contribute to this problem. To illustrate this point, FS1 revealed that '*To find a person who believes in the same values and could dedicate himself to the case as much as I did is very hard*' (FS1). FS23 agreed, adding, '*I look back and I won't hand things over to just anyone*' (FS23). FS14 also offered some poignant advice to those who may follow in the FS' footsteps:

> They should also remember and take care about their own coping, if they get tired, who is going to keep working? We should remember to share workload and responsibilities among others. That way we can make new activities. We need to learn to say no sometimes. I am not so good at that, but I keep going. (FS14)

The sentiment of sharing the overall responsibility and not trying to do everything themselves to avoid 'FS burnout' was also discussed in other interviews, with FS34 also offering this valuable advice, '*we need to remember that it is easy for one stick to break but difficult for a collection of sticks to break'* (FS34). Interestingly here the FS's challenge is supported by literature on the importance of Human Resource Development (HRD) (Philip *et al.*, 2023). Although the FS describe their intention to search out their future replacements, they were not able to provide any specific examples of training or support, other than being able to share their experiences, despite this being described in the literature as a key tenant of successful operations (Keane *et al.*, 2021).

(ii) Changing behaviours. The challenge of trying to change the behaviours was discussed in various contexts. Much of this related to motivation and especially the barriers to getting involved in, and then sustaining sports participation activities such as access, finance and relational issues (Pink and Cameron, 2013), as well as the obstacles faced by rural communities such as the lack of human and physical resources (Edwards, 2015; Sherry *et al.*, 2017). It should be noted too that impacts from the restrictions imposed during the COVID-19 pandemic had severely affected the FS' clubs so, the effects of restrictions in sport clubs' activity were very present in the interviewees' minds, as was the problem of how to re-engage and inspire their local population to get active again. For example, *'The hardest thing for me to do is to make activities good and attractive to a wide circle of people in our local community… Maybe the hardest thing for me [after Covid restrictions] was to motivate the local community to do recreational sports'* (FS1).

While sharing their experiences, FS talked about the decreased motivation of sport club members. One of the reasons mentioned was the inactivity of the community itself to engage in physical activity.

> Convincing people who sometimes react too emotionally and endangered, to convince them that this story we set ourselves has a wider meaning and that it is good for the surroundings. To convince people that it is a great way to connect with each other and that the club is worth it, is not a short process. (FS40)

The struggle to involve children in physical activities due to the lack of motivation was also remarked upon.

> To attract new people especially young people. They are very much bound by the world of ICT and it's hard to move them out of their online world. It's also difficult to attract middle aged people as they are busy with keeping up their family. (FS8)

(iii) Lack of physical resources. To address this issue the FS were actively seeking out new activities to motivate their communities into action, but often this relied upon the physical resources, location and equipment to deliver.

> We need to start seeking for a place that will meet our current needs and the needs of what we do, i.e. the variety of activities and sports, different classes for each level, separated classes for adults and the emphasis on the quality. We wanted to offer this to the kids joining us and to their families. (FS28)

Unfortunately the lack of physical resources, whether equipment, buildings, transport or infrastructure, continue to challenge the FS' creative skills and limit their sports clubs' activities. This is challenging given the work the FS are engaged in to recapture their community's interest.

> Indeed, we have plans to establish something of our own. We planned to do it later on and not immediately but based on the current situation and the current developments, it is probably the only solution. Start creating our own place, as soon as possible, will be the solution to our current situation. (FS28)

This need to innovate and be creative resonates with recent research into how SFD initiatives are evolving to survive (Svensson and Cohen, 2020). In line with previous research material however, financial issues are commonly reported as a main barrier when organizations are trying to develop and improve (Lower and Czekanski, 2019). These challenges are clearly reflected too in the FS' responses. The lack of funding for their clubs is a concern for many, as is the bureaucracy that often accompanies and hinders many of their new initiatives. To illustrate this point, FS42 noted that, *'There are difficulties because there are always budget issues. Every step and everything you need or want to do has a certain budget required'*, whilst FS34 bemoaned the bureaucratic burden slowing him down,

> Bureaucracy! This is a major issue! Some years back, things might have been simpler, you had the money, and you could go ahead and implement your plans! There are many certificates and paperwork needed nowadays. (FS34)

To summarise the theme of Challenges to get going and sustain, the problems identified by the FS are generally in line with the literature. In particular, our results almost mirror Seippel *et al*'s. (2020) findings that exposed difficulties relating to the recruitment and retention of volunteers at different organization levels, the lack of sports facilities, finances, and rigorous legal requirements that SFD innovators need to overcome.

Major Theme 3: Overcoming issues and maximising resources

The final major theme was overcoming issues and maximising resources. This related to three sub themes that emerged from the data: (i) Critical supporters to make it happen, (ii). Asking for and finding help, and (iii) Changed actions

(i) Critical Supporters to Make it Happen. In a fascinating twist, many Fire Souls noted the positive impact that the recovery from the COVID-19 pandemic had had, energising the community and providing a catalyst for the resurgence of their work. As FS2 commented, *'Interestingly, lockdown made us want to get out and acknowledge the benefits of nature. All of a sudden, we all wanted to see at least a tree'*. Encouragement from their significant others was another beneficial factor for the FS. The interviewees emphasised the significant impact that the people who taught and worked with them had had on their professional development and careers.

For example, FS9 explained, *'I had a very wonderful physical education teacher who was the soul of the school. It meant that I wanted to be myself, to work on something similar'* (FS9). *'Now my PE teacher colleague (X) is wonderful and supportive, he never shuns my ideas and is making suggestions and developing ideas with me'* (FS40). When talking about the people who helped them the most, the FS naturally underlined the importance of family and their support in the form of encouragement and understanding. As FS17 recounted, *'the most important person has been my wife who understands me and also understands why I am away from home a lot or need to go again'* (FS17).

Family members constitute key socializing agents (Kay and Spaaij 2011; Wheeler and Green, 2014). Our findings therefore reflect previous research that identify key socializing agents (i.e., teachers, peers, family) as playing significant roles in shaping coaching behaviour (Perényi, 2010) yet adds the critical role that partners and spouses also play.

> The most important and closest person is my partner, when I got some questions then he is the first person I address them to. Together we then discuss and think of how we can solve certain things and challenges. (FS15)

The data analysis also revealed the help from the community and volunteers as being extremely important, thus supporting the literature that has shown volunteers to provide essential services to community sport organizations (Wegner, Baker and Jones, 2021). This reflects the SFD literature in relation the critical impact of volunteers in their various roles either as the 'core' FS or the 'peripheral' helpers (Ringuet *et al.*, 2014). As FS25 exclaims, *'of course volunteers! Our own volunteers! We do not have paid employees, so we really need a lot of volunteers when organizing events'*. The rural locations of the FS work make sourcing volunteers more difficult than for other SFD projects (Smith *et al.*, 2014). The lack of access to a local university student population and/or easy transport links to facilitate volunteer tourism as can operate elsewhere, which compound the FS challenge.

(ii) Asking for and finding help. FS described how important the parents were in supporting their projects. *'The biggest support for me is the parent. The first thing I do is to try to win the parent. They seem to me younger and younger. There are parents whose grandparent I used to teach!* (FS6). FS10 agreed, stating that his *'fantastic help is the 'crew'. This is a group of parents from our members, who put in a huge effort... They are a huge help'* (FS10).

With regards to children's activities, the FS' accounts supported Dyck's (2012) work on how involving families, facilitating their contribution so that they play an active role in helping to organize events, help at the events and even contributing financially evidences the strong social connection between the sports club and the families (Dyck, 2012). Regardless of their different location and/or activity focus, all FS openly discussed how they got the help they needed from their wider social network and community assets (Bates and Hylton, 2021). What was evident in this rural context too was that their sport clubs do not operate in isolation as they receive help from their immediate social environment (family, friends, neighbours, parents, local businesses), from further away (clubs, partners implementing similar activities) or from formal structures such as associations, foundations and so on.

In particular, the FS promoted the valuable input from sporting associations, government agencies and commercial sponsors. FS10 recognised that he receives *'a lot of support from the gymnastics federation in Flanders. They provide lessons (content, materials) and training programmes which in the future can take place in our own hall'* (FS10). FS16 confirmed this point when he described the support he receives from his Sports Union for, *'questions such as legal help, education, professional help, and financing of the projects we turn to the Sports Union of Slovenia and for co-financing to the municipality of Kranj and the Sports Foundation'* (FS16). FS19 agreed with the positive input from the government and explained, *'Today you have more support from the City Halls and the government to those goals, to support and encourage cycling and sports in general'* (FS19).

The data did reveal, however, that in some circumstances FS felt a lack of support from the authorities. At these times, the importance of local sponsors and business support was vital.

> But obviously our sponsors have been boosting our survival. Without it there was no chance. People helping us deserve our thanks and I think it is is the most important jump. But it is not only about money, it is the help and advice they offer too. (FS39)

The different experience of government support has been described by other projects around the world. In particular, Rich and Misener (2020) described how government funding priorities had influenced the sport and recreation programme delivery in rural Canada with both positive and negative results. With respect to learning about new ideas and initiatives to drive their projects forward, the FS described the importance of learning from others who already had a track record of success, both those who worked at different clubs but also mentors and role models in their own environment.

> The director, X, loves basketball and already supports other local projects and activities in different areas. Part of that certainly helped that we were previous acquaintances, but he also definitely listened to us, liked our vision and plan and decided to cooperate and show support. His recognition gave us a big impetus for the future. (FS30)

In an emotionally uplifting tone, FS highlighted the benefits of collaboration with colleagues who are more like friends to them.

Although leadership might change (like presidents etc) but old colleagues in this sector who take youth important are always there and supporting you. like X, who always kept telling us - no problem, let's keep on doing. (FS6)

They also gave specific examples of friends' help from other professional fields in solving legal or accounting issues. For instance, FS31 spoke about one person,

X, who is also a member of the board is a treasure for us, because his contacts and relations locally help us to get sponsors and funding easier. He has been working for the club longer than I or anybody else can remember. He is an irreplaceable resource for the club, because if he didn't want to continue in the club, part of the club culture would disappear. He's the one who knows how the things were done in the previous times.

Finally in this theme, the FS described how important it was to get support from other more external forces, to learn from how others in distant and different contexts solved the problems that they now faced, and to make the effort to seek out such learning. For example, FS2 noted that,

I try to travel abroad every year... I get to see how other countries manage to face the problems they encountered. How they manage to solve the problems we consider to be problems, because, at times, to them, these are not problems... (FS2)

[FS14 agreed]: It is true that is important to see different people, places and activities to be able to mix and find new ideas. And of course give (our) own tips and ideas to others.

(iii) Changed actions. The FS' stories revealed that the most important support to attract was human rather than financial, especially when received from their close social environment. Indeed, the opportunity to develop social networks and promote social equality has been identified as an important factor for those working in this SFD space (Wadey, Day and Howells 2020). It is how to sustain the support networks that leads into the final sub-theme, that focusses on the learning that has taken place and how this will help develop the FS' work by changing their future actions. One of most important areas to support the sustainability and future growth is how the FS will engage with technology. FS3 explained,

Of course, now we all have become IT specialists, because media and chat platforms are already necessary. They help to communicate to meet people quickly within a few hundred kilometres. We also have ambitions to further improve our knowledge in the distance learning process so that we can more easily exchange practical ideas, create a programme that teachers can use in their daily work and show to children. (FS3)

Key to the future plans is the need to communicate better and market the work that is happening in their communities. As FS13 realised,

We need to use a lot of marketing awareness, try to promote what we do. Try to have some reflection on what you do. Show it on social media, talk about it to people, try to get more people involved. People really want to do sports. They want to come along they want to come around. They do not know how to get the right information. They do not know where to go. They do not know where to fit in. (FS13)

The need to develop practices and processes as well as the motivation to develop new activities and opportunities for their communities demonstrates the FS' innovation. This supports recent SFD literature which highlights how successful projects around the world are being underpinned by the creativity and innovation of their activity leaders (McSweeney, 2020; McSweeney *et al.*, 2022; Neuvonen and Weaver, 2021; Neuvonen-Rauhala and Weaver, 2022; Svensson and Cohen, 2020).

A large part of this learning was accredited to the collaborations the FS had facilitated with other sports clubs and organisations. However, this was an area that still needed development, with FS recognising that much more needed to be done. *What we really need to do more of, as an organisation, is try to work with other organisations as well'* (FS13). The lack of this type of partnership and support was surprising given the importance that the FS afforded it, but is definitely a key development area for the future. Potentially the plethora of other challenges the FS face had just pushed this desire aside. As FS14 described, *'Cooperation with other local sport clubs is something that was discussed a lot in the past, but nothing really happened, not enough has been done'* (FS14).

A summary of practical learnings

Reflecting this study's aim to provide practical learning from the FS' stories and to guide future project across rural European communities, figure 4 below provides a brief overview of the learning relating to the challenges and solutions to be applied.

Figure 4: Practical learnings from the Fire Souls' stories

Project Element	Challenge	Solution
Fire Souls	To sustain and develop own work and skills	Honest skills appraisal. Seek out collaborators and mentors. Seek and value family members' support and input. Source professional development courses. Be realistic about size and scale of project and activities. Recognise when pressure starts to get too much. Ask for help. Accept bureaucracy is involved in getting things done. Engage with new technologies to learn how to promote, deliver and evaluate activities.
User groups- children and young people	Need to attract new participants	Assess what are the best information channels – e.g. Social Media / visiting schools to promote activities / targeting parents. Utilise Active School Communities EU Toolkit to engage schoolteachers as key agents for change. Engage parents – involve them as helpers, provide joint activities or parallel activities

		Promote benefits of activity and beauty of nature especially post-COVID-19. Engage community to co-design activities. Offer choices and variety of activities available Consider motivation of competition, and of providing high profile events to bring others to the area.
Volunteers	To attract, train to independence, and retain new volunteers	Promote benefits of volunteering. Help them learn by doing, get them involved straight away. Pair with mentor to help develop their own leadership skills. Give them responsibility. Get them hooked. Link to motivation factors – help them feel good, feel useful, moral valuing - create a good atmosphere, organise extra activities, excursions, parties, celebrate successes.
	Lack of knowledge, coaching and teaching skills	Sport federations and education associations (schools, colleges, universities) can help provide resources, volunteers, and training.
Parents	To keep engaged and positive about their children's activity	Joint activities and events linked to parent's days and holidays. Run parallel activities at delivery site. Ask for feedback whilst in attendance. Engage in volunteering and support roles.
Wider Stakeholders (businesses, local government and national bodies)	Gain 'buy in' to project that will lead to resource support (finances, authorisations, information)	Appreciate age and experiences of key decision makers. Explore any concerns and agree joint actions to overcome them. Work to co-create future activities. Create a trusted and transparent profile to increase reputation. Provide range of competition and charity events to raise awareness
Physical Resources	To gain finances to secure, develop and maintain physical delivery location and equipment	Learn from others – networks - where and how to access support. Create strategic partnerships. Identify key advocates and champions. Lobby stakeholders – link to profile and reputation
Sustainability and the Sustainable Development Goals	To ensure activities enhance social and environmental impact	Promote quality education, inclusion, equality, skill development in volunteering, importance of natural environment, green-blue space benefits. Ensure direct promotion to all diverse social groups Link the outdoor environment to positive health care. Consider the language and communication strategy in order to target all those that can benefit.

Conclusion

The study sought to explore the work of rural community activity leaders, our Fire Souls, and provide practical insight that could guide the creation, resilience, and sustainability of similar projects in rural European settings and positively impact the lives of children and young people living in those communities. In doing so, we conducted in-depth and semi-structured narrative interviews with 42 FS from seven European countries to investigate how they have established, maintained, and developed their clubs and activities, as well as exploring their future plans.

Our findings reinforce much of the existing SFD literature specifically in the areas of motivation, capacity building and social entrepreneurship. With regard to studies highlighting SDT this is specifically poignant given the FS' geographical location, personal ties, and lack of resources ensure that their practice is built upon the 3 areas of autonomy, competency and relatedness (Deci and Ryan, 2008). The FS are problem solvers and utilise their skills, experience, contacts, and additional social capital to navigate through the varied challenges that they face. They all demonstrate altruistic characteristics within their work and a humanistic philosophy of individual and society development as they try to positively impact the children and families living in their communities.

The FS' stories revealed a multitude of factors that shaped their journey and promotion of sport and physical activities. These stories can act as an account of human capital (Bailey et al., 2015) related to sport and PA participation that can help others develop. Their stories and actions contribute to efforts in the direction of improving health and well-being, promoting social inclusion and community development, and fostering positive social values. The FS appear to act as key socializing agents who can help to build capacity and empower individuals and communities to achieve their development goals. This aligns with the broader goal of SFD, which is to harness the power of sport to promote positive social change and contribute to global development efforts.

As noted above, our findings reinforce existing research on motivation, activity, and outcomes of SFD workers. Interestingly, the study also supports previous studies that demonstrated how sport and activity leaders act as active social agents and community developers by bringing to society beneficial forms of PA and opportunities to participate (Rich and Misener, 2020; Rich et al., 2022; Van der Veken et al., 2020). The FS in this study were certainly committed to creating opportunities for social networking, and new friendships and connections, along with promoting healthy lifestyles and the wider social values evident within sport activities. Their stories emphasised the value of their SFD activities in facilitating the safety, wellbeing, and welfare of the people with whom they work (e.g., children, parents, athletes, coaches, volunteers and supporters) as well as their motivation to create positive change for their communities (Wadey, Day, and Howells, 2020).

In summary our FS are highly motivated individuals, sometimes what Coalter (2013) would describe as evangelical, and heavily invested in the rural communities in which they serve. They face many similar challenges to other SFD workers around the world but have additional considerations due to their remote location and limited population and support networks. FS find innovative and creative solutions to problems they encounter as they attempt to create a 'ripple effect' (Sugden, 2010) which will attract more volunteers, engage more stakeholders, and reap wider benefits for their communities. This learning is being collated so it can be shared through the VOMGO project with others working in this domain.

This study gives voice to the unheard, in this specific context those invaluable sport and PA leaders who operate in rural and sometimes difficult to reach communities – our Fire Souls. It offers a European multi-country, multi-site, and multi activity/sport investigation into their work which, to our knowledge, is the first of its kind. Finally, our study substantiates links to previous research on motivation, activity leadership, volunteerism, and SFD whilst providing additional insight and areas for future development.

Of particular interest here is the FS' use of their natural environment. Green sustainability is a worldwide focus (see SDGs) but FS' work offers linkages to contemporary concepts of Learning in Nature, Ecotherapy, and Blue-Green Social Prescribing (Gascon *et al.*, 2017; Jordan and Chawla, 2019), and the associated benefits for children (Stangierska *et al.*, 2023; Wells and Evans, 2003; White, 2004). What this could look like, and the training required for FS and their helpers would be a worthwhile investigation (see Keech and Gray, 2023 for a similar innovation around Nature-Based Learning). This professional development consideration links into 2 further points and areas of future research. 1) What and how training / CPD is offered to FS as well as 2) what training they can provide helpers/volunteers. Human Resource Development could be the lens by which to explore these in more detail. HRD is a key area to cultivate the assets present in rural communities and build community capacity (Bates and Hylton, 2012; Edwards, 2015; Philip *et al.*, 2023).

In recognition of this focus the final VOMGO project will produce a series of guides and handbooks to help other rural activity leaders in Europe to start and to sustain their project ideas. This study's data will inform the content and delivery mechanisms, but more research is needed into the resources required for volunteers and wider stakeholders to engage more effectively in rural areas. Finally responding to calls for a more holistic study of Community Sports Partnerships (Yu *et al.*, 2023) the whole community needs to be involved in evaluating the FS work ensuring the macro and meso level data feeds into this process (Keane *et al.*, 2021). Despite the numerous challenges of gaining authentic feedback from children, the end user experience is key if FS are to provide the services they believe their communities need. This may also lead the FS to engage in more co-creation of programmes and even adopt more of a critical pedagogy which would help address the growing social inclusion agenda and reflect some of the more contemporary approaches to research in this domain (Luguetti *et al.*, 2023; Meir, 2022; Smith *et al.*, 2021).

The study presented here does however have some limitations. The interviews were conducted by researchers from seven different European countries. The personal characteristics of the interviewers and the peculiarities of communication could therefore have had an impact on the how the FS were interviewed. The analysis in this study is based on the FS' self-reported perceptions and reflections of their own activities in their own communities. The findings are therefore difficult to generalise to different sports, clubs, and/or geographical locations to provide lessons and guidance for others to follow. Nevertheless, naturalistic generalisations are possible. Those reading the stories and learning about our FS' motivations, challenges, and support, will hopefully recognise and appreciate the FS' circumstances and reflect upon how they too may face similar scenarios and learn from the findings presented here.

References

Albrecht, J., Elmose-Østerlund, K., Klenk, C. and Nagel, S. (2019) Sports clubs as a medium for integrating people with disabilities. *European Journal for Sport and Society*, 16, 2, 88-110.

Bailey, R., Cope, E. and Parnell, D. (2015) Realising the benefits of sports and physical activity: the human capital model. *Retos: Nuevas Perspectivas de Educación Física, Deporte y Recreación*, 28, 147-154.

Barkley, C., Sanders, B. and Barkley, G. (2018) A systematic review of the evidence of Sport for Development (SfD) and youth development interventions at contributing to life outcomes among South African youth. *Laureus Sport for Good*, 1, 1, 10-25.

Bates, D. and Hylton, K. (2021) Asset-based community sport development: putting community first. *Managing Sport and Leisure*, 26, 1-2, 133-144.

Bloemen, M., Van Wely, L., Mollema, J., Dallmeijer, A. and de Groot, J. (2017) Evidence for increasing physical activity in children with physical disabilities: a systematic review. *Developmental Medicine and Child Neurology*, 59, 10, 1004-1010.

Coakley, J. (2015) Assessing the sociology of sport: on cultural sensibilities and the great sport myth. *International Review for the Sociology of Sport*, 50, 4-5, 402-6.

Coalter, F. (2007) Sports clubs, social capital and social regeneration: ill-defined interventions with hard to follow outcomes. *Sport in Society*, 10, 4, 537-559.

Coalter, F. (2013) *Sport for Development: what game are we playing?* Routledge, London.

Coburn, A.F., MacKinney, A.C., McBride, T.D., Mueller, K.J., Slifkin, R.T., Wakefield, M.K. (2007) Choosing rural definitions: Implications for health policy. *Rural Policy Research Institute* Health Panel (Issue 1, Brief #2).

Conrad, P. (1987) The experience of illness: recent and new directions. *Research in the Sociology of Health Care*, 6, 1-31.

Conroy, D.E., Coatsworth, J.D. (2006) Coach training as a strategy for promoting youth social development. *Sport Psychology*, 20, 2,128-144.

Corbin, J. and Strauss, A. (2015) *Basics of Qualitative Research*. Sage, Thousand Oaks, CA.

Council of European Union (2016) *The European Sport Charter* [online]. Available at: http://www.coe.int/t/dg4/epas/resources/charter_en.asp (Accessed 26th January 2023).

Cronin, O. (2011) *Mapping the research on the impact of Sport and Development interventions*. Comic Relief Review [online]. Available at: https://www.orlacronin.com/wp-content/uploads/2011/06/Comic-relief-research-mapping-v14.pdf (Accessed 29.11.2023).

Darcy, S., Lock, D, and Taylor, T. (2017) Enabling inclusive sport participation: effects of disability and support needs on constraints to sport participation. *Leisure Sciences*, 39, 1, 20-41.

Darnell, S.C. and Hayhurst, L. (2012) Hegemony, postcolonialism and sport-for-development: A response to Lindsey and Grattan. *Journal of Sport Policy and Politics*, 4, 1, 111-124.

Deci, E.L. and Ryan, R.M. (2008) Self-determination theory: a macrotheory of human motivation, development, and health. *Canadian Psychology*, 49, 182-185.

Dix, S., Phau, I. and Pougnet, S. (2010) 'Bend It like Beckham': the influence of sports celebrities on young adult consumers. *Young Consumers*, 11, 1, 36-46.

Dyck, N. (2012) *Fields of Play*. University of Toronto Press, Toronto, Canada.

Edwards, M.B. (2015) The role of sport in community capacity building: An examination of sport for development research and practice. *Sport Management Review*, 18, 1, 6-19.

Eime, R.M., Charity M.J., Harvey J.T. and Payne, W.R. (2015) Participation in sport and physical activity: associations with socio-economic status and geographical remoteness. *BMC Public Health*. 15, 1, 434.

European Union (2020) *Resolution of the Council and of the Representatives of the Governments of the Member States meeting within the Council on the European Union Work Plan for Sport* (1st January 2021 to 30th June 2024). *Official Journal of the European Union*, C 419/01.

Francis, D.W. (2020) Excavating Freytag's Pyramid: Narrative, identity and the museum visitor experience. Doctoral thesis (Ph.D.). UCL, University College London.

Galbraith, M.W. (1992) *Education in the rural American community: a lifelong process*. Krieger, Malabar, Florida, USA.

Gascon, M., Zijlema, W., Vert, C., White, M.P. and Nieuwenhuijsen, M.J. (2017) Outdoor blue spaces, human health and well-being: A systematic review of quantitative studies. *International Journal of Hygiene and Environmental Health*, 220, 8, 1207-1221.

Giulianotti, R. (2011) *Sociology of Sport #3. Social identities and sites of sport*. Sage, London.

Guthold, R., Stevens, G.A., Riley, L.M., and Bull, F.C. (2020) Global trends in insufficient physical activity among adolescents: a pooled analysis of 298 population-based surveys with 1·6 million participants. *Lancet Child Adolescent Health*, 4, 1, 23-35.

Howie, E.K., Guagliano, J.M., Milton, K., Vella, S.A., Gomersall, S.R., Kolbe-Alexander, T.L., *et al.* (2020) Ten research priorities related to youth sport, physical activity and health. *Journal of Physical Activity and Health*, 17, 920-929.

ICSSPE (2021) *International Council of Sport Science and Physical Education*. Annual Report, Berlin, Germany.

ICSSPE (2022) *International Council of Sport Science and Physical Education: Let's get moving together! A toolkit for grassroots sport leaders*. Berlin, Germany.

Järvinen, M. and Mik-Meyer, N. (2020) Analysing qualitative data in social science (pp. 1-27). In, Järvinen, M. and Mik-Meyer, N. (Eds) *Qualitative Analysis: Eight Approaches for the Social Sciences*. Sage, London.

Joens-Matre, R.R., Welk, G.J., Calabro, M.A., Russell, D.W., Nicklay, E. and Hensley, L.D. (2008) Rural-urban differences in physical activity, physical fitness, and overweight prevalence of children. *Journal of Rural Health*, 24, 1, 49-54.

Jordan, C. and Chawla, L. (2019) A coordinated research agenda for nature-based learning. *Frontiers in Psychology*, 10, 3, 766-768.

Kalb, R., Brown, T., Coote, S., Costello, K., Dalgas, U., Garmon, E., Giesser, B., *et al.* (2020) Exercise and lifestyle physical activity recommendations for people with multiple sclerosis throughout the disease course. *Multiple Sclerosis*, 26, 12, 1459-1469.

Kay, T. and Spaaij, R. (2011) The mediating effects of family on sport in international development contexts. *International Review for the Sociology of Sport*, 47, 1, 77-94.

Keane, L., Negin, J., Latu, N., Reece, L., Bauman, A. and Richards, J. (2021) Governance, capacity, communication, champions and alignment: factors underpinning the integration of sport-for-development within national development priorities in Tonga. *Sport in Society*, 24, 4, 493-514.

Kellstedt, D.K., Schenkelberg, M.A., Essay, A.M. *et al.* (2021) Youth sport participation and physical activity in rural communities. *Archive of Public Health,* 79, no:46.

Kidd, B. (2008) A new social movement: sport for development and peace. *Sport in Society*, 11, 4, 370-380.

Kumaat, A.D. and Zulkarnain, A. (2021) The use of Freytag's pyramid to adapt 'positive body image' book into a motion graphic structure. *IMOVICCON Conference Proceedings,* 2, 1, 77-82.

Langer, L. (2015) Sport for development – a systematic map of evidence from Africa. *South African Review of Sociology*, 46, 1, 66-86.

Lee, I.M., Shiroma, E.J., Lobelo, F., Puska, P., Blair, S.N. and Katzmarzyk, P.T. (2012) Effect of physical inactivity on major non-communicable diseases worldwide: An analysis of burden of disease and life expectancy. *Lancet,* 380, 219-229.

Lower, L.M. and Czekanski, W.A. (2019) Effective management of scarce resources: a case study of American collegiate sport clubs. *Managing Sport and Leisure*, 24, 1-3, 119-40.

Luguetti, C., Jice, N., Singehebhuye, L., Singehebhuye, K., Mathieu, A. and Spaaij, R. (2023) 'I know how researchers are [...] taking more from you than they give you': tensions and possibilities of youth participatory action research in sport for development. *Sport, Education and Society*, 28, 7, 755-770.

Lyras, A. and Welty Peachey, J. (2011) Integrating sport-for-development theory and praxis. *Sport Management Review*, 14, 4, 311-326.

Malterud, K. (2001) Qualitative research: Standards, challenges, and guidelines. *The Lancet,* 358, no:9280, 483-488.

May, T., Chan, E.S., Lindor,E., McGinley,J., Skouteris,Hl, Austin,D., McGillivray,J. and Rinehart, N.J. (2021) Physical, cognitive, psychological and social effects of dance in children with disabilities: systematic review and meta-analysis. *Disability and Rehabilitation,* 43, 1,13-26.

Maxwell, J. (2012) *A Realist Approach for Qualitative Research.* Sage, London.

McCormack, L.A. and Meendering, J. (2016) Diet and physical activity in rural vs urban children and adolescents in the United States: a narrative review. *Journal of the Academy of Nutrition and Dietetics*, 116, 3, 467-480.

McSweeney, M.J. (2020) Returning the 'social' to social entrepreneurship: Future possibilities of critically exploring sport for development and peace and social entrepreneurship. *International Review for the Sociology of Sport,* 55, 1, 3-21.

McSweeney, M. (2021) Looking beyond the 'intended beneficiary': parent experiences and perspectives of child participation in sport-for-development programs at an inner-city Toronto sport facility. *Managing Sport and Leisure,* 26, 6, 524-540.

McSweeney, M., Svensson, P., Hayhurst, L. and Safai, P. (2022) *Social innovation, entrepreneurship, and sport for development and peac*e. Routledge, London.

Meir, D. (2022) A qualitative systematic review of critical pedagogy in Physical Education and Sport for Development: exploring a dialogical and critical future for Sport for Development pedagogy. *Sport, Education and Society*, 27, 3, 300-319.

Moore, J.B., Jilcott, S.B., Shores, K.A., Evenson, K.R., Brownson, R.C. and, Novick, L.F. (2010) A qualitative examination of perceived barriers and facilitators of physical activity for urban and rural youth. *Health Education Research*, 25, 2, 355-367.

Mountjoy, M., Andersen, L., Armstrong, N., Biddle, S., Boreham, C., Bedenbeck, H., van Mechelen, W. (2011) International Olympic Committee consensus statement on the health, fitness of young people through physical activity and sport. *British Journal of Sports Medicine*, 45, 11, 839-848.

Neuvonen-Rauhala, M.L. and Weaver, C. (2021) Xamk Beyond 2021: Sustainable Development and Social Responsibility. South-Eastern Finland University of Applied Sciences. Kotka, Finland.

Neuvonen-Rauhala, M.L. and Weaver, C. (2022). Xamk Beyond 2022: Impacts. South-Eastern Finland University of Applied Sciences. Kotka, Finland.

Nicholls, S., Giles, A. and Sethna, C. (2011) Perpetuating the 'lack of evidence' discourse in sport for development: Privileged voices, unheard stories and subjugated knowledge. *International Review for The Sociology of Sport*, 46, 2, 249-264.

Nowell, L.S., Norris, J.M., White, D.E., and Moules, N.J. (2017) Thematic analysis: striving to meet the trustworthiness criteria. *International Journal of Qualitative Methods*, 16, 1, 1-13.

OECD (2021) *Tackling the mental health impact of the COVID-19 crisis: An integrated, whole-of-society response. Policy Responses to Coronavirus (COVID-19)*. OECD Publishing, Paris.

OECD (2023) *Step Up! Tackling the burden of insufficient physical activity in Europe. World Health Organization. Regional Office for Europe and Organisation for Economic Co-operation and Development* [online]. Available at: https://iris.who.int/handle/10665/366327 (Access 2.1.2023).

Pedersen, B.K. and Saltin, B. (2015) Exercise as medicine - evidence for prescribing exercise as therapy in 26 different chronic diseases. *Scandinavian Journal Medical Sci-Sports*, 25, 3, 1-72.

Peralta, L. and Cinelli, R. (2016) An evaluation of an Australian Aboriginal controlled-community remote sports-based programme: a qualitative investigation. *Sport in Society*, 19, 7, 973-989.

Perényi, S. (2010) The relation between sport participation and the value preferences of Hungarian youth. *Sport in Society,* 13, 6, 984-1000.

Philip, B., Seal, E. and Philip, S. (2023) Human resource development for community development: lessons from a sport-for-development program in rural India. *Asia Pacific Journal of Human Resources*, 61, 2, 442-461.

Pink, M. and Cameron, M. (2013) Motivations, barriers, and the need to engage with community leaders: challenges of establishing a sport for development project in Baucau, East Timor. *International Journal of Sport and Society*, 4, 1, 15-29.

Rich, K.A. and Misener, L. (2020) Get active Powassan: developing sport and recreation programs and policies through participatory action research in a rural community context. *Qualitative Research in Sport, Exercise and Health*, 12, 2, 272-288.

Rich, K., Nicholson, M., Randle, E., Donaldson, A., O'Halloran, P., Staley, K., P., Nelson, R. and Belski, R. (2022) Participant-centered sport development: A case study using the leisure constraints of women in regional communities. *Leisure Sciences,* 44, 3, 323-342.

Ringuet-Riot, C., Cuskelly, G., Auld, C. and Zakus, D. H. (2014) Volunteer roles, involvement and commitment in voluntary sport organizations: Evidence of core and peripheral volunteers. *Sport in Society*, 17, 1, 116-133.

Ritchey, J.A. (2006) Negotiating change: adult education and rural life in Pennsylvania. *Pennsylvania Association for Adult Continuing Education Journal of Lifelong Learning*, 15, 1-16.

Ritchie, J., Spencer, L. and O'Connor, W. (2010) Carrying out qualitative analysis (pp 219-262). In, Ritchie, J. and Lewis, J. (Eds.) *Qualitative research practice: a guide for social science students and researchers*. Sage, London.

Ritchie, J. and Spencer, L. (1994) Qualitative data analysis for applied policy research (pp 173-94). In, Bryman, A and Burgess, R.G. (Eds.) *Analysing Qualitative Data*. Routledge. New York.

Robinson, J.W. and Green, G.P. (2010) *Introduction to community development theory, practice, and service-learning*. Sage. New York.

Rottensteiner, C., Laakso, L., Pihlaja, T. and Konttinen, N. (2018) Personal reasons for withdrawal from team sports and the influence of significant others among youth athletes. *International Journal of Sports Science and Coaching*, 8, 1,19-32.

Ryan, R.M. and Deci, E.L. (2000) Intrinsic and extrinsic motivations: Classic definitions and new directions. *Contemporary Educational Psychology*, 25, 1, 54-67.

Schuch, F.B., Vancampfort, D., Firth, J., Rosenbaum, S, Ward, P.B., Silva, E.S., Hallgren, M., Ponce De Leon, A., Dunn, A.L., Deslandes, A.C., Fleck, M.P., Carvalho, A.F. and Stubbs, B. (2018) Physical activity and incident depression: a meta-analysis of prospective cohort studies. *American Journal of Psychiatry*, 175, 7, 631-648.

Seippel, Ø., Breuer,C., Elmose-Østerlund, K., Feiler, S., Perenyi, S., Piątkowska, M. and Scheerder, J. (2020) In troubled water? European sports clubs: their problems, capacities and opportunities. *Journal of Global Sport Management*, August, pp:203-225.

Sherry, E., Schulenkorf, N., Seal, E., Nicholson, M. and Hoye, R. (2017) Sport-for-Development in the South Pacific Region: macro, meso and micro perspectives. *Sociology of Sport Journal,* 34, 4, 303-316.

Skille, E.Å. (2015) Community and sport in Norway: between state sport policy and local sport clubs. *International Journal of Sport Policy and Politics,* 7, 4, 505-518.

Smith, B. (2018) Generalizability in qualitative research: misunderstandings, opportunities and recommendations for the sport and exercise sciences. *Qualitative Research in Sport, Exercise and Health*, 10, 1, 137-149.

Smith, J. and Firth, J. (2011) Qualitative data analysis: the framework approach. *Nurse Researcher,* 18, 2, 52-62.

Smith, N.L., Cohen, A. and Pickett, A.C. (2014) Exploring the motivations and outcomes of long-term international sport-for-development volunteering for American millennials. *Journal of Sport Tourism,* 19, 3-4, 299-316.

Smith, R., Spaaij, R. and McDonald, B. (2019) Migrant integration and cultural capital in the context of sport and physical activity: a systematic review. *Journal of International Migration and Integration,* 20, 3, 851-68.

Smith, R., Danford, M., Darnell, S.C., Larrazabal, M.J.L. and Abdellatif, M. (2021) 'Like, what even is a podcast?' Approaching sport-for-development youth participatory action research through digital methodologies. *Qualitative Research in Sport, Exercise and Health*, 13, 1, 128-145.

Somerset, S. and Hoare, D.J. (2018) Barriers to voluntary participation in sport for children: a systematic review. *BMC Pediatrics*,18, 1, 47-48.

Sparkes, A.C. and Smith, B. (2014) *Qualitative research methods in sport, exercise and health: From process to product.* Routledge, London.

Spencer, L., Ritchie, J. and O'Connor, W. (2010) Analysis: practice, principles and processes (pp: 199-218). In, Ritchie, J. and Lewis, J. (Eds.) *Qualitative research practice: a guide for social science students and researchers*. Sage, London.

Sport-for-Development (n.d.) *Achieving more together: the sport for development resource toolkit* [online]. Available at: https://www.sport-for-development.com/home#:~:text=Welcome%20to%20the%20Sport%20for,projects%2C%20workshops%20and%20training%20sessions (Accessed 27th January 2022).

Stangierska, D., Fornal-Pieniak, B., Szumigała, P., Widera, K., Żarska, B. and Szumigała, K. (2023) Green physical activity indicator: health, physical activity and spending time outdoors related to residents' preference for greenery. *Environmental Research and Public Health*, 20, 2, 1242 [14].

Steinmayr, A., Felfe, C. and Lechner, M. (2011) The closer the sportier? Children's sports activity and their distance to sports facilities. *European Review of Aging and Physical Activity*, 8, 1, 67-82.

Storm, R.K. and Eske, M. (2021) Dual careers and academic achievements: does elite sport make a difference? *Sport, Education and Society*, April pp:1-14.

Svensson, P.G. and Cohen. A. (2020) Innovation in sport for development and peace. *Managing Sport and Leisure*, 25, 3, 138-145.

Sugden, J. (2010) Critical left-realism and sport interventions in divided societies. *International Review for the Sociology of Sport*, 45, 3, 258-272.

Sumption, B. and Burnett, C. (2021) A framework for capturing active participation in structured physical activity across the lifespan in Sub-Saharan Africa. *Journal of Physical Education and Sport,* 21, 3141-3148.

Taylor, S.J., Bogdan, R. and DeVault, M. (2016) *Introduction to qualitative research methods a guidebook and resource* (4th ed.). John Wiley and Sons Inc., Hoboken, New Jersey.

Tobin, G. and Begley, C. (2004) Methodological rigour within a qualitative framework. *Journal of Advanced Nursing,* 48, 4, 388-396.

Treadwell, S.M. and Stiehl, J. (2015) Advocating for change in rural Physical Education: a middle school perspective through Photovoice and student SHOWeD analysis. *Journal of Qualitative Research in Sports Studies,* 9, 1, 107-162.

Umstattd Meyer, M.R., Perry, C.K., Sumrall, J.C., Patterson, M.S., Walsh, S.M., Clendennen, S.C., Hooker, S.P., Evenson, K.R., Goins, K.V., Heinrich, K.M., O'Hara Tompkins, N., Eyler, A.A., Jones, S., Tabak, R., Valko, C. (2017) Physical activity-related policy and environmental strategies to prevent obesity in rural communities: a systematic review of the literature, 2002-2013. *Preventing Chronic Disease,* 13, 3, E03.

United Nations (2022) *Youth Strategy 2030.* United Nations [online]. Available at: https://www.un.org/youthenvoy/youth-un/ (Accessed 2nd June 2022).

UNESCO (2022) *Fit for life: Sport powering inclusive, peaceful, and resilient societies.* UNICEF Office of Research, Florence, Italy.

UNICEF (2019) *Getting into the Game: Understanding the evidence for child-focused sport for development.* UNICEF Office of Research, Florence, Italy.

UNICEF (2021) *Playing the Game: A framework for successful child focused sport for development programmes. Understanding the evidence for child-focused Sport for Development.* UNICEF Office of Research, Florence, Italy.

Van der Veken, K., Lauwerier, E. and Willems, S. (2020) To mean something to someone: sport-for-development as a lever for social inclusion. *Int. Journal for Equity in Health,* 19, 1, 11-11.

VOMB (2019) *Villages on the Move Baltic. Erasmus+ Sport European Union Project* [online]. Available at: https://ec.europa.eu/programmes/erasmus-plus/project-result-content/bf21238d-6349-47f7-b23e-6dce3a1457db/Links%20to%20videos.pdf (Accessed 10th September 2023).

VOMNet (2020) *Villages on the Move Network. Erasmus+ Sport European Union Project.* [online]. Available at: https://ec.europa.eu/programmes/erasmus-plus/project-result-content/df1f0a07-08a1-4ff8-a809. c4f22d0d287f/Seminar%20report_Kaunas_meeting%204.pdf (Acc: 1.9.2023).

Wadey, R., Day, M. and Howells, K. (Eds.) (2020) *Growth following adversity in sport a mechanism to positive change.* Routledge, London.

Wells, N.M. and Evans, G.W. (2003) Nearby Nature: A buffer of life stress among rural children. *Environment and Behaviour,* 35, 3, 311-330.

Welty Peachey, J., Cohen, A., Borland, J. and Lyras, A. (2013) Building social capital: Examining the impact of Street Soccer USA on its volunteers. *Int Review for Sociology of Sport,* 48,1, 20-37.

Welty Peachey, J., Lyras, A., Cohen, A., Bruening, J. E. and Cunningham, G.B. (2014) Exploring the motives and retention factors of sport-for-development volunteers. *Nonprofit and Voluntary Sector Quarterly,* 43, 6, 1052-1069.

Welty Peachey, J., Musser, A., Shin, N.R. and Cohen, A. (2018) Interrogating the motivations of sport for development and peace practitioners. *Int Review for Sociology of Sport,* 53, 7, 767-787.

Welty Peachey, J., Cohen, A. and Musser, A. (2016) 'A phone call changed my life': Exploring the motivations of sport for development and peace scholars. *Sport for Development,* 4, 7, 58-70.

Welty Peachey, J., Schulenkorf, N. and Hill, P. (2020) Sport-for-development: An analysis of theoretical and conceptual advancements. *Sport Management Review,* 23, 5, 783-796.

Wheeler, S. and Green, K. (2014) Parenting in relation to children's sports participation: generational changes and potential implications. *Leisure Studies,* 33, 3, 267-84.

White, R. (2004) Young children's relationship with nature: its importance to children's development and the earths future. *White Hutchinson and Learning Group,* 1, 9, 215-219.

Whitley, M.A., Massey, W.V., Camiré, M., Blom, L.C., Chawansky, M., Forde, S., Boutet, M., Borbee, A. and Darnell, S.C. (2019) A systematic review of sport for development interventions across six global cities. *Sport Management Review*, 22, 2, 181-193.

WHO (2018a) *Physical activity factsheets for the 28 European Union member states of the WHO European region: an overview.* World Health Organization, Geneva.

WHO (2018b) *Global action plan on physical activity 2018–2030: more active people for a healthier world.* World Health Organization, Geneva.

Wicker, P., Breuer, C. and Pawlowski, T. (2009) Promoting sport for all to age-specific target groups: The impact of sport infrastructure. *European Sport Management Quarterly*, 9, 1, 103-118.

Wilke, J., Mohr, L., Tenforde, A.S., Edouard, P., Fossati, C., González-Gross, M., Sánchez Ramírez, C., Laiño, F., Tan, B., Pillay, J.D., Pigozzi, F., Jimenez-Pavon, D., Novak, B., Jaunig, J., Zhang, M., van Poppel, M., Heidt, C., Willwacher, S., Yuki, G., Lieberman, D.E., Vogt, L., Verhagen, E., Hespanhol, L. and Hollander, K. (2021) A pandemic within the pandemic? physical activity levels substantially decreased in countries affected by COVID-19. *International Journal of Environmental Research and Public Health*, 18, 5, 2235.

Yousefian, A., Ziller, E., Swartz, J. and Hartley, D. (2009) Active living for rural youth: addressing physical inactivity in rural communities. *Public Health Management and Practice*, 15, 3, 223-31

Yu, J., Ding, M., Wang, Q., Sun, W. and Hu, W. (2023) Community sports organization development from a social network evolution perspective: structures, stages, and stimulus. *IEEE Transactions on Computational Social Systems*, 10, 3, 878-889.

Ethics statement: Each international partner gained ethics approval via their own institution and government office. The coordination of approvals was managed by the lead partner - South Eastern Finland University of Applied Sciences, XAMK and reported to the Erasmus+ (Sport) administrators.

JQRSS Author Profile

David Grecic[1] [corresponding author] is the Head of Research and Innovation in the School of Health, Social Work and Sport. His research specialisms include coaching consultancy, Physical Education and International partnerships in Higher Education.
ORCID-ID https://orcid.org/0000-0003-1487-8327 Email: dgrecic1@uclan.ac.uk

Reviewer Comments

This international team of researchers have pooled their resources, shared their expertise and overcome barriers which can often make academic publication of such valuable research difficult. In so doing, now it is published, it becomes clear how the endeavours of the researchers share similar characteristics with those of the Fire Souls in their community settings. Not least, those of reconciling language differences, seeking funding and even succession planning for implementing long-term ideas come to mind, all are pivotal to promoting health and social wellbeing through sport and exercise (and a lot more besides in this instance). What the Fire Souls are achieving is real success on the ground across Europe, in communities that need and value their efforts. This article does not describe a pipe-dream or ideal, it is not a funding bid for what *might* become, it is a true account of genuine efforts of 'community coaches' to make a difference on a huge scale, to many 1000s of people. This excellent research, and report into the activities of the Fire Souls should become part of the funding case for further investment to support this excellent work, and therein celebrate the impact that an academic voice can have on real-world outcomes.

Milton Keynes UK
Ingram Content Group UK Ltd.
UKHW051515100324
439088UK00004B/24